The Essential Guide TO

A Lasting Marriage

by Martin Tashman, Ph.D., and
Karla R. Dougherty

ALPHA

A member of Penguin Group (USA) Inc.

ALPHA BOOKS

Published by the Penguin Group

Penguin Group (USA) Inc., 375 Hudson Street, New York, New York 10014, USA

Penguin Group (Canada), 90 Eglinton Avenue East, Suite 700, Toronto, Ontario M4P 2Y3, Canada (a division of Pearson Penguin Canada Inc.)

Penguin Books Ltd., 80 Strand, London WC2R 0RL, England

Penguin Ireland, 25 St. Stephen's Green, Dublin 2, Ireland (a division of Penguin Books Ltd.)

Penguin Group (Australia), 250 Camberwell Road, Camberwell, Victoria 3124, Australia (a division of Pearson Australia Group Pty. Ltd.)

Penguin Books India Pvt. Ltd., 11 Community Centre, Panchsheel Park, New Delhi—110 017, India

Penguin Group (NZ), 67 Apollo Drive, Rosedale, North Shore, Auckland 1311, New Zealand (a division of Pearson New Zealand Ltd.)

Penguin Books (South Africa) (Pty.) Ltd., 24 Sturdee Avenue, Rosebank, Johannesburg 2196, South Africa

Penguin Books Ltd., Registered Offices: 80 Strand, London WC2R 0RL, England

International Standard Book Number: 978-1-61564-089-8
Library of Congress Catalog Card Number: 2011901232

13   12   11   8   7   6   5   4   3   2   1

Interpretation of the printing code: The rightmost number of the first series of numbers is the year of the book's printing; the rightmost number of the second series of numbers is the number of the book's printing. For example, a printing code of 11-1 shows that the first printing occurred in 2011.

Printed in the United States of America

Note: This publication contains the opinions and ideas of its authors. It is intended to provide helpful and informative material on the subject matter covered. It is sold with the understanding that the authors and publisher are not engaged in rendering professional services in the book. If the reader requires personal assistance or advice, a competent professional should be consulted.

The authors and publisher specifically disclaim any responsibility for any liability, loss, or risk, personal or otherwise, which is incurred as a consequence, directly or indirectly, of the use and application of any of the contents of this book.

Most Alpha books are available at special quantity discounts for bulk purchases for sales promotions, premiums, fund-raising, or educational use. Special books, or book excerpts, can also be created to fit specific needs.

For details, write: Special Markets, Alpha Books, 375 Hudson Street, New York, NY 10014.

Publisher: *Marie Butler-Knight*	**Copy Editor:** *Jan Zoya*
Associate Publisher: *Mike Sanders*	**Cover Designer:** *Rebecca Batchelor*
Executive Managing Editor: *Billy Fields*	**Book Designers:** *Rebecca Batchelor, William Thomas*
Senior Acquisitions Editor: *Paul Dinas*	**Indexer:** *Tonya Heard*
Senior Development Editor: *Christy Wagner*	**Layout:** *Ayanna Lacey*
Senior Production Editor: *Kayla Dugger*	**Senior Proofreader:** *Laura Caddell*

Dedication

This book is dedicated to the two women whom I am privileged to have in my life, my mother and my special lady, Roberta, and to my son, Gidalya. Thank you for teaching me about relationships and love. —Martin Tashman, Ph.D.

Contents

Part 1	An Enduring Marriage: The Dream and the Challenge	1

1	Happily Ever After 3

What Is a Happy Marriage? 4
    Complementary Goals 4
    The Importance of Shared Values 5
    Compatible Views on Children 6
    A Similar Sense of Humor 6
    Religious Beliefs 8
Lasting Marriage Territory 8
    An Evolving Definition of Love 9
    Change Is Part of the Equation 10
    Realistic Expectations 10
    Lasting Marriages Take Work 11

2	Here Come the Bumps 15

Challenges Over Time 15
    Financial Ups and Downs 16
    Declining Health 18
    A Shifting View of the World 19
    The In-Laws 19
    Personal Habits: Too Much Sharing? 20
Rumblings in Paradise? 21
    Silent Days and Nights 21
    Churning Emotions 22
    Denial 23
    Too Many Excuses 23

3	The Myths and Realities of Marriage 25

Marriage Myths 26
    Myth: A Lack of Sex Means a Lack of Love 26
    Myth: The Odds Are Stacked Against You 26
    Myth: Men and Women Are from Different
       Planets 27
    Myth: If Someone Has an Affair, the Marriage
       Is Over 27
    Myth: Never Go to Bed Angry 27

Myth: A Baby Will Make Things Better 28
Myth: Mental Problems Can Erode a Marriage. 28
Myth: Common Interests Are the Key to a
   Lasting Marriage 29
Myth: A Lasting Marriage Is All About Quid
   Pro Quo. 29
Myth: Too Many Fights Mean the Marriage
   Is In Trouble 30
How Strong Is Your Marriage? 30
Finding Solutions Together 33

Part 2   **The Four Stages of Lasting Marriage**   **35**

4   **Stage 1: The Honeymoon Days**
(and Nights!) 37
The First Few Months. 37
   Ain't Love Grand 38
   Passion and Romance 38
A Strong Attraction. 39
   "I Hate to Say Good-Bye" 40
   Great Sex—and Lots of It! 41
   Idealizing Your Mate 41
Everything Is New. 42
   Making Your Own Rules 42
   Necessary Guidelines 43
The First Fight 43
   Forgiving and Forgetting 44
   Avoiding Catastrophic Thinking 45

5   **Stage 2: Settling In.** 47
The Day-to-Day Realities. 47
   No Relationship Is Perfect 48
   Everything Evolves and Changes. 49
   Avoiding Disillusionment—Then and Now 49
Setting Emotional Goals. 50
   Financial and Career Changes 51
   Mortgages and Parenthood 52
   Using Maslow's Hierarchy of Needs. 53

6   Stage 3: Facing Life's Challenges 57
Learning What to Expect from Each Other 57
In Crises *58*
In Daily Life *59*
Establishing a Life Together 60
Balancing Home and Work *61*
Building a Home and Community *62*
Creating Short- and Long-Term Goals *63*
The Child Factor 65
Rules and Expectations for Raising Children *65*
Handling Extended Family Issues *66*
Compromise Is Critical *66*

7   Stage 4: Growing Old Together 69
Been There, Done That 69
Been There, Done That, Still Together *70*
Getting Comfortable with Compromise *70*
The Aging Factor 71
Vulnerability May Breed Temptation *72*
Fantasizing About Past Loves *72*
Fear of Mortality *72*
Accepting Your Spouse 73
Knowing the Real Person You Married *73*
Accepting and Respecting the Differences *74*
Minimizing Resentment *74*
Focus On What's Right About Each Other 75
Managing Anger or Hurtful Triggers *75*
Agreeing to Disagree *76*
Enjoying Each Other's Company *76*

Part 3   Building a Strong Foundation   77

8   Acceptance Is a Two-Way Street 79
Putting the Value in Validation 80
The Flexibility Factor 80
Tolerance Builds Acceptance 81
Laid Back and "In the Moment"? *82*
Can Drama Equal Excitement? *82*

The Art of Acceptance 82
   First, Accept Yourself 83
   When Acceptance Is a Challenge 84
   Circumstantial Acceptance 85
Disagreeing in an Agreeing Way. 86
An Acceptance Inventory. 87
Does Your Spouse Accept You?. 88

9   **Beyond Empathy** 91
Different Points of View. 91
Respecting Each Other's Opinion. 93
   Keeping Judgmental Thinking to a Minimum 94
   Vive la Différence!. 95
Establishing Boundaries. 95
   Everyone Needs Some Space 96
   Emotional, Physical, and Financial Boundaries . . . 96
Your Spouse's Needs or Moods 97
   Don't Cling 98
   You Can't Always Make It Better 98
   Respecting Each Other's Needs 99
The Importance of Influence 100
   Influence Between Spouses 101
   Empathy Helps Foster Influence 102
Dealing with Contempt 102

10   **In You I Trust.** 105
A Cornerstone of Marriage 105
Trust Has Many Layers. 106
   Trusting Yourself 107
   Repeating the Past 108
   Between the Two of You. 108
   Developing Trust 109
   How Much Trust Exists Between You? 109
What's Yours Is Mine 111
   Money Matters. 111
   Sharing Spaces 112
   Being There. 112

11   The Importance of Good Communication . . 115

Communication: More Than Talk 115

The Difference Between But and Yet. 116

The Do's and Don'ts of Communication 118

Recognize the Mars/Venus Aspect of Your
    Marriage 121

What You Say Might Not Be What He Hears 121

*Your Intention Might Not Get the Right
    Reception.* 122

The Receiver Determines the Real Meaning 123

Plan Effective 30-Minute Meetings. 124

Preparing for the Conversation 124

During the Meeting 125

Keeping Lines of Communication Open 126

Opening the Curtain on Denial 127

Enhancing Your Conversations 127

12   Fighting Is a Fact of Life. 129

Anger Has Many Faces 130

Not Feeling Loved or Necessary. 130

The Aggressive Shape of Feeling Helpless 131

Depression Turns Anger Inward 132

Resentment and Passive-Aggressive Behavior 133

Anger Uses a Lot of Energy 134

The Anger Diluter 135

Listen, Don't React. 136

Meaningful Input in a Situation 137

Strive for Clarity. 137

Try Laughter. 138

It's Not the Fight, but *How* You Fight 139

Talking Through Problems. 140

Taking Time-Outs 140

Avoiding Words and Behaviors That Hurt 141

Strategies for Fighting. 142

Take a Deep Breath 142

Choosing Words That Taunt, Not Haunt 143

Postmortem Analysis 144

13   Playfulness Is Key **145**
Laughter Helps You Cope 145
Laughing Can Be Erotic. *146*
Laughter Brings You Closer. *147*
A Smile Brightens Anyone's Day *147*
Making Dates and Keeping Them. 148
Plan Fun Events *148*
Schedule Date Nights *148*
Share Hobbies and Sports *149*
Take a Class Together *149*
Take a Hike. *150*
Learn to Play Your Spouse's Game *150*
Play Does Not Have to End in Sex 151

14   Lasting Romance and Sex **153**
Keeping Lust Alive 153
Communicating Sexual Needs 154
Sex Is Good for You *155*
Familiarity Means Safety. *155*
Free to Be Uninhibited. *156*
Keeping the Flame Alive 157
Reminisce About the Early Years. *158*
Intimacy Changes Over Time *158*
Romancing Your Marriage. 159
Don't Take Each Other for Granted *159*
Be Thoughtful. *160*
Being—and Feeling—Sexy as You Mature. 161

Part 4   The Marriage Land Mines   163

15   The Seven Deadly "I Don'ts" **165**
Criticism: "You Never Do It Right" 166
Criticism Versus Complaining. *166*
Criticism Is Global, Not Situational *166*
Contempt: "You Are a Jerk" 167
Laughing at Your Spouse's Expense: "You're
Crazy, but I Love You". 167
Insults *169*
Dismissive Body Language *169*

Being Defensive: "Why Is It Always *My* Fault?" 170
   Turning the Tables on Your Spouse. *170*
   Making False Assumptions *171*
Denial: "There's Nothing Wrong!" 172
   Reality Versus Need *173*
   Avoiding Responsibilities *173*
Mentally Removing Yourself: "Huh?" 174
   No Reaction Is Not Staying Calm *174*
   Muttering Is Not an Answer *174*
Negativity: "We're Doomed" 175
   Catastrophic Thinking *175*
   Part of the Problem, Not the Solution. *176*
Martyrdom: "It's Me, Not You" 177

16   And Baby Makes Three 179
Adapting to Change 179
   Shifts in Time Management. *180*
   Coping with Fatigue. *180*
   Kids Come First *181*
   Added Responsibilities *182*
Identity Shifts. 182
   From a Couple to a Family *182*
   Who Stays Home *183*
   Changing Routines. *183*
The Joys of a Family 184
Sustaining Your Marriage as Your Children Grow. . . 184
   Avoiding Blame *185*
   Take Time-Outs *185*

17   Money Changes Everything 187
Finances Are Not Static 188
   Wealth Can Grow or Dwindle. *188*
   Compromise, Not Sacrifice *189*
When You See Different Shades of Green 190
Creating a Budget Together 191
Debt and More Debt. 192
   Realizing There's a Problem. *192*
   Getting Out of Debt *192*
Career Moves. 193
Making Money Work with You, Not Against You . . . 194

18   Intimacy Interference 197

Intimate Relations Can Erode with Time 197

Familiarity Doesn't Have to Breed Contempt 198

Less Time for Sex 198

Life Problems Dampening Desire 199

Do You Need More Time Together? 199

When Desire Is Absent 200

Menopause 202

Manopause 203

Underlying Medical Problems 203

Psychological Factors 204

Getting Back in the Groove 204

Medication 205

Making Time for Love 205

Where There's a Will, There's a Way 206

19   The Empty Nest and Beyond 207

Just the Two of You … Now What? 207

Revisiting Old Issues 208

Are You Living with a Stranger? 209

Growing Apart 210

Living with Empty Nest Syndrome 210

Avoiding Marital Burnout 211

Some Grief or Loneliness Is Normal 212

Coping with an Empty House 212

Just When You Thought It Was Over … 213

20   The Parent Trap 217

When Your Parents Grow Old 217

Two Families for the Price of One 218

The Desire to Do What's Right 218

Taking Care of Aging Parents 219

Making It Work with Your Family 220

Making Hard Choices 220

How Does Your Spouse Feel? 222

Devote Time to Discuss Events 223

Finding a Solution—Together 223

Are You on the Same Page? 224

21   The Marriage Sea Changes 225
Overcoming Infidelity 225
The Conflict-Avoidance Affair. *226*
The Intimacy-Avoidance Affair. *226*
The Sexual Addiction Affair *227*
The Split-Self Affair *227*
Give Yourself Time to Heal *227*
Barriers to Falling Back in Love *228*
The Challenges of Substance Abuse 228
Helping Your Partner. *229*
Getting Through to a Troubled Child *230*
Making Your Family Whole Again *231*
Coping with a Debilitating Illness 233
You're in This Together. *234*
Enlisting Help from Family and Friends. *234*
Handling Bankruptcy. 235
Stopping the "Blame Game" *235*
Changing Money Habits *235*
When the Unspeakable Happens: A Child's Death . . . 236
The Stages of Trauma Recovery. 236

**Part 5   Repairing, Reconnecting, and
Renewing   239**

22   Healing Old Wounds 241
Repairing Deteriorated Trust 241
Rebuilding Trust Takes Time. 243
Spend Time Together *244*
Use Positive Self-Talk. *244*
Share Your Thoughts *244*
Acknowledgment *245*
The Role of Faith 245
An Effective Replay Technique 246
Set Aside Two Hours *246*
Identify Problem Issues *246*
Identify an Insight *247*
Recognize What Really Hurts Your Partner. *247*
What Could You Have Done Differently? 247
Develop a Plan. *248*
Three Scenarios: An Exercise for Healing. *248*

23   Falling Back in Like .251

A Complicated Emotion 251

Back to the Beginning 252

Take Responsibility for Your Actions 252

Explain the "Why"s 253

The Devil's in the Details 253

Analyzing the Situation 253

Finding Solutions 254

Using Positive Self-Talk 255

Remember What You Loved About Your
Partner 257

Remember a Time When You Were Happy 257

Visualize the Memory 257

Working with a Positive Mind-Set 258

Acknowledge Your Partner's Value 259

Have a Positive Experience 259

Speak Positively Without Patronizing 259

Reinforce Good Feelings 260

Perform Random Acts of Kindness 260

24   It's Okay to Ask for Help 261

When to Seek Couples Therapy 262

When Your Relationship Is Falling Apart 263

Some Good News About the "Last Resort" 264

The Rejection Factor 265

Even in Rejection, There Is Hope 265

Rejection Testing 266

When Your Spouse Isn't Ready 267

What to Expect from a Marriage Counselor 268

A Safe, Comfortable Environment 269

Problem-Solving Techniques 269

Finding a Good Therapist 270

Support Groups: You're Not Alone 271

Do You Need Sex Therapy? 272

25   Renewing Your Commitment 275

Celebrating Your Life Together 275

The Good Times, the Bad Times 276

Reasons to Renew Your Vows 277

Finding the Words *277*
Vow Renewals "I Don'ts" *278*
Romantic Renewals. 279
Daily Affirmations. 279

Appendixes

A   Glossary 281

B   Resources 285

     Index 289

Introduction

Your wedding is the most exciting and romantic day of your life. It's a time when everyone you care about is in a room or backyard, a chapel, or on the beach, bearing witness to you and your soon-to-be spouse. It's the day when life is brimming with possibilities and you know, deep in your heart, you are with the one person you want to grow old with, the one person with whom you will have children, the one person you want to hold your hand when things get tough and love you, really love you, forever. And when you're swirling around the dance floor dressed to the nines, drinking champagne, and eating wedding cake, you're so happy, it's like a dream come true.

Sometimes that ecstatic love can last well after you have unpacked your bags from your honeymoon. But whether it's a few months or a few years, your love will definitely change. Your marriage will evolve. And life will have a way of throwing up obstacles to that love you felt so completely sure about on your wedding day.

There are the times when your marriage is truly tested: when money becomes an issue, if you have a sick child, or if you start to grow in opposite directions. Then there are the times when the crises are more subtle: the changes that come when you have a baby, when that baby grows up, when you grow old and feel less attractive, when your marriage together becomes boring or stale and you wonder how you ever married him or her in the first place.

How did it happen? When did your love erode? When did you—or your spouse—decide it isn't working? Is your marriage strong enough to last? That's what this book is all about: making your marriage a lasting one; making your marriage stronger, better, and happier than ever; and keeping alive that love you pledged on your wedding day.

I've been a marriage counselor for more than 35 years, and in that time, I've seen couples with no hope of getting back together again become close. I've seen the tragic, the ugly, and the painful side of marriage and have helped couples address these issues and find new ways of connecting and renewing their love.

It's not easy. A lasting marriage takes work. But the beauty of this work is that the results can be wonderful. You can stay together through thick and thin, better and worse, failings and joy.

Within these pages, you find the insights and strategies I've used in my practice and which I can now bring to you. You'll find exercises that help you determine where your marriage can use work and where things are simpatico. You learn the foundations that all good marriages need and the ways to rekindle love, sex, romance, and fun.

I hope this book brings you and your spouse closer. I hope it helps you rekindle and renew your love. And most of all, I hope it gives you the insights, information, and knowledge you need to make your marriage one of those that last: a marriage that stays strong from those early heady days of young love through the sweet, sweet joys of growing old together.

How to Use This Book

I've divided this book into five distinct parts, each one building on the other, and each one containing quizzes, important information, and case studies of couples just like you:

Part 1, An Enduring Marriage: The Dream and the Challenge, offers an overview of marriage—from its ideals to its realities. It offers insights into the elements that make a marriage happy, the challenges you can expect over time, and some of the myths that can sabotage your idea of a happy marriage.

Part 2, The Four Stages of Lasting Marriage, is all about the stages every marriage goes through—from the honeymoon years to the golden days. I've included descriptions of the four main stages as well as the roadblocks that may crop up along the way, and advice for handling them.

Part 3, Building a Strong Foundation, is the core of this book, where you find the foundations that will make your marriage a strong and lasting one. Here you find the elements that all lasting marriages have, from empathy and trust, to playfulness and sex, from respect and validation, to communication and the art of fighting well.

In **Part 4, The Marriage Land Mines,** you find the potential land mines that marriages may face, from the problems that may arise when you have children to those you may face with an empty nest. You find ways to cope with intimacy difficulties, in-law issues, money pitfalls, and even such changes as infidelity and illness.

Finally, in **Part 5, Repairing, Reconnecting, and Renewing,** you find the ways to repair a broken marriage or renew a marriage that may have gotten stale. I offer strategies for healing old wounds, re-creating trust, and rekindling romance. I even include a special section on renewing your vows to celebrate your lasting love.

Throughout the book, you will find exercises for both you and your spouse. I'll ask you to write down your answers so you can refer to them later, or to simply see them with more clarity in black and white. Just jot down your answers—and any other thoughts that come to mind—in a notebook or journal.

Extra Advice

Throughout this book, I've sprinkled extra information about a particular subject or some wise words to enhance the nearby text. Here's what to look for:

Definition	These sidebars offer definitions of words or phrases that may be unfamiliar to you.
Love Letters	Look here for short and sweet tips on making your marriage work even better.
Marriage Trap	Heed these warnings to take notice of behaviors or actions that may be harming your marriage.

You'll also see a fourth, name-changing sidebar that presents anecdotes, interesting facts, case histories, or other extended background information you should know.

Acknowledgments

I would like to acknowledge my teachers, Drs. John Gottman, Brent Atkinson, and Bill Miller, for their research and insights, and for allowing me to stand on the shoulders of their genius.

I would also like to acknowledge my co-author, Karla Dougherty, who has made this process both easy and enjoyable.

Trademarks

All terms mentioned in this book that are known to be or are suspected of being trademarks or service marks have been appropriately capitalized. Alpha Books and Penguin Group (USA) Inc. cannot attest to the accuracy of this information. Use of a term in this book should not be regarded as affecting the validity of any trademark or service mark.

An Enduring Marriage: The Dream and the Challenge

It's hard to believe, but you've been married 10, 20, maybe 45 years! In some ways, it feels like you've been together forever. Sometimes, it's as if no time has gone by at all.

You've been through so much together: the honeymoon years, the birth of your children, the everyday ups and downs of life, and even the heart-breaking crises.

As you'll find in the following chapters, marriage is not just about love. It's about living together, meeting challenges together, and sharing a life—with all the glory, messes, joys, and changes that brings.

Think of Part 1 as an introduction to the rest of your life together. You'll find insights into the way marriage works and learn what marriages need to endure. At the end of this part, you'll find a quiz to help you determine how strong your marriage really is.

chapter 1

Happily Ever After

A picture of a happy marriage

Necessary compatibilities

Love over time

The work of marriage

Reality, not reality show

"I do."

These two small words signify a powerful commitment: for better or for worse, a lifetime together, a journey filled with love. For some people, the implication of "I do" means never feeling alone. For others, the words mean financial security. And for still others, "I do" means roots, a family, the timeless progression of the human race.

Whatever your ultimate expectations in the words "I do" initially, the meaning is the same for almost everyone: "I love you, and I pick you to share my life with. I am happy and scared and filled with excitement. I am, and I do!"

Sealed with a kiss, these two little words launch you into a marriage, a lifetime filled with hopes and dreams and happiness. You will always love this person. Yours will be a marriage that lasts.

What Is a Happy Marriage?

Couples who are happily married don't have supernatural powers. They aren't necessarily smarter than other folks. Nor are they just plain lucky. What happy couples do have, however, goes deeper than love: they respect and validate each other. They care deeply about each other's happiness. They communicate.

Sounds easy. But as anyone who has been or is currently married knows, these qualities can go out the window when life takes a left turn or even when it just stays on such a straight path for so long it just gets boring.

So how do you make a marriage that lasts?

Complementary Goals

We all start out with life goals, some realistic and some flights of fancy. (What teenager doesn't fantasize about being a famous movie star or music diva?) Hopefully, as we mature, the decisions we make lead us to fulfilling those dreams. But as we all know, not everyone becomes a rock star. The majority of us make plans to go to college, focus on a field of work we find interesting, begin to date, and think about marriage.

MISC.

It's a Wonderful Life

There's a reason so many are taken with George Bailey in the holiday classic *It's a Wonderful Life*. George spent his life putting off his dreams. He compromised everything to do what's right for *other* people to the point where he almost took his own life. But thankfully, George comes to realize he's had a rich, successful life all along. Like George, we make compromises in life, especially when we marry. Those compromises may make us feel resentful in the moment, but looked at later, those compromises helped make a wonderful life.

Marriage doesn't have to sidetrack or even cancel your goals. (If it did, none of us should get married!) But it might mean they must be amended. Do your goals "fit" both of you? Does your spouse support your goals, and do you support his? Have you made newer goals as a married couple?

These days, many marriages are composed of two career-driven individuals who sacrifice personal time and put a lot of energy into climbing the corporate ladder. However, if one of you is less focused on that climb, you may be in trouble if you start missing your spouse when she's always at the office or out of town on business. Worse, you might start resenting her for not doing her part around the house. But if your goals are complementary, or they're in sync with each other, these problems shouldn't arise.

It's great to have shared interests, leisure activities, and hobbies. Chances are, when you were dating, you figured out which of these you can share and what you need to pursue on your own. It's wonderful if you both love to ski; it makes planning a winter vacation easy. But you both don't need to love skiing to enjoy each other and have a great time on vacation. If you don't share your mate's passion for scuba diving and your idea of heaven is sitting on a pristine beach under an umbrella … Aloha! Still a great vacation. On the other hand, if the idea of a week-long yoga retreat makes you twitch or the thought of a casino with flashing lights and its bing, bing, bings gives you a headache, you'll need to talk about your vacation some more.

Some alone time can be good for a marriage, too. Time spent with your own interests can bring you back to the relationship refreshed and relaxed, having nurtured a personal part of yourself. If you love to paint or are an avid reader and if your partner builds scale models, no problem. The time you spend apart on your different activities can translate to quality time when you are together.

The Importance of Shared Values

Leisure activities, interests, and hobbies are one thing, but values are another. Values are our core beliefs and guiding principles, and they help ensure a marriage stays solid. They're what we think are truly important in life. Family, children, friendship, community, religion, or whatever we hold dear, these are the ideas and attitudes you should agree on as a couple. And if not 100 percent, you should at least give your spouse's values the same understanding and respect you want for yours.

For instance, Marcia thought education should be a life-long pursuit. Her husband, Ken, on the other hand, thought a good education was what one needed to get started on a career path. However, Ken understood Marcia's attitude and never resented her for it. In fact, he was actually proud his spouse was "always working on some sort of degree."

Marcia placed a high value on formal learning, and Ken didn't, but he respected how important it was for her. Not only that, Ken hoped their children would take after their mother when it came to education.

Compatible Views on Children

This one is almost a no-brainer. If one of you wants children but the other doesn't, I guarantee you will have problems down the road. True, life changes things. You both might start out never wanting children, especially if you marry young, but, say 8 years later, one of you wants to start a family while the other is still content to feel untethered. The result? A potential marriage-breaker, unless some sort of compromise is reached. (See Chapter 16 for more information on the issue of children.)

But let's say you both agree you'll have children. Maybe you agree three is the perfect number and you even agree that one boy and two girls would be spectacular. Perfect compatibility! Unfortunately, that's just the start.

After you decide on bringing a new life into the world, you and your mate must decide on how to go about raising that child. Of course, you want to raise a physically and mentally healthy baby, well-adjusted and confident, who will be equipped to cope with the world and lead a good life. But how do you do that?

Compatibility regarding children is not just about wanting children, or even how many, but agreeing—or compromising—on everything from affection to nutrition, from education to discipline.

Definition

Compatibility is what married couples hope to achieve. It's not necessarily agreeing on *everything,* but feeling comfortable with each other's values and goals, likes and dislikes.

A Similar Sense of Humor

Nineteenth-century wit Oscar Wilde once said, "Life is too important to be taken seriously." So don't waste your life worrying and fretting. Instead, live your life with a certain *joie de vivre,* or lightness and joy.

The same holds true with marriage. Lightness and joy can go far in making marriage last. In fact, according to a *Reader's Digest* survey of more than 1,000 couples, 47 percent of both husbands and wives valued humor as a real positive in their marriage.

Is this because they envision marriage as a lifetime of belly laughs and knock-knock jokes? Or is it that we know on a primal level that having a similar sense of humor—and the accompanying lightness and joy—is an ingredient in a successful marriage?

Two scenes in the Academy Award–winning movie *Annie Hall* help illustrate my point. In one, the lead characters cook lobster, with hysterical results. When the couple broke up, the man took another woman on a "lobster-cooking date," only to find that she thought the whole situation was stupid. She was definitely not amused. Those two scenes, identical except for the cast of characters, are so telling about the role of laughter in a marriage and how humor needs to be compatible in order for a relationship to last. (By the way, the reason the laughing couple broke up had nothing to do with humor.)

Humor is personal; it has to do with the way we were raised; our social, economic, ethnic, and religious background; and even our level of education. What we as individuals find funny encompasses our whole life experience and our personalities.

A sense of humor can be the number one coping device a person draws on during difficult times. It's crucial that a couple is able to share a laugh to relieve some of the stress of a situation. The couple in tune with each other's way of looking at the bumps is way ahead of the game—in both good times and bad.

The Best Medicine

MISC.

When you laugh, chemicals in the brain associated with well-being are released, reducing your stress levels and strengthening your immune system. Laughter has also been found to help reduce blood pressure, relieve tension, and bring you and your spouse closer together.

Religious Beliefs

The importance of religion in your marriage can become an issue if you are from different faiths or if one of you is more religious than the other.

Say you're from a Jewish household but you don't practice the religion. You don't keep a kosher home, and you don't go to temple. The man you love is Catholic, but he isn't religious either. Sounds like religion won't be too much of an issue when you marry, right?

Wrong. You may not feel religious now, but what about when you have a child? Will you want to raise that child as a Jew or a Catholic? Will it be important that your child is raised with some sort of faith?

Families can put a wedge in a marriage, too. If you're close with your parents, who go to temple during the High Holidays even if they're not religious, they might not be too pleased with you marrying a Catholic—and vice versa.

> **Love Letters**
>
> I once talked to a couple who were from different religions, and fights were already brewing among their families on where the marriage should take place. The couple found the perfect solution: they got married on the beach by a nondenominational minister (in this case, a licensed ethical culturist).

Religion can become a sore spot in a relationship, and it's important that you and your spouse discuss raising children, family values, and faith before you say "I do."

Lasting Marriage Territory

Elizabeth and George came to me so full of resentment for each other they couldn't even say "hello" without it provoking a fight. They had been married 14 years, but they were ready to call it quits. Coming to me was their last chance at saving their marriage.

Before we could fix the problem, we first had to determine what each one resented in the other. It turned out George had promised that once he finished law school and got a job, it would be Elizabeth's turn to stay home and write the novel she'd been dreaming of. But along the way, they had two children and life became very busy. Elizabeth no longer went to work, but she didn't have the time to write anything, let alone carve out any time to think.

Rather than discuss the situation with George, Elizabeth quietly built up resentment: "George never stays home with the kids." "I have to do everything." "He got to go to law school, but I never got my chance to write." "He reached his goal, but I never reached mine." George, on the other hand, couldn't understand why Elizabeth was so upset—he kept up his end of the bargain.

After several sessions, Elizabeth began to understand that she was the one preventing herself from reaching her goal. No one, including George, was stopping her from writing. George was willing to get a nanny and any household help Elizabeth needed to get her novel done. But Elizabeth had lost her ambition. Her goals had changed, but she hadn't realized it. She didn't want to write a novel anymore, but she'd spent so many years wishing for it she couldn't give it up.

The solution to Elizabeth and George's lasting marriage was re-evaluation. They both needed to re-evaluate their goals. Marriage is not made of stone. It's a flexible and malleable territory made up of many different elements.

An Evolving Definition of Love

Believe it or not, marrying for love wasn't always the main reason to tie the knot. For millennia, people more often married as a way to consolidate power or money. Today, though, love is the main reason we get married. We lust after each other; we want to spend time together; we want to share our lives together.

Unfortunately, that kind of love fades over time. But it's replaced with a different definition of love, one that's just as profound as time goes by.

MISC.

Saturday Night Fever

Saturday was just another day until the Roaring Twenties, when date night on Saturdays became the newest craze. It was a way to get away from the family and have some fun. In fact, many Americans were afraid dating was becoming so popular marriage would become extinct.

Change Is Part of the Equation

"The only thing we can be sure of in life is change." It may be a cliché, but it doesn't make it less true. Change is constant, and unless you're flexible, it can blindside you.

Love takes on a new guise with every marriage milestone. During the first years, everything is new, and your love is passion and lust. Over the next 10 years, babies come and life shifts. During this time, your intimacy deepens. Up to 25 years into your marriage, you work on settling in and establishing routines. Closeness becomes more important than sex. Finally, during your golden years, you grow old together, best friends.

Yes, love changes over the years, but as I've learned over my years as a marriage counselor, it's still profound at any stage.

Realistic Expectations

The old saw about the knight in shining armor who sweeps you away on his white horse might still have a home in romance novels, but most of us know it's more make-believe than reality. In today's world, few women want to be saved—they can save themselves, thank you very much. But there's still a vestige of hope in the words "happily ever after." We want—and need—to believe we'll be happy with our spouse. Otherwise, we wouldn't be getting married!

However, wanting a long-lasting marriage is different from living in a fantasy. Many marriage counselors believe that overblown expectations can cause unhappiness, and that a marriage has a better chance of making it if both parties have a more realistic view of who they've married.

It sounds logical: less expectation equals less disappointment. But researchers have found this isn't true. Dr. Donald Baucom put this equation to the test in his studies at the University of North Carolina. He found that those couples who had the highest expectations of each other also had the happier marriages!

I've found this to be true in my work as well. When a couple's standards for each other are high, they help each other meet those standards; they bolster each other when things get tough. On the other hand, those couples who have lower standards tend to let things slide; they end up ignoring or denying a problem because they don't expect anything else.

Marriage Trap	High expectations are one thing, but they do have to be realistic. If your husband doesn't have a head for numbers, don't expect him to become a CEO. Similarly, if your wife doesn't like motorcycles, don't expect her to jump for joy when you buy her one for her birthday.

This might sound counterintuitive, but think about it. If you have low expectations in your marriage, down the road you'll end up feeling bitter and unsatisfied. But those couples with high expectations refuse to let life bring them down. Like the "Unsinkable Molly Brown" on the *Titanic*, they won't give up—in life or in their marriage. If there's a problem, they won't shove it under the rug for long. It will be discussed, aired, and solved. These couples have marriages that last.

Expectations are often based on your parents' marriage. If they had a good marriage, you'll expect a happy one yourself. If they fought a lot and barely seemed to talk, you might not even want to get married in the first place!

Lasting Marriages Take Work

It's true that a happy marriage requires work from both spouses, but it's not the kind of work you hate to set your alarm clock for. It's not like washing the dishes or taking out the trash. The work you do to sustain your marriage should not be labor-intensive. In fact, sometimes you won't even realize you're "working" on it.

But just as you give certain hours to your job, your children, or your chores, it's a good idea for both of you to take some time, a half hour every week, or even every other week, to take your "marriage temperature."

Let's review an exercise I use in my practice. Rate the statements on a scale of 1 to 5. It's good if you both want to answer them, but don't force your spouse. Just ask. Your results alone will show you if you have a problem that needs to be addressed or if life in your marriage is good. And be honest when you answer—that's one of the foundations of a good marriage!

1. My partner is judgmental.
   (very little) 1 2 3 4 5 (a great deal)

2. My partner has a valid point of view.
   (often) 1 2 3 4 5 (rarely)

3. My partner is my friend.
   (true) 1 2 3 4 5 (not true)

4. I consider my partner's point of view.
   (often) 1 2 3 4 5 (rarely)

5. My partner tells me when she feels close to me.
   (often) 1 2 3 4 5 (rarely)

6. My partner knows what's really important to me.
   (true) 1 2 3 4 5 (not true)

7. I understand what's really important to my partner.
   (true) 1 2 3 4 5 (not true)

8. My partner is interested in things that are important to me.
   (true) 1 2 3 4 5 (not true)

9. My partner sees my positive qualities.
   (true) 1 2 3 4 5 (not true)

10. I think about my partner's good qualities often.
    (true) 1 2 3 4 5 (not true)

11. My partner tells me how much he cares for me.
    (true) 1 2 3 4 5 (not true)

12. I tell my partner how much I care about him.
    (true) 1 2 3 4 5 (not true)

13. I trust my partner.
    (true) 1 2 3 4 5 (not true)

14. My partner and I share the same goals for our future.
    (true) 1 2 3 4 5 (not true)

Now add up your score:

26 or less: Your relationship is strong.

27 to 36: Your relationship has some problem areas.

37 or more: Your relationship needs a lot of work.

If you have 37 or more as your score, don't despair. It just means you really need to dig in and focus on your marriage. Get to know your partner. Talk. When you discover you have problems, it's best to deal with them as soon as possible. This book will help!

Essential Takeaways

- Complementary values don't mean exactly the same, but rather values you can both respect.
- It's important for you both to agree on raising a family.
- The definition of love changes as your marriage grows.
- High expectations can make your marriage stronger as you help each other reach your goals.

chapter 2

Here Come the Bumps

Dealing with changing world views

The impact of financial troubles

In-law intrusions

Potential marriage roadblocks

Think back to those first few months of wedded bliss: first your wedding day—the beautiful ceremony, the champagne, the dancing, the joy! And it didn't stop with the wedding. The glorious honeymoon, just you and your beloved, with no cares in the world. Reliving it all while looking through photographs. The dinner parties for your friends and families with your new china and crystal. Oh the glow!

You might have spent an entire year planning your wedding, deciding on the cake, the guest list, and the decorations. And now it's over. The honeymoon tan has faded, everyone has seen your photos, and you're now sharing a bathroom, a bed, a life, with the person you married.

Now comes the serious part: life together.

Challenges Over Time

Online dating services ask specific questions to help you find your perfect match, ranging from your looks to your hobbies to the things you find important in a relationship. But where are the "what ifs"? What if your husband was laid off from his job? What if you became chronically ill? What if you couldn't get pregnant? And on and on.

I'm not saying these "what ifs" will happen to you and your spouse, but they are real situations and do come up in many marriages. Sometimes they can even happen during the first year. These are scenarios we're often ill-prepared to handle.

As the song says, "Into every life a little rain must fall," but being forearmed is being forewarned. Some of the following situations may have already occurred in your marriage, or they might never happen. But each can be a potential roadblock that needs to be dealt with.

Financial Ups and Downs

If we've learned anything in the last few years, it's that financial situations can and do change. The loss of a job, a business, or nest-egg investments can shake us to the core and put tremendous stress on even the best marriage.

Why? For one, anger. All that hard work, frugality, sacrifice, and planning—out the window! There's also fear. In less than a heartbeat, your financial situation can change and put you in a place of uncertainty and insecurity. Where will you go? What will you do?

> **Marriage Trap**
>
> The problem with money—and the lack thereof—is that money is more than the material goods and services it can provide. Money has an emotional component that goes to our very core needs: security, power, and freedom. Couples need to recognize that when they're fighting about money, it's much deeper than whether or not they can afford to take a summer vacation.

But the financial problems most couples face in their daily lives are less dramatic than losing a home or a retirement fund. For most couples, it's deciding what to spend money on and when. (See Chapter 17 for the potential problems money can create and Chapter 21 for the more dramatic financial sea changes that befall some marriages.)

Philip and Barbara weren't wealthy, but over the years they'd saved enough for their daughter to go to a good college of her choice. When the housing market dropped, Philip saw it as an opportunity to buy their dream retirement home by a lake, but they'd have to dip into their daughter's college fund to afford it. In Philip's mind, the problem was easily solvable: their daughter could go to a cheaper state school for a year or two and transfer to an Ivy League university for her junior and senior years.

Barbara had a very different take on the situation: she didn't want her daughter to have to settle. She wanted her daughter to experience college life from start to finish on a single campus. How could Philip be so selfish?

The problem seemed like an easy one to fix. Barbara had been a licensed nurse and could easily go back to work. Together, they'd make enough to have their dream house and the best school money could buy for their daughter.

But the situation was complicated by the fact that Barbara's mother lived with them and needed around-the-clock care. To save money, Barbara had been handling the nursing herself. If she went back to work, they'd have to pay someone, which would take most of Barbara's weekly salary.

When they came to see me, they'd been arguing so much they were concerned their marriage was going to end up in divorce. I helped them find a compromise in a calm and logical fashion: Barbara would go back to work, but only part time so she could still help her mother. Philip would talk to his boss about working at home two days a week so he, too, could pitch in. This would cut the need for home health care drastically, and their daughter would be able to go to the college of her choice. In a year or two, the extra money coming in would help buy the house of their dreams.

Love Letters	Is it better to be broke and together or broke and divorced? Being broke can be fixed, even though it may seem improbable or almost impossible from where you're sitting now. But if money breaks up your marriage, it isn't as easy to fix. Besides, being a team can help you solve your financial problems in a more objective—and supportive—way.

You can't always predict financial ups and downs, but working on the problem together can help you weather the storm.

Declining Health

"In sickness or in health"—it's such an important component in a good marriage, it's part of the marital ceremony. But when you're reciting your vows, smiling at your soon-to-be spouse, the last thing you're thinking about is the possibility you might get cancer or she might die.

In most cases, health doesn't become an issue until later in the marriage as couples approach middle age. But whether it's you or your spouse with a chronic disease and declining health, it's important to realize that the disease happens to *both* of you. Both of you are affected.

A temporary health crisis is one thing. It's easier to be supportive to your spouse if the situation has a finite end, when you see her healing and becoming her old self. But what if, God forbid, she has a stroke that leaves her paralyzed or cognitively impaired? You'll love her, of course, but you'll also go through myriad emotions—all of which are normal and all of which can be successfully handled. But what if she develops a condition that results in continuously declining health? That's another matter.

Two decades ago, psychologist Elisabeth Kübler-Ross came up with her now-classic six stages of grief when handed a diagnosis of cancer. She was talking about the actual person with cancer, but it could easily apply to his or her spouse:

Stage 1—denial. Shock on hearing the news; it's unreal.

Stage 2—anger. The initial "why me?" shock leads to rage at the situation.

Stage 3—bargaining. If I pray really hard and promise to be a better person, the condition will go away. If I can just have 5 more good years, I'll leave my life savings to charity.

Stage 4—depression. Reality sets in; life will never be the same. This is the way it is, and this is how I will feel to the end.

Stage 5—acceptance. When the rage and sadness dissipate, you can begin to be rational, see things the way they really are, and integrate the situation into your life experience.

Stage 6—hope. Not "pretend" hope that things will be different, but hope that, together, you and your spouse can enjoy the life you have now.

These stages can happen as a progression, with a clear ending of one and beginning of another, but they don't necessarily have to. A person can skip a stage, or not experience one at all, while another person may get stuck on an emotion and not seem able to move on. Whatever the experience, a counselor can help.

A Shifting View of the World

It's a fact of life: people change. You both might begin your marriage with the romantic notion that you can easily live in a world without much money. After all, how perfect does living in a studio apartment and cuddling up at night with Chinese takeout sound?

But the idea of that studio apartment gets old really fast—especially when you factor in kids. If you both change your life philosophy, that's fine. But what if your husband is still content to live in the studio apartment because it's in the heart of the city while you're ready to pack up and move to the suburbs? This may spell trouble.

Politics. Money. Living arrangements. Career. All these can be potential marriage hot spots, but as long as your fundamental values remain the same—your sense of integrity, your respect for each other, and your honesty—there should be no problem getting through these issues.

As your world views change, however, it's important to discuss them with your spouse. Opposites may continue to attract, but they need a smooth landing to connect.

The In-Laws

There's an old joke, "Take my wife … please!" In reality, as married life settles in, the joke could change to, "Take my wife *and* my mother-in-law … please!"

Although we live in modern times wherein men and women have pretty much the same opportunities and goals, the mother-in-law situation is still very much woman versus woman. As I've found in my practice over and over again, wives and mothers battle over their husband and son, respectively—sometimes unconsciously, sometimes very much on the surface in a screaming match.

Aaron's mother seemed like the perfect mother-in-law. She embraced Jill from the get-go and was excited about having "the daughter she never had." Jill even boasted to her friends that her mother-in-law was a gem and she loved her very much.

But things changed when Jill and Aaron had their first child. All of a sudden, Aaron's mother started calling three or four times a day. She made up excuses to come to the house and play with her grandchild. She kept telling Jill and Aaron "to go out to dinner, have fun, go away. I'll watch the baby."

Sounds perfect: a built-in babysitter you don't have to pay. Unfortunately, the cost was even higher than an hourly rate. Aaron's mom started to complain about Jill to Aaron when she wasn't home. She told him she noticed that the baby needed more face time or that Jill was too lenient—anything and everything that portrayed Jill as a poor parent.

Aaron was stuck in the middle, torn between his love and loyalty to his wife and to his mother. When he told Jill what his mother said, she went ballistic. Aaron found himself playing referee. He was miserable—and so were his wife and his mother.

MISC.

We-Ness

Psychologist John Gottman, Ph.D., has studied couples for years in his Seattle, Washington, "Love Laboratory." Gottman coined the word "we-ness" when it came to in-law issues. He told the couples who participated in his studies that the husband must side with the wife. He can be nice about it, but as cold and as harsh as it sounds, his wife comes first.

How did Aaron and Jill handle their problem? Simple. Aaron told his mother he didn't want to hear any complaints. He loved her, but he had his own family now. It made his mother cry a little, but today, all five of them—yes, Jill and Aaron had another baby!—get along great.

Personal Habits: Too Much Sharing?

When you were first dating, you were at your best. Your soon-to-be spouse never saw you on the toilet; no unshaved legs were ever spied. Dirty socks piling up to towerlike heights or the candy wrappers and plates migrating to under the bed were nonexistent when the other was around.

But once you get married, things change. You might still keep the bathroom door closed, but both of you will see each other's personal habits up-close and personal, and it might not be nice. Not to mention what it can do to romance!

Marriage Trap

It's true that you may not know certain things about your partner until you live under the same roof. That's when you discover you hate the way he doesn't put the cap on the toothpaste—ever! Or when he discovers you take up the whole bed when you're in a deep sleep. These, of course, are little things, but they can blow up if you don't talk about them, minimize them, and laugh at them.

I suggest to my clients that they make an attempt to look good in front of each other. That doesn't mean full makeup and suit and tie, but a little effort in personal hygiene—and bathroom privacy—can go a long way in keeping romance alive.

Rumblings in Paradise?

It's easy to spot trouble when the drama is high. A huge fight, a few days of silence, a nasty remark, one partner staying out late—alone, these are all signs a marriage is in trouble.

But wouldn't it be so much better if the trouble was caught and dealt with in the early stages? You don't want to "fix it if it's not broken" as the saying goes, but you don't want to wait until the roof falls in to patch up the leaks.

It's best if you locate those marriage land mines before they blow up. The following sections offer some advice on treading carefully and de-activating the problem before it gets worse.

Silent Days and Nights

Here's a common thread between husbands and wives I frequently find in my practice: silence. But the term *silent treatment* is arbitrary. One of you may feel all alone and isolated, while the other is happily doing her thing, thinking all is well.

Don and Rhoda, for example, have a wide discrepancy on what the term means. Rhoda feels like she is alone and on her own. She gets up before her husband because she has a long commute to her advertising job. She gets home before her husband and is busy most evenings helping their young daughter with her homework and catching up on personal correspondence. Don is a corporate executive and travels quite a bit. When Don comes back from a trip or when he comes home after a hard day at work, he is happy to see Rhoda. The first thing he wants to do is hang out with Rhoda, and he's filled with anticipation until his daughter falls asleep.

But Rhoda is in a very different place. She rejects him constantly; she's too tired, she has a headache, she has to get some work done. Don's resentment begins to build. "What's wrong with her?" he asked me one visit. "Most wives would be wildly happy their husband finds them attractive!"

Rhoda, on the other hand, feels like a single girl with none of the perks. She and Don don't talk—they rarely even see each other!

I suggested they try synching their weekends and break the silence by asking what the other one wants—but not defensively. This will spark a conversation.

Churning Emotions

Although we get gray hair and age spots, when you get angry at your spouse, the 4-year-old in you comes out. "I want this!" "It's not fair!" "It's all your fault!" Sound familiar?

One of the biggest signs these churning emotions will eventually explode, possibly ending in divorce, is if you never argue or disagree. Most couples disagree to a certain extent. But not reacting to conflict or participating in a discussion is a sign of emotional check-out.

Marriage
Trap

Waiting for tomorrow quickly becomes today. Avoiding reality won't stop a problem from happening. You can't stop a pencil from falling to the ground if you let go. You won't make the calendar turn the pages any slower. Deal with any current issues in the present—today.

Denial

Agreeing to disagree—I can't tell you how often I've heard this when a new couple comes into my office. They think this is a positive thing; they accept that they're two adults who have their own opinions and everything's okay.

In reality, these couples are simply pushing their problems under the rug—until they can't anymore. Instead of agreeing to disagree, they're avoiding any conflict. They aren't talking about their problems because they're afraid it will lead to a huge fight, they'll end up in a nasty tie, or both.

Don't get me wrong—when you're in the midst of a life crisis, pushing away negative thoughts can help you cope and get past it. But most of the time, denial is problematic. By not discussing your problems, the distance between the two of you gets wider, and the more alone you may feel. Air your differences and talk about the situation—and then you can agree to disagree.

Too Many Excuses

Talking too much is as bad as talking too little. If you find your spouse constantly making excuses for, say, not doing the laundry, not changing a diaper, or not having sex, you may be headed for trouble.

Everyone can be excused, and oftentimes those excuses are legitimate. But if your spouse is using excuses over and over again, you need to address the underlying reasons—together. (Learn about rebuilding a strong relationship in Part 3.)

Essential Takeaways

- Denying a problem will just make it a bigger problem later on.
- Respect each other's boundaries.
- Life will bring change. The way you handle this will make your marriage stronger—or weaker.
- Some of the early danger signs in a marriage are silence, denial, and unreleased resentment.

chapter 3

The Myths and Realities of Marriage

Marriage myths debunked

Marriage barometer quiz

Problem-solving as a couple

For some of us, the idea of marital bliss has been partly concocted by the media. When we see a couple fall in love and marry on the big screen, we dream that one day, we, too, will find our true love, marry, and live happily ever after, married for a lifetime, like those characters. Or we may look at the couple, glowing with love, and think, *What's wrong with me? Why can't my life be like that?*

The problem is, the version of marriage most often depicted in movies is completely idealized. Think about it: Why is it that in the movies a character can always get a parking spot, at midday, in front of their favorite coffee shop on a busy city street? Or how come even twenty-somethings, waiting tables and going on auditions, live in huge, beautifully decorated apartments? Because it's the movies, where life is easier and less drab, everyone is attractive, and when people fall in love, it's with a capital L and marriages last forever.

Even though part of you knows what you're watching is fiction, another part might yearn for the fantasy on the screen to be real, especially the love and marriage part. But fantasies can get in the way of real happiness; by separating myth from reality, you can avoid disappointment and grief and move toward a relationship that can bring you real joy.

Marriage Myths

The following sections highlight marriage myths that have been around for decades. However, they're not true, and they can undermine a marriage that, in reality, is doing just fine.

Myth: A Lack of Sex Means a Lack of Love

As we all know, sex can be an expression of love, but sex does not *mean* love. And just because the raging flames have changed to smoldering embers doesn't mean the fire has gone out. It's physically impossible to have the same libido you had when you were 17 and making out in the backseat of a car when you're twice or three times that age. If "twice a night" has turned into "twice a week" and eventually "twice a month," it really isn't cause for concern if you or your partner don't feel deprived.

Sex is important in marriage, but it's not the definitive test of a good marriage. It's the intimacy that counts. Touching, hugging, holding hands— these all contribute to physical closeness.

However, if you haven't had sex in say, over a year, it may mean a real psychological or even physical problem. It's important to speak to your doctor. Don't be embarrassed; he or she has heard it all.

Myth: The Odds Are Stacked Against You

We've all heard the divorce rates: 50 percent of all marriages … 60 percent of all marriages …. These statistics can be shocking. An article in *Newsweek* in the mid-1980s, for example, stated women over 40 were more likely to die in a terrorist attack than get married.

Happily, this is the twenty-first century and the news is good. In a January 2010 article, *The New York Times* reported that 86 percent of women over 40 who'd gone to college remained married in 2008—and college-educated women were most likely to stay married. A 2010 Reuters survey found that approximately 75 percent of all marriages between men and women over 26 years old last at least 10 years. In other words, lasting marriages are not a dying breed!

Myth: Men and Women Are from Different Planets

Although men and women do think differently about certain things, they basically connect on a very primal level. John Gottman, in his ground-breaking research on married couples, found that both 70 percent of men and 70 percent of women agreed on the importance of friendship above all else in their relationship—above passion, sex, and romance. There are differences, of course, in genders, but they don't create marital strife.

Love Letters	We live in an age when being pulled in all directions is the norm. Even sex can become a chore, something else you "should" do. Try to keep sex playful. You don't have to go all out with a romantic, candlelit dinner. A 10-minute quickie can be fun, too.

Myth: If Someone Has an Affair, the Marriage Is Over

False. You might not believe this if your spouse has cheated on you, but the truth is, an affair by itself doesn't destroy your marriage. Researchers have found that only 20 to 25 percent of divorces are caused by infidelity and, even more importantly, 75 to 80 percent of couples stay together after the affair is over.

The real reason people get divorced is that they feel distant from one another and don't know how to reconnect. They feel ignored by their partner and not cared about; they feel angry and don't know what to do with their strong feelings. They feel so alienated, they end their relationship.

Myth: Never Go to Bed Angry

Sure, no one wants to go to sleep upset. Not only will you have a poor night's sleep, but being tired can make you extra cranky and fuel your anger the next morning.

But if you are genuinely angry, "kissing and making up" won't work; it will be a lie, which can make you even angrier! Instead, give yourself the night to think of all the positive things you love about your spouse. Tabling your fight until the next day may also bring you more perspective on the problem at hand.

Too angry to sleep next to each other? Someone hit the sofa!

Myth: A Baby Will Make Things Better

True, a baby seals the bond between husband and wife, and the moment you see this little miracle, all is forgiven. You are a family and love begins anew … until the first night the baby cries.

Children bring added responsibility and added pressure. Hopefully, the joy you get from them supersedes all that, but the fact does remain that your priorities—and goals—change. Never have a baby to save your marriage. It just won't work.

Myth: Mental Problems Can Erode a Marriage

Wrong. Over time, mental problems and neurotic behavior can add pressure to your marriage if one of you is *clinically depressed* or *bipolar* and doesn't seek help. But the "seeking help" part of that sentence is what's key. It's the recognition that something is wrong and the willingness to do something about it.

> Definition
>
> **Clinical depression** is different from the normal ups and downs people go through in life. It's a chemical imbalance in the brain that can make a person feel helpless and hopeless to the point where he or she can't get out of bed. **Bipolar** is a mental disorder caused by chemical imbalances in the brain. Here, a person swings from being very manic (spending money, not sleeping, "over the top") to very depressed.

We all have our eccentricities and peculiarities. The question is not that both of you are "normal" but that both of your neuroses connect.

Myth: Common Interests Are the Key to a Lasting Marriage

Common interests are great—it's most likely one of the things that brought you together. And isn't it nice not to have to *drag* your spouse kicking and screaming to a ballet or a ball game? But common interests alone won't make your marriage last.

Let's say you both love baseball but your husband loves to wear face paint and hold up signs. You, on the other hand, find that embarrassing. You just want to cheer on your team, eat hot dogs, and enjoy the day. In fact, you're so humiliated by your husband's behavior you won't even sit next to him.

So you both might want to see the Red Sox beat the Pirates, but to say your common interest brings you closer is a stretch. It's not just the common interest; it's the way you view the common interest that counts.

Myth: A Lasting Marriage Is All About Quid Pro Quo

Many couples treat marriage like ongoing negotiations. "I'll do this for you if you'll do that for me." But happy marriages are about compromises, not negotiations.

A perfect example of this comes from Susan and Todd, a couple who'd come to see me. Todd loved his wife and wanted to give her something really special to show it. So he bought her a $54,000 BMW. Talk about generosity! Susan was delighted, and Todd figured he got a free pass for the next decade. But two weeks later, Todd asked Susan to plan a weekend to entertain some of his friends he hadn't seen in a while, and she said no. Her back was acting up again, she was frazzled from her work, and the kids were driving her crazy. She asked Todd if his friends could stay in a hotel. Todd went ballistic: didn't he just buy Susan an expensive car?

They were headed for real trouble, but with my help, they worked out a compromise. Todd would postpone his invitation to his friends for a few weeks until Susan felt she could take on the role of gracious hostess.

Myth: Too Many Fights Mean the Marriage Is In Trouble

Actually, it's not the number of fights, but the *way* you fight. You need to air your differences, but there's a way to do it that won't cause irrevocable damage. (See Chapter 12 for more on fighting.)

MISC.

The Exception to the Rule

Each of my clients is an individual, and there's no "one size fits all" answer. Each must recognize his or her individuality even while they work on their marriage. Saul and Jessica, for example, never fought. When one or the other was angry, they'd each do separate things. Saul would take the dogs for a walk, and Jessica would go upstairs and read a book. They both created their own time and space to calm down and sort out their feelings. Eventually, they'd discuss the problem that caused the anger, but this time they discussed it without the emotion. This "backing off" technique wouldn't work for everyone, but it's been successful for Saul and Jessica—they've been married 45 years!

How Strong Is Your Marriage?

Before you can see where you need to improve your marriage to make it last, you need to recognize its strengths. The following Relationship Satisfaction Scale (RSS) is a questionnaire I developed for my initial session with a new couple. Using it honestly helps you find the positives in your lives together so you can tackle the negatives in the most constructive way.

If both of you want to take the test, so much the better. Be sure to openly discuss your answers.

The Relationship Satisfaction Scale

Part 1:

Read the following statements, and rate how accurately each statement describes how you're feeling on a scale of 1 to 5, where 1 means "strongly agree," 2 means "somewhat agree," 3 means "don't know," 4 means "somewhat disagree," and 5 means "strongly disagree."

   1. I feel heard and understood by my partner.

   2. I feel respected by my partner.

3. I like my spouse.

4. We deal with issues well.

5. The relationship is right for me.

Repeat this exercise, this time thinking about how your partner would respond to each statement. Use the same scale: 1 (strongly agree), 2 (somewhat agree), 3 (don't know), 4 (somewhat disagree), or 5 (strongly disagree).

This is a good exercise to return to occasionally to see how you're coming along. Each time, rate your progress and make a note of any changes and/or insights you find.

Part 2:

Part 2 gives you a deeper look into your relationship so you can gain further insight into how you're feeling about your partner and your relationship.

Read each of the following statements, and note how each statement best fits how you feel based on a scale of 1 to 5, where 1 means "strongly agree," 2 means "somewhat agree," 3 means "don't know," 4 means "somewhat disagree," and 5 means "strongly disagree."

1. Knowing what I know now, I would have a relationship with my partner.

2. I like my partner.

3. I trust my partner.

4. I seek out my partner's opinion.

5. I'm ready to do what I need to do to create a lasting relationship.

Add up your total: _____

Repeat this exercise, this time thinking about how your partner would respond to each statement. Use the same scale: 1 (strongly agree), 2 (somewhat agree), 3 (don't know), 4 (somewhat disagree), or 5 (strongly disagree).

Add up your partner's total: _____

Your and your partner's combined total: _____

Now let's look at what the numbers mean: If you had …

> 17 or higher: your marriage is well on its way to being a lasting one.
>
> 12 to 16: your marriage is still in sync, but utilizing the information in this book will help it get stronger.
>
> 8 to 15: make time for you and your partner to discuss any issues using the guidelines in this book.
>
> 7 or less: you and your partner might want to get professional help to really work on your marriage.

Part 3:

Your ultimate goal is to ensure your marriage is an enduring one, but you first need to define what you consider are the qualities of a good marriage so you know what you're working toward. Many people have never really taken the time to think about the qualities they'd like in a relationship. Take a few minutes to think about the kind of partnership you'd like and the qualities important to you.

The following list identifies specific qualities I believe make up a good relationship. Take a look at them, and compare them to your own list. Add any additional ones from your list. When you're satisfied you've listed the qualities of a lasting marriage that are important to you, rate them on a scale of 1 (not at all important) to 5 (very important). Do *not* rate the level of satisfaction you're feeling with each quality, only how important that quality is to you.

The Qualities of a Good Relationship

1. Open lines of communication

2. Feeling supported

3. Bringing valuable insights

4. Balancing personal welfare and the relationship's welfare

5. Trustworthiness

6. Personal resilience

7. Bringing optimism to the table

8. Flexibility

9. Being caring

10. Setting a positive tone for the relationship

Now go back and redo this exercise, rating each quality for how you think your partner would respond.

Filling out the RSS should give you a good idea of how you feel about your marriage. By seeing in black and white what you've identified as important to you—and what you think is important to your partner—helps you use the material in this book to its fullest potential. If your partner has been willing to also go over the RSS, it's an even better jumping-off place for discussion. That is exactly how I use it with my new clients.

Finding Solutions Together

Building an enduring relationship is more than filling out a form, of course, but it gets you thinking. So often, many of my clients haven't really thought about what they really want out of the relationship. They've only considered what they're feeling now.

Even if your spouse isn't willing to fill out a questionnaire, you can still set aside time during the week to talk about your hopes and plans. It's important for both of you. (See Part 3 for strategies for creating a lasting marriage.)

Essential Takeaways

- Real marriage is very different from the fictionalized depictions on television and in the movies.
- There's no "norm" for a good marriage, just what you both want from it.
- Understanding what you want from your marriage can help you better identify the areas you need to work on with your spouse.
- The Relationship Satisfaction Scale gives you and your spouse a solid jumping-off point for discussing what you need to work on— together.

Part 2

The Four Stages of Lasting Marriage

When you think of your marriage, it's usually broken up into "before kids" and "after kids" sections. You probably think of your marriage as the early years, the parental years, and the senior years.

In reality, marriage is much more fluid, and there's no hard-and-fast start or stop on its journey. My 35 years of experience as a marriage counselor has helped me formulate four stages every good marriage goes through. There are no set time limits for any of them, but all good marriages experience these stages in some form or another.

I call these four stages "The Honeymoon Days (and Nights!)," "Settling In," "Facing Life's Challenges," and "Growing Old Together." In Part 2, you discover some interesting insights into each of these four stages—one or two you most likely have experienced, the one you're living through right now, and the one or two stages yet to come. By understanding more about the different stages marriages go through, you can help make your marriage a solid one.

chapter 4

Stage 1: The Honeymoon Days (and Nights!)

Love and lust forever

Separation anxiety

Getting to know you

Fighting and forgiving

There's nothing so heady, so exhilarating, and so dramatic as the weeks leading up to the wedding, the wedding itself, and the honeymoon. Even if you had to postpone your honeymoon for financial, work, or education reasons, you're still probably awash in the glow of the "honeymoon phase" of love. You hold hands. You kiss in public. You call or text each other several times a day. You can't bear to be apart.

Who would ever doubt that this marriage will last forever? Who doesn't get married thinking, *This marriage will be the exception to the D word—divorce. He (or she) is my soul mate, and I will love him (or her) until the day I die.*

The First Few Months

You're just back from your honeymoon, fresh from that wonderful week of being alone together, enjoying being husband and wife, filling your days and nights with each other, and making love whenever you want. Now you're back in the real world again.

If you've been co-habitating and you've already staked out your side of the medicine cabinet, returning from the honeymoon simply means you go home, unpack, make some calls to share your fabulous trip with your friends and family, and go back to the way things were. You prepare to resume your life.

If you've put off the moving-in-together part until after the wedding and honeymoon, you're now faced with the monumental task of getting your new household in order.

But whether back to a routine or starting a new one, the upshot is you're starting a new life as a married couple.

Ain't Love Grand

When you first get married, you're hopeful, full of passion, walking around with stars in your eyes. The sex is good, and there's plenty of it. This doesn't happen for all couples, but generally, this strong attraction stage is laced with thinking about and wanting to be with your new love.

During these first few months, you'll most likely want to share your memories of your wedding and honeymoon, making friends and families sit through slide shows and browse through albums. You'll want to show off your home and entertain with all the new gifts you received.

Face Time

Friends and families of couples today: consider yourselves lucky! Thanks to Snapfish, you no longer need to spend the better part of a dinner party looking at photos of a newlywed's trip to Hawaii. You can choose to browse through their uploaded pictures at your own time and place.

Passion and Romance

If only life could remain a chain of lustful weekends with nary a worry in the world!

That's what Jo and Henry believed. When they married 12 years ago, they both declared this was the happiest they had ever been in their lives. As Jo told me when they began couples therapy, "It was like the stars were aligned. Everything was perfect. And I was so happy I felt giddy."

It was very difficult for them to go back to work after the honeymoon. They wanted to stay in bed forever, forgetting everything and everyone except themselves. But they needed to pay their rent, and life had to go on.

"I felt like my right arm was torn off," Jo said. "I called Henry like 10 times a day." And vice versa. Henry would call and tell Jo he loved her. He'd put sexy notes in her briefcase the night before. If they'd been newlyweds today, their text message bills would be off the charts.

Henry and Jo wanted to recapture those days. They didn't realize that the *honeymoon stage* is just that—a stage. As life goes on, other stages come into play. These other roles aren't necessarily worse, just different. I explained that passion and romance evolves, and that just as their bodies age, so does their marriage mature.

Definition	The **honeymoon stage** is those first few months of marriage, before routines become boring and sex is still hot. It's when marriage is more consumed by fantasy than reality.

A Strong Attraction

I always say that the reason puppies are so cute is to make training them easier. Without the adorableness factor, no one would want to go through the frustration of training. I'm not equating marriage to dogs, but if a couple saw the reality of married life without the rose-colored lenses, they might not want to tie the knot.

Is this a wonderful period? Yes. And for more reasons than lust. Here are some of the reasons why those first few months are so perfect:

- You present your very best self, and vice versa. You want to show your spouse how wonderful you are, and part of that means keeping your dirty little habits private.

- Your spouse is idealized. For now, your souls are united. Your spouse is perfect and wonderful, and you are the luckiest man or woman in the world.

- Conflict is only a blip on the life together radar. Your husband wants Chinese. You want Italian. Who cares! Whatever makes the other one happy is the end goal.

- Fighting becomes foreplay. As you yell at each other, cry, or slam doors, one look or one half-smile, and all is forgiven—and all end up in bed.

- Routines are novelties. The day-to-day chores are brand new. Making dinner is so much fun. Going grocery shopping together is high entertainment. Cleaning is exciting … and all end up in bed again.

It's easy to see why these first few months are special in a relationship!

"I Hate to Say Good-Bye"

I remember a story Ellen, one of my clients, told me: she and her husband, Dan, had been married a few months when he was relocated to Maryland from New Jersey. Unfortunately, Ellen had to remain behind until she could find a new job. She went to Maryland with Dan to help set up an apartment, but much too soon it was time to say good-bye. It was painful, and they missed each other before they'd even separated. In fact, they hated saying good-bye so much, Dan got on the train with Ellen. They were embracing each other so tightly they didn't realize the train had already left the station.

But there's another type of "good-bye" that's not about physical separation. Take the story of Joanne and Bob, for example. They had been together for 23 years. They'd come to see me when they were having troubles with their adult child. They found themselves arguing a lot, and there was a lot of tension at home.

What Joanne and Bob didn't realize in all these years was that they hadn't let go of the idealization of the other. They couldn't say "good-bye" to the unconscious belief that they could save each other. Joanne wanted Bob to be like her father before he died—to take command of the situation and make everything all right. Bob, on the other hand, wanted to be nurtured, something he never got from his mother. He wanted Joanne to make everything all right with a kiss and some soup. It sounds like a cliché, but the truth is that couples do think, down deep, that the person they marry will heal old wounds and, for the first time, they truly will be safe.

Great Sex—and Lots of It!

In the honeymoon stage, sex is wonderful and you can't keep your hands off each other. Part of why sex is so exciting during this time is because you can explore things together. After you're married, there's an unwritten "safety" in your relationship. Inhibitions can roam free because you are a couple. You can experiment and have fun.

Part of the reason for all that delicious sex is chemical, more specifically a chemical in the brain called *dopamine* that's responsible for experiencing pleasure—and increasing sexual drive. In other words, the more dopamine, the more you'll want sex and the more pleasure you'll get out of it.

Dopamine levels can stay high for several months after a marriage, but eventually things simmer down a little bit. Part of that is getting back to your real life. You can no longer just hang out in bed listening to the ocean outside your hotel room. You have to get up in the morning, get dressed, and go about your day. But even with time restrictions, you'll still look and feel great—and want sex a lot. You might not be having sex four times a day, but you're still attracted to each other.

Definition	**Dopamine** is one of the chemicals in the brain responsible for pleasure. The more dopamine, the better you feel, and the more you'll want sex.

Idealizing Your Mate

It's natural during these months of domestic bliss to put all your hopes and dreams on the other person, to believe, at last, you have found someone who loves you for who you are. In fact, you want to believe so much that the person you married is right for you that you'll forgive any erosion of that perfect ideal. If your husband withdraws occasionally, so what? He loves you! If he didn't tell you how beautiful you looked before you went to that party, so what? You know he thinks you're gorgeous!

Feeling you found your perfect mate is part of the enchantment of marriage. And it isn't a bad thing! But it's important to understand that eventually things will change; they won't be constant. In these early months, it's more important than ever to discuss anything that may upset you.

Love Letters	Getting married is not just about love and commitment. It's also about courage. Think about it: you're taking the risk of sharing your life with another person! That "I do" is a badge of bravery.

Everything Is New

The honeymoon stage of your marriage is like your very own private Discovery Channel. It's the time when you find that adorable way she curls into a ball when she sleeps. That time when you make cute noises when you're concentrating. It's a time when you learn the byways of your spouse: what makes him tick, what makes him think, why he dresses the way he does, if he picks up after himself, if his hygiene is up to par.

It's also a time for new beginnings: a new joint tax return, a new bank account, a new name for the mailbox, a new address. In short, it's like visiting a foreign country for the first time.

Making Your Own Rules

The best way for you to start your life together as a married couple is to ignore what everyone is telling you and do exactly what you as a couple want to do. That means, among other things …

- You don't need to immediately create a 5-year plan.
- You don't have to double-date with other married couples.
- You can spend alone time without each other.
- You can keep separate bank accounts, separate tax returns, and even separate names.

None of these means you love each other less. It just means you're being yourself—together.

Necessary Guidelines

Although you should live your lives the way you want without worrying what other people think, some rules are critical for newlyweds to follow:

- Fight fair. Beware of using hurtful words that aren't easily forgiven.

- Encourage your individuality. It was each of you as separate people that first attracted each other. Don't lose that unique personality in the guise of being a married couple. *Together* doesn't mean "fused."

- Draw lines. If your partner doesn't feel like talking, don't force him. If he doesn't want to talk in the morning, don't talk! On the other hand, if your partner needs a hug, give it to her.

- Let go with love. Don't let past grievances get in the way of the present. Then was then and now is now, and resentment has a way of building up.

- Respect each other. This is the most important rule of all. (See Chapter 9 for more information about respect in a marriage.)

By Any Other Name

Should you take your husband's name? Should you attach your last names with a hyphen? Or should you maintain your single surname? There are so many options—and equally as many answers. Obviously, if one way is more important to one of you than the other, go that route. If people at work know you by your single name, you might want to keep it professionally. Sometimes you each have such long last names that using a hyphen is impractical. Ideally, it should be something you both agree on—happily.

The First Fight

It's bound to happen. That first real fight when neither one of you wants to back down. You aren't performing angry foreplay, and you are feeling angry, hurt, and shocked. Yes, shocked. Suddenly, that honeymoon stage when everything was blue skies and rainbows seems to stop in its tracks. Everything turns bare, cold, and ugly. You are fighting! It's over!

Of course, it isn't, and you know that somewhere in your heart even though you're afraid it is. You will get over the first fight, but it's inevitable that it will happen. It happens to every couple.

Forgiving and Forgetting

People start fighting for several major reasons—and it has nothing to do with not making the bed or taking out the garbage. Common reasons for fighting include the following:

Finances. It's not only love that makes the world go 'round. It's money, too. Hopefully, you've discussed this before the wedding, but if not, now's the time. I strongly recommend sitting down and figuring out a budget that satisfies both of you.

Lifestyles. Okay, maybe you aren't as bad as the Odd Couple, but if one of you is more concerned about the dishes, the best thing to do is take care of it yourself. Or better yet: hire a housekeeper to come twice a month!

Kids. At this point, you probably know whether or not you want children. But fights can occur when it comes to timing and child-rearing values, which you might not have discussed before. Relationships evolve, and so will these decisions.

Family and friends. There are ways around dislike. If you or your spouse dislikes each other's family or a particular friend, compromise. See them alone most of the time, and limit the number of get-togethers where you're all required to attend.

Careers. It's difficult to keep that work-life balance, but that doesn't make it impossible. Devote at least one night a week to each other. It doesn't have to be a Saturday "date night."

You can probably think of more reasons to fight—there are probably as many as there are reasons not to fight! But these are the most common, so if you haven't already talked about these issues with your new spouse, I suggest you do so, soon.

Avoiding Catastrophic Thinking

It's important to remember that one fight doesn't mean the end of your marriage. Some people tend to think in black and white, but in reality, life is full of grays.

I remember Mavis and Paul, for example. Mavis was always terrified Paul was going to leave her. Every time they had a fight, she'd try to stop it—even at the sacrifice of what she believed. But that fear ended up driving a wedge in their marriage. Instead of being closer, as Mavis wanted, they began to move further and further away. What Mavis didn't realize is that it's better to let it "all hang out" and dry, than leave the dirty laundry damp.

Marriage is a pact between two people, and, hopefully, you'll grow with each other and be each other's best friend. But while your spouse may be "everything" to you, know that no one person can fulfill all your hopes and dreams. Only you can do that.

Essential Takeaways

- The first few months of marriage—the honeymoon stage—are wedded bliss, when passion is at its highest.
- It's important to live your lives by your own rules, but some rules—like respect for each other—always need to be in place.
- Fights, even as newlyweds, are normal.

chapter 5

Stage 2:
Settling In

Reality rears its head

When habits get annoying

Stress of life changes

Goal-searching

Maybe it'll be a few months, or maybe a year or two, but eventually you and your spouse will leave behind the glow of the honeymoon stage. This doesn't mean you don't love each other; it's just a different stage of love.

Real life has its ups and downs. You have to unpack your bags from your honeymoon and replace them with other "baggage"—your hopes and fears, your insecurities and your guilty pleasures. Add to that the stress of work and paying bills, and, if you don't settle into a routine, you could be on rocky ground.

The Day-to-Day Realities

I call this stage *accommodation*. It's the time in your marriage when you realize love isn't perfect. It doesn't mean you don't love your spouse or cherish her with all your heart, but after a few months, you realize there are things you may not exactly love about your partner.

Accommodation is the time when you establish your roles, set expectations, and make compromises.

At this point, disillusionment may step in—but it doesn't mean the marriage is in trouble. Disillusionment is perfectly normal in an imperfect world.

No Relationship Is Perfect

The first day John and Ashley had to go off to their respective jobs was heart-wrenching. They'd been married for a little over two weeks, and they didn't want to leave each other. But little by little, they established their new routine. Instead of 20 texts to each other a day, it dropped to 3: "Have a good day!" "Call me later." "What do you want for dinner?"

In the evenings, they watched television and, although the sex was still great, they dropped from over seven times a week down to twice a week.

Mornings were quiet. John and Ashley went about their routines. Previously, when Ashley gave John a hug while he was shaving, he'd stop and they'd kiss, both of them getting shaving cream on their faces. When John traced Ashley's lips while she was putting on her makeup, they'd both end up back in bed. Now they'd just get dressed, grab a cup of coffee, and the last one leaving locked the door.

The worst part of "settling down" was the bickering: "I don't want to watch that. It's boring!" "I did the laundry last time!" "I hate it when you grab all the covers." "Why do you insist on talking to me when we're both in the bathroom? And speaking of that, why can't we take turns?"

I was glad when Ashley and John came to see me. They recognized they were developing a pattern that wasn't healthy, and they saw themselves getting further and further apart. Instead of continuing on their downhill slope, they wanted to learn how to stop the nagging, the fights, and the distance. Getting help so early in their marriage meant they could avoid bigger problems in the future.

Those first few weeks or months after the honeymoon can be stressful. The other person's habits, needs, anger, and neuroses become uncomfortably clear. Even if you lived together and already recognize your spouse's patterns, it's different: you are now linked to this person "until death do us part," and you may feel trapped. It's important to avoid the problems by talking about them with your spouse, not pretending that the at-one-time adorable habit doesn't annoy or irritate you now.

Marriage Trap	It might sound hard to believe, but those first few months are critical to a lasting marriage. That's the time you learn how to problem-solve and manage conflict. It's when you learn that being a partner means compromise and communication.

Everything Evolves and Changes

A longitudinal study (a study that researches the same people over a long period of time) published in 2001 in the *Journal of Personality and Social Psychology* compared the same couples married for 2 years and again later, at 15 years. The findings showed that the way the couples handled the dynamics of their relationship in those first 2 years foreshadowed whether or not they were still married 13 years later. It wasn't the negative feelings about each other that drove the couples apart, but the inability to express those feelings. Disillusionment—the erosion of love, spouse unresponsiveness, and ambivalence—was the difference between the couples who remained married and those who divorced.

Things change when the honeymoon is over, but if you talk about the differences, especially those you dislike, you have a better chance of your marriage surviving over the years.

Avoiding Disillusionment—Then and Now

Knowing that you should have talked about your problems early on doesn't help what's going on now—10 or more years later. But you can still practice avoiding further disillusionment today—and help erase any disillusionment that currently exists. Here's how:

- Talk about what you want from your partner: "I would like you to …."

- Think about what you need and then make it concrete for your partner: "I need more intimacy" is not as clear as "I need you to tell me more about how you're feeling about me."

- Avoid focusing on what your spouse has done wrong. Instead, remember what he's been doing right.

- Putting a positive spin on your requests makes things clearer for your partner. "Let's stay calm while we talk" feels less negative than "I don't want you to yell at me when you're angry."

- Talking about what you don't like will be heard as criticism and is more likely to trigger a defensive response.

As these suggestions show, the way you communicate is as important as the communication itself in order to avoid the negative feelings and ambivalence that come with disillusionment. Learning how to effectively communicate in the early years can help prevent problems in the future.

Marriage Trap	It's a quick step from being *right* to being *righteous*. How can you see your spouse's point of view if your thinking is rigid? Learning you don't always have to be right is an important lesson all young married couples need to know.

When you first get back from your honeymoon and your life settles back to being routine, it's easy to get depressed. I call it "the honeymoon blues," and it's perfectly normal. After all, you've gone from the excitement of planning a wedding and honeymoon to getting dressed and going to work … again.

Being prepared for when "the honeymoon is over" can go far in keeping your marriage viable throughout the years. In fact, many married couples say the first few years of their marriage were the most joyous! After all, you are discovering new things about each other, the sex is good, and there's an added bonus in your routine: you will be with your partner when you get home.

Setting Emotional Goals

A majority of people make goals about their finances, their careers, their lifestyles, even how and who they will marry, but very few set goals about their marriages. I'm not talking about when to have children, when to buy a house, or even when to retire, but the more intrinsic goals in marriage, such as ...

- Nurturing your spouse in some way every day—whether it's something simple like saying "I love you" or something more elaborate like a "just because" gift.

- Taking the time to feel grateful that your spouse loves you—and you love her.

- Making a list of ideas to keep the romance alive—from planning a monthly getaway to a small bed and breakfast to a hug and a kiss before going to sleep.

- Writing down what you'd both like to accomplish—on an emotional level—in 5 years. Add items like still having sex twice a week to finding new ways to make anniversaries special every year.

Making these love goals is just as important as setting goals about when to have children and how much to save!

Love Letters	I know a couple who keeps their marriage strong with a simple goal: every anniversary they plan a trip to a different state. It adds excitement and acknowledges their love for one another. So far they have been to 20 states, including Alaska and Hawaii!

Keeping love alive by making goals sounds fairly easy, but it can become a challenge when real life enters the picture. Careers, money, and parenthood change goals. Nothing is engrained in stone. What kept your love alive in the first few months can be very different when you have your first child.

Financial and Career Changes

Rose and Joseph came to see me when they found that the spark was gone in their marriage. They used to be inseparable on weekends, and they missed each other terribly when one of them had a business trip. But Joe's career had become very demanding within a short time; he was traveling more, and he was becoming distracted at home. They enjoyed having more money and prestige, but what good was it if they were falling out of love?

I suggested that Rose and Joseph sit down and make a new set of goals for themselves. Because finances and careers can change perceptions and life choices, it's important to revisit your marriage goals whenever an important element of your lives together changes.

Rose and Joseph used to spend every Friday night either going out to dinner or going to a movie. But with Joe's new schedule, it was becoming impossible to get together. Rose not only found herself fending for herself on Friday nights, but she was also feeling lonely—and a little resentful of Joe's not being there.

Joseph was also beginning to feel resentful. Here he was, a good provider making a lot of money, and what thanks did he get? None. All he got was complaints from Rose that their Friday nights together weren't happening.

It only took one session for Rose and Joseph to realize that with a simple shift in their goals, they could recapture the love they felt for each other on their wedding day. They decided that every Friday night was too much. They planned on getting together at least one night every month—it didn't matter which day—and go on a date. Rose also decided to use her newly free Fridays to catch up with her friends, either going to dinner or to a movie— which also meant she could see a "chick flick" without feeling guilty!

Mortgages and Parenthood

Mortgages are a fact of life if you want a house. And parenthood is a fact of life if you want children. How can you ensure these stressful situations don't erode your love? Simple: address your goals and change them where needed.

MISC.

100% Mortgage Free

Friends of mine decided they never wanted to be saddled with a mortgage, even if it meant they'd never own a house. Today, while many people are scrambling to pay their mortgages, this couple just has to be sure they can make their rent every month. Is this for everyone? No. But it's another strategy for couples who may see having any kind of debt as a real buzz kill.

Every marriage is different, and every couple will address their goals and issues in different ways. Communication is key. Goals change as we grow. Spend one evening a month to go over your plans. Renew your commitment by renewing your goals—or changing them. If one of you wants to buy a house right away and the other wants to wait until you can pay cash, compromise. Buy a retirement home or vacation home with cash, for example, and continue to rent an apartment.

When I work with younger clients who have just had children, I advise them to find a great babysitter (or a doting grandparent) who can take over once a month while the couple can escape together for some alone time.

Getting time away from young children can be a challenge for couples. My suggestion: go to a hotel for a few hours. Getting a hotel room in the middle of the day or for a night has an erotic feel to it—and can help keep romance alive in between changing diapers and warming bottles!

Using Maslow's Hierarchy of Needs

One of the psychology disciples of the twentieth century was Abraham Maslow. In 1954, he wrote a book on motivation and personality in which he created a Hierarchy of Needs pyramid. According to Dr. Maslow, humans are not just motivated by the need for food and shelter, but by higher goals as well. When the needs at the bottom are met, we're motivated to move up the pyramid, fulfilling needs until reaching the very top—which Maslow called self-actualization, the pinnacle of one's individual needs and the ultimate goal in life.

These same needs can be reflected in your marriage. Once your basic needs in marriage are met—your safety, your home, your life—you can look for respect in a spouse. You will feel confident that your marriage will continue to be a happy, healthy union.

Recently, Douglas Kenrick, a professor at Arizona University, along with Vladas Griskevicius of the University of Minnesota and Mark Schaller from the University of British Columbia created a new pyramid that put parenting at the very top. Kenrick's argument is that parenting helps keep the species going, whereas self-actualization is only a means unto itself and does nothing to help the human race grow. This new pyramid can still be used as a model for lasting marriage: until your basic needs in marriage are met, you cannot become a good parent.

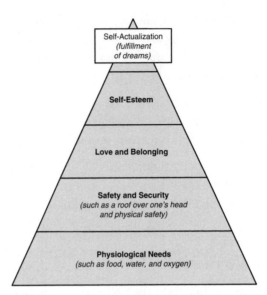

Maslow's Hierarchy of Needs describes how humans are motivated and how our basic needs need to be filled before we move up the pyramid to higher needs.
(Adapted from Motivation and Personality *by Abraham Maslow, New York: Harper & Row, 1954.)*

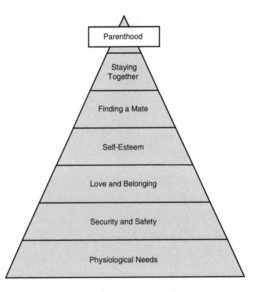

This is today's modern hierarchy of needs, with parenting at the very top in importance.
(Adapted from Kenrick, D.T., Griskevicius, V., Neuberg, S.L., and Schaller, M. "Renovating the Pyramid of Needs: Contemporary Extensions Built Upon Ancient Foundations." Perspective on Psychological Science. 2010; 5(3):292–314.)

Times change, but whether or not parenting is seen as the ultimate goal, it is indeed a goal. But couples need to have all their needs met before good parenting can occur—and that means having a happy and healthy marriage. Ultimately, that means knowing your needs and communicating them, and also knowing your partner's needs and communicating them back.

With that in mind, settling in can be a wonderful stretch on the road to a lasting marriage.

Essential Takeaways

- There's no such thing as a perfect relationship. Relationships grow, evolve, and change over time.
- Start good communication habits early in your marriage to help ensure it lasts.
- As with any other goals, couples need to set emotional goals in order to live happily in their day-to-day routines.
- In marriage, as in life, basic goals must be met before you can go on to the higher goals—whether it be fulfilling your dreams as a couple or becoming a parent.

chapter 6

Stage 3: Facing Life's Challenges

Coping with crises together

Creating goals as a couple

Balancing individual routines with home life

Raising children with similar values

The "new" in *newlyweds* was a reality back when you were first married: every day, every night, every errand, every chore, every evening in or out—everything was new. The years have come and gone, and by now that newness is just a memory. You've learned to cope with daily routines and individual personalities. You've gone through the ups and downs of married life.

And now? Maybe you're celebrating 10 or 15 years married. Maybe you're coming up on your twenty-fifth anniversary soon. Whichever it is, congratulations! You've gone through a lot, and you're still together.

Many of life's challenges are still in front of you. In this chapter, I help you traverse some of the potential land mines in your continued journey as a couple.

Learning What to Expect from Each Other

A couple doesn't really know how strong their relationship is until they deal firsthand with the challenges life brings. Whether it's starting a new job, facing unemployment, or coping with an unfortunate accident or family illness, we all face challenges in life. In this stage of your marriage, you will learn what you can expect from your partner during these difficult times—and what he can expect from you.

An important truth before we go too far: you will feel a certain amount of disillusionment in this stage. The relationship might not be quite what you expected when you said "I do."

Disillusionment doesn't have to turn into disaster, though. Recognizing what you can expect from your partner—who he or she really is—can actually bring you even closer. From disillusionment, a newly formed intimacy can grow.

Marriage Trap	When one or both of you feel the marriage isn't what you dreamed it would be, it's possible to become increasingly attracted to *other* people. It's during this "facing life's challenges" stage when the relationship is very vulnerable to unfaithfulness, which makes the tools in this book even more important to use.

In Crises

There's nothing like the first time you face a challenge together to really see your mate with new eyes. Sometimes what you find out is great and reinforces your love for each other.

Take Dave and Jane, a couple I was working with a few years ago. They had gone to the grand opening of a new shopping mall near their home. It was packed on opening day, and they were excited to see what was being offered—so excited, in fact, that they forgot to make note of where in the six-story parking lot they parked.

Once they got over the initial "I thought you knew! ... No, I thought you knew!" shock, Dave calmly began thinking and asking questions out loud: "Did we park near a stair or an elevator? Did we park on an incline? If we got off the elevator on each floor and tweaked our car alarm, would we hear it? ..." and so on. Finally, Dave decided to go to the security office to see if they could help; one of the guards offered to drive them through all six decks until they found their car.

"I was so impressed with how Dave didn't panic, that he didn't blame me or himself," Jane told me. "He wasn't even upset! Instead, he made a joke about how next time he'd be in charge of making a note of where they parked."

This was a small challenge, and Jane told me she even felt silly talking about it, but it showed her early on how the guy she married could cope with life's challenges. It gave her a clue as to how Dave would handle himself when a big crisis happened.

Jane and Dave had come to see me during one of those big crises: when Dave lost his job, they lost their house; it was so overwhelming to both of them they needed to talk to someone as a couple. I helped them through this difficult time, and today they live in a new home in a new city and have a new life.

One of the things that saved their marriage was Dave's attitude. Once he was able to discuss his fears and disappointments about their mutual loss, he was able to approach the problem as he always did, logically and calmly: "Okay, how do we fix this?"

Love Letters	Practicality is not the only asset in a challenge. You want to be able to share the shock and the grief with your partner; every emotion you feel, you want her to feel. Ultimately, you want to come through the crisis together, knowing you both did your best to have the best outcome.

When a crisis occurs, you want to know, or at least have a sense of, how your mate will handle herself. You want to believe she won't fall apart and you won't have to get through it alone. Ideally, you want your partner to be strong, stable, and capable of handling the situation with you, side by side.

In Daily Life

In most marriages, it's life's daily challenges that can separate a couple, that can make one of you think about having an affair or fantasize about a long-lost love. Why? Because the daily challenges can provoke boredom and resentfulness that, if not addressed, can grow.

Here are a few of the daily challenges that can throw a wrench in the works:

- Getting up and going to work no matter how you feel

- Paying bills—the same ones over and over again

- Planning, cooking, and eating meals

- Doing household chores

- Making sure the children are dressed and ready to go to school

Do you see a pattern here? These activities are ongoing and make up the daily ebbs and flows of life. If your marriage is strong, if you always remember to communicate with each other, if you let each other know when you need something different, the daily grind doesn't have to be a problem.

MISC.

Consistency's the Thing

There's an upside to the daily ups and downs of life. If your mate is consistent, you can count on him to hold up his end of the bargain, to take care of his responsibilities, and to take care of himself. This consistency is invaluable—it provides a sense of stability and safety every marriage needs.

Establishing a Life Together

You are husband and wife. You are a couple. But do you have a life together? There's a difference. Do you communicate, share goals and dreams, make plans, and play together?

When couples in this "challenge" stage come to see me, I ask them to rekindle their togetherness, to take the boredom of daily life out of the equation. The following exercise is one of the tools I use to help.

The following statements reflect behaviors that strengthen a relationship. Rate each statement on a scale from 1 to 10, with 1 being "rarely" and 10 being "often":

1. I ask my spouse about his day.

2. My partner asks me about my day.

3. I spend at least 15 minutes a day alone with my partner, just talking about things.

4. I look forward to my weekends so I can spend time with my spouse.

5. My partner is curious about my life in general.

6. I'm curious about my partner's life.

7. We have meaningful conversations.

8. I talk to/e-mail/text my spouse on a daily basis.

Do most of your answers range in the 1 to 5 range? If so, see if you can improve your score within the next 2 weeks and take the quiz again.

Balancing Home and Work

Famed psychiatrist Sigmund Freud once said the two things that make a healthy individual are work and love. You have to have both. But having work and love in your life isn't enough. You must *balance* them to be happy.

Here is an all-too-typical scenario: the husband works 100 hours a week to be able to afford a nice home in a good neighborhood, a private school, piano lessons for his kids, and so on. The wife is alone with the responsibility of running the household and raising the kids and all the activities that entails. The husband doesn't understand why his wife resents him when he comes home and just wants to relax. Doesn't she understand that he's doing it all for the family?

Or let's say it's the wife who works the 100+ hours a week and the husband who takes care of the kids. It doesn't matter who's doing what. The fact remains that the children virtually grow up in a single-parent home. The husband and wife are both exhausted and frustrated, and the whole family is stressed. Talk about a recipe for disaster!

It's very difficult, especially in these uncertain economic times, to get the right balance between work and home. It's especially difficult when both partners work very hard to provide economic stability and security for the family.

Here are some suggestions for achieving that sought-after balance:

- Ask your boss if you can work at home one or two days a week.

- Become more efficient at work by taking a 5-minute break every 2 hours and, if your office allows it, listening to relaxing jazz or classical music on your earphones to help you focus.

- Schedule one day a week when you have to leave at 5—no questions asked. If necessary, you can always do the last-minute crisis work at home.

- Turn off your work cell phone and e-mail when you're at home.

Misc.

Let Ringing Phones Lie

Let your cell phone go to voicemail when you're home. Give yourself 15 minutes, say, from 9:00 to 9:15, after the children are asleep, to check your voicemail and e-mail very quickly. If there are no emergencies, turn off your phone—and then relax and enjoy spending time with your partner!

- Share the chores—and keep to it. You'll get done in half the time.

- Maintain a healthy lifestyle. Eating right and getting enough exercise relieves stress and provides energy.

- Take a personal day now and again. That's what they're there for!

Building a Home and Community

When you put down roots as a married couple, you're not only building your lives together, you're also becoming a part of the bigger picture: your community. Humans have evolved within a tribal framework, and we've not lost the basic instinct to socialize. We know on a gut level that to survive, we need each other—and that includes friends, extended family, and the community at large.

Some families center their activities around their churches, synagogues, or mosques. Other families may be active in their PTAs or coach their kid's soccer teams. Others may join the local YMCA-YWCA as a family. Still others may do all the above!

The point is that your marriage doesn't exist in a vacuum. The social aspect of marriage and family is important for a number of reasons. Having friends and neighbors helps relieve stress and provides support. That community gives your kids a sense of belonging. It gives all of you roots.

MISC.

Welcome to the Community

In 1928, Thomas Briggs from Memphis, Tennessee, recognized families' need to assimilate. He created the Welcome Wagon to help couples settle in when they moved to a new community. A Welcome Wagon hostess would visit new homeowners with a gift basket containing samples, coupons, and newsletters from local businesses. Today, Welcome Wagon International, Inc., still markets to new homeowners through direct mail, phone calls, and online.

Creating Short- and Long-Term Goals

As Lewis Carroll wrote in *Alice in Wonderland,* "When you don't know where you are going, any road will do." But as successful married couples will tell you, to take "any" road still requires directions, gas for the car, and food and lodging along the way. In other words, not having goals is actually another goal!

We need to set goals, both as individuals and as couples. These goals can change over time. They can be crossed off the list and new ones added in their place. They can be divided into short-term and long-term.

But why do we need goals? Goals define what we want for ourselves and for each other. They help us see if we're going in the same direction and if or when we need to change gears.

A couple I know told me about their 30-year wish list. As a young couple, right after they were married, they bought their first house. It was a fixer-upper Cape Cod on a cul-de-sac, and they got it cheap. They planned to turn it into their dream house.

During the first month in their new home, the couple sat down at the kitchen table and wrote down all the dreams they had for their house. The list had everything from adding a second story to hanging French doors in the dining room. That original list hung on their refrigerator door for

30 years (even when they upgraded their fridge), and every year or two they crossed off something. They kept at it through the births of their three children, through four White House administrations, through their first big career moves, and through their retirements. As the sapling trees they planted grew into tall shade trees, the list got shorter and the paper it was written on yellowed and faded. Two years before the mortgage was paid in full, the list was finished!

They had the list professionally framed, and it now hangs in the kitchen of their new retirement condo: a testament to making plans and setting goals. Did the goals help make their marriage successful? Or did their successful marriage give them the ability to make the list? Probably a little of both.

> **Love Letters**
>
> Without goals, the challenges you will face as a couple can become insurmountable. They not only feel overwhelming, but they can push you apart. With goals, these challenges can be dealt with one by one, all within the context of what you want your life together to be.

Goals are necessary for a happy life—and marriage. Here are some hints for setting your own goals, whether they're 30-year long-term wish lists or 1- or 2-month short-term plans:

- Think your goal through before you commit to it. Be sure it's optimistic but realistic. Don't set a goal of "living in the French countryside" if neither one of you sees yourself mastering another language.

- See yourself at that goal. Visualize what it will feel like when you reach it. Smell it, taste it, use all your senses. If you can't imagine how you will feel, it might not be what you really want, and you and your spouse might need to compromise.

- Break down big goals into little ones so you can measure your progress and give both of you a chance to celebrate early on.

- Write down your goals. Be as elaborate and as detailed as you want, and add dates and timelines if they will help you reach your goals. Or like the couple with the 30-year list, make simple line items and stick it on your fridge or put it somewhere you can both find it easily.

- Reward yourself as you tick off your accomplishments.

Every month or so, go over the list with your partner. Make changes, if necessary, and cross off those goals you've reached.

The Child Factor

As I discussed in Chapter 1, it's important for couples to agree on the values and morals they want to instill in their children. But when you become parents, you don't suddenly stop being spouses. Instead, you now have a dual role: parents and mates. You must learn to balance these roles as well. How can you be both successful parents and still have a viable marriage?

Children and family crises are important factors during this "challenge" stage. Each partner sets his or her own rules and expectations for raising children and how extended family issues should be handled. It's important to be aware of this fact and find a successful compromise in meeting each other's rules and expectations.

Rules and Expectations for Raising Children

It's inevitable that you won't see eye to eye on every issue that comes up with your children. You are two different people raised in two different households—how can you possibly be in synch on everything?

But even if you disagree wholeheartedly with your spouse on a particular issue, you must be supportive of him; you must strive to be a united front. It's a guaranteed disaster if you don't.

Here are some ground rules to keep in mind:

- Do not undermine your mate's authority and side with your child against your mate.

- Do not fight in front of your children.

- Do not use your children as pawns to get what you want.

- Do not use hurtful words you can't take back—whether you're talking to your children or to your spouse. They can create challenges you won't be able to master.

MISC.

Fighting for a Good Cause

It's actually beneficial for your children's growth and development if they see you and your spouse have a disagreement—if you are discussing ways to resolve the conflict. But a no-holds-barred yelling contest can cause irreparable damage. Keep that private.

Handling Extended Family Issues

Those in-laws and cousins and nephews can create a bountiful family circle—along with challenges you need to address. In most cases, I've found extended families to be both a blessing and sometimes a curse.

The solution? Create ground rules early on in your married life about aging parents, lending money to troubled family members, and seeing which families for which holidays. If it's too late for these ground rules to be made early, make them *now*. You can still avoid some potential problems down the road.

Compromise Is Critical

As you might have noticed already, I use the word *compromise* a lot. Compromise is critical for any successful marriage, especially when it comes to raising children or handling extended family. During this "challenge stage," there are three common negative patterns you can find yourself in:

- Being resigned to sticking with a bad decision just to make peace
- Becoming emotionally withdrawn and distant
- Trying to force your spouse into being different from who she is

As you'll discover when you recognize and change these behaviors, compromising is the solution to these trouble spots. Compromise is not impossible. Nor is it a "necessary evil." It's a crucial fiber in the fabric of your marriage. Make compromise as painless as possible by respecting your mate, understanding her point of view, and offering your point of view calmly.

Love Letters

When your partner compromises in your favor, reciprocate by compromising on another issue in his favor! That give and take works wonders.

Essential Takeaways

- These are the years in which you will learn what to expect from each other during a crisis.
- Making goals is a crucial component of maintaining a successful life together.
- Balancing your work and home life isn't impossible, but it is vital.
- Circumvent future problems by setting ground rules for raising children and dealing with extended family as soon as possible.

chapter 7

Stage 4: Growing Old Together

Familiar actions and reactions

Vulnerability as you age

Seeing your spouse for who he or she is

Focusing on the good

You've come a long way together. You've weathered the ups and downs, the joy, the love, the fun, the pain—in short, almost everything life as a married couple has to offer. But just when you think it's smooth sailing from here on out, you still have a few challenges to face.

Been There, Done That

The mortgage was paid off years ago, the children are out living their lives, and the house seems too big for two people. You look at each other and sigh. You've done it! You've been through the big challenges in life—finding a nest, making a living, raising children.

You flip though the old photo album and reflect on the passage of time. Here are photographs from the newlywed years, the salad days, the first big job, the new home, the first child, the promotion, the second child, the bigger house, the teenage years, the aging parents, the birthday parties, the graduations, the weddings, and the funerals. Whew! All those years spent together ....

Been There, Done That, Still Together

When you look at the pictures of your younger selves, beaming as new parents or at a family reunion, it's mostly the good times you remember. However, the events in a marriage that strengthen it are quite the opposite: it's the challenges you both faced that have brought you closer.

One of my clients told me she and her husband might have split up after only a few years of marriage if their youngest son hadn't become schizophrenic in his freshman year at college.

"We seemed to have reaffirmed our commitment to our marriage," she said. "We clung to each other over this tragedy and drew strength from each other." With their sick son, they were like young parents again, focusing all their energy on their only child and his illness. "We rediscovered each other in the midst of coping."

Misc.

Sharing Husband Stories

In a *Reader's Digest* survey of 1,001 couples, some husbands described their happiest and most cherished moments in their marriage as "kissing in the snow," "when she walked down the aisle," and "my wife's face when she saw our first baby."

Getting Comfortable with Compromise

It's simple: the more life challenges you face together, the more you learn about compromise. One of the nice things about growing old together is that you come to know what's important to your spouse. You've learned how to pick your battles—or at least the ones you know you'll win. For a marriage to stay healthy, the scales have to balance somehow. Each partner must feel he or she is getting as much as they put in over the long haul.

Here's what Betty, happily married for 30 years, said about her mate, Charlie: "Charlie never made a lot of money, but he always provided for me and the kids. He never missed a day of work, and he was a wonderful father."

In essence, Betty is saying Charlie didn't put her in the lap of luxury, but he was a good husband and father. Betty feels like she did just fine in the long run and picked a good life partner.

The Aging Factor

Although we all know it to be true, aging is still difficult to accept as a fact of life. Unfortunately, with aging, our bodies change. We are not as healthy as we once were. We still do things—but at a slower pace. And if we're lucky enough, we can be married well into our senior years.

Some couples cope with aging better than others. While a gray hair can freak out one of you, it's possible that the other sees it as no big deal. Going bald might make some men rush to the Hair Club for Men, while others will accept it and only occasionally wear a baseball cap outside.

> **Love Letters**
>
> Chances are, you can see how your husband or wife is aging, but it's more difficult to see it in yourself. You can see that he's losing hair to his comb, and he can see your laugh lines even when you aren't smiling. But when you look at yourself in the mirror, you know you're still sweet 16 inside.

Carol and Brian have been married a long time and still love each other very much. But Carol has a thing about getting older. She winces every time she sees a new wrinkle. She hates her crêpy neck. More than anything, she wants a face-lift.

Brian, on the other hand, loves Carol just the way she is. They have grown old together, and he is happy. He doesn't want Carol to have surgery. He's terrified he'll lose her on the operating table. Why should she take such a risk when he thinks she's beautiful exactly the way she is?

Unfortunately, they quickly got to an impasse. Carol was annoyed that Brian didn't want her to have it. He actually came out and told her that if she had surgery, it would prove she didn't love him enough, that his opinion didn't count. Carol tried to explain to Brian that she didn't want surgery to look better for him, but to look better for herself. She was miserable when she looked in the mirror.

It got so bad that Carol and Brian came to see me. The good news is that we worked out a compromise. Carol would not go under the knife, but she would have less-invasive Botox injections. She would look and feel better without the surgery risk.

Vulnerability May Breed Temptation

It's the classic cliché: the husband in his late 40s or early 50s who suddenly goes out and buys a flashy red sports car. Or the wife who absolutely needs a brow-lift. Some say these are examples of a middle-age crisis.

The truth is, when you're in the throes of middle age, you're vulnerable. You see your appearance change. You see your mate getting older, too—and it can really scare you! Being afraid of growing old is so common, it even has a name: gerascophobia.

It's possible that you may panic and try to recapture some of the excitement of your youth or, worse, you may refuse to see that you are getting old. When that happens, it's possible for wandering eyes to look for someone other than your mate who will desire you, to affirm that, "Yes, you might be a cougar, but I think you are hot!" You may not act on these feelings, but you may stray into dangerous territory and toy with the idea of having an affair.

Fantasizing About Past Loves

As you age, the possibilities become fewer and the regrets a little stronger. Maybe you think about the career path not taken (who knows, maybe you would have been a brilliant lawyer, even a judge by now!) or about that trip to Europe you promised yourself after graduating but never took.

Or you may find yourself wondering about someone you haven't seen or even thought about for years. How strange to be thinking about what would have happened if you had married Ed instead of George! Or if Ed is happily married. Or what he looks like. This is the stage in life we think a lot about the "what ifs."

Fear of Mortality

It isn't just looking old that can give you a mid-life crisis. It's the fear of dying, too—or the fear of your spouse dying. This fear can sometimes take over, creating panic attacks, anxiety, and smothering of the one you love.

Marriage Trap

Believe it or not, the majority of seniors are happy. True, growing old is no picnic, but depression is not the norm. If you are depressed, seek professional help.

The more you worry about dying, the less living you're doing. Enjoy the fact that you're both together, right now, in the moment. No one knows what the future will bring.

The brilliant psychologist Erik Erickson proposed the theory that the personality develops through eight different stages as we age, and each stage is represented by a crisis. The last stage is called "Integrity versus Despair." This stage is initiated when an individual experiences a sense of mortality, as a response to a death of a close friend, retirement, or growing old. It's in this crisis stage when a person starts to review his or her life. Was it a success or a failure?

According to Erickson, Integrity versus Despair is most productive when you share it with your significant other. Integrity results from sharing a life with someone you love. But if you're not happily married, your view of life will be very different. You might feel you wasted your life with your partner. That's the despair.

Ensure that your final "crisis" stage is full of integrity: communicate with your spouse, respect him, and enjoy each other's company to the fullest.

Accepting Your Spouse

With wisdom comes acceptance—of growing old or your spouse growing old. If you don't accept your spouse exactly as she is, you're headed for trouble because you can't change anyone; you can only change yourself. If you're feeling uncomfortable about getting old, talk to each other. Being close has no age limit.

Knowing the Real Person You Married

In my opinion, the best two words of wisdom are "know thyself." Lengthy tomes have been written on these two little words, in fact—from the foundation of Buddhism to Shakespeare's *Hamlet*.

Do we really ever know our true selves? And do we really ever know the "real" person we married? The answer quite simply is no. We can never know *everything* about ourselves and about each other. But by having spent 10, 20, or 30 years together, you certainly have more than a clue about how your spouse ticks, how he sees the world, and what his basic sense of right and wrong is.

MISC.

Summing It Up

"Infatuation is when you think he's as sexy as Robert Redford, as smart as Henry Kissinger, as noble as Ralph Nader, as funny as Woody Allen, and as athletic as Jimmy Conners. Love is when you realize that he's not as sexy as Woody Allen, as smart as Jimmy Connors, as funny as Ralph Nader, as athletic as Henry Kissinger, and nothing like Robert Redford—but you'll take him anyway."

—Humorist Judith Viorst, *Redbook,* 1975

Accepting and Respecting the Differences

Here's an anecdote a couple described to me about their first date. The husband said, "I just don't understand how you could possibly eat that … I mean, they are slimy and slippery and raw! And you just gulp it down. GAD! How can you do it?"

"I love oysters," was his wife's reply.

That was on their first date—more than 50 years ago. And you know what? After 50 years, they're both of the same opinion about oysters.

"But even after all these years," he told me, "no one is more excited than me to see fresh oysters on the menu when we sit down in a restaurant. Nothing gives me more pleasure than to see my wife enjoy what I consider the most disgusting thing a human being could eat!"

Vive la différence!

Minimizing Resentment

At this point in the marriage, most couples have figured out the real person they've married, as much as anyone can. They've learned to compromise and, most importantly, they truly, deep down, accept areas of differences with minimum resentment. This means …

Laughing things off. Instead of getting angry at the jokes your spouse tells everyone over and over again, you have a sense of humor about it. "Here it comes again," you might say, not with contempt, but with fondness.

Acting, not reacting. It's that ubiquitous Friday night again—and your husband will come through the door cranky. Instead of waiting to see his grimace, you leave him a note that you're going to the movies with some friends. You also leave a pizza in the freezer for his dinner.

Counting your blessings. Not everyone gets to be in this fourth stage of marriage. Whether because of death, sickness, or divorce, most couples just don't get this far. You're the lucky ones, and you're grateful.

Having a life outside the marriage. Having a social circle puts less pressure on your spouse to be all things to you. You have a full life—whether it be continued work, volunteer work during retirement, or getting together with old friends for a reunion.

Focus On What's Right About Each Other

When you've reached this stage in your relationship, it's almost as if you have a new marriage. You've learned to re-appreciate and re-love each other and give each other the benefit of the doubt in conflict situations.

This marriage rebirth can be a wonderful time. Imagine those early years of marriage, but with comfort, ease, and wisdom tossed in.

Managing Anger or Hurtful Triggers

When Joanne and Peter were first married, they learned early on how to push each other's buttons. When Peter was angry with Joanne, he'd watch a game on TV really loud. When Joanne was angry with Peter, she'd talk on the phone while he was trying to read.

But now, after 32 years, they laugh about their patterns. When Peter gets angry, he'll say, "Gee, are there any games on tonight?" And Joanne will make a big deal of trying to find her cell phone. "I haven't spoken to Susan in years!" The difference today is that they don't actually turn on the television or make a call. They laugh about it.

Agreeing to Disagree

Ellen was fully aware that John was a Republican when she met him. A diehard Democrat, she almost stopped dating him when their arguments were so heated. Sometimes they'd stop talking for days. Ellen would try to get John to see reason, and vice versa. Of course, neither one would change his or her opinion. They were who they were.

Today, they each know whom the other is voting for on Election Day, but they have agreed to disagree. They loved each other, and it wasn't worth losing what they have for an elected official. They'll still argue, but with fondness and respect.

Enjoying Each Other's Company

"These are the best years of our lives," Selma told me when I ran into her at the mall. She and her husband, Patrick, had come to see me several years ago when they were having some marital problems.

I was glad to see how happy Selma was. She and Patrick had gotten over their disagreements; the disagreements weren't important anymore. Instead, they wanted to be with each other. They fully valued each other and never ran out of things to talk about. And when they did stop talking, it was a comfortable silence, the kind born out of respect and love.

Essential Takeaways

- Getting old is natural—accept it and count your blessings you have someone to grow old with.
- Letting go of old resentments and anger is key to a happy marriage in your golden years.
- You can never know the "real" person you marry, but after many years of marriage, you can come close.

Part 3

Building a Strong Foundation

What makes an enduring marriage? What are the secrets that make some marriages successful and others less so? The truth is, there are no secrets, no hidden words or actions that can make all the difference in your marriage. There's no lucky charm that can make your marriage one of the lifelong ones.

Every good marriage contains some common elements, and some parts of every marriage could be stronger. As you read through the following chapters, the elements might sound so simple. But as with anything in life, it's the simple things that count.

From the obvious foundations like communication and trust to the subtler building blocks like empathy and acceptance, you can learn something with each one. In Part 3, you'll find insights, tools, and quizzes for each of these foundations, all designed to help make your marriage a stronger one and one you'll celebrate for a long time.

chapter 8

Acceptance Is a Two-Way Street

Roles of flexibility and tolerance

Feeling valued

Avoiding neediness

Roadblocks to acceptance

We all want to be accepted. We want to feel secure and comfortable, whether it be at work, within a circle of friends, or in a marriage. We want to be valued for what we "bring to the party," our unique set of strengths and skills, fears and foibles, that make us who we are. In fact, one of the main reasons we stay married is because we feel accepted and valued. We feel safe and secure in the knowledge we are loved for who we truly are: a less-than-perfect human being.

But acceptance is a two-way street. It's not only important for you to feel that your eccentricities and moods are accepted by your spouse; you must also be accepting of his personality, his likes and dislikes, his quirks—and, equally important, make him aware of that acceptance.

In this chapter, you learn how to make your spouse feel good about his sacred Tuesday poker nights, even though they drive you nuts, and how he can reciprocate by accepting the fact that you *must* see every episode of *Grey's Anatomy*.

Putting the Value in Validation

Acceptance cannot be faked. If you only pretend to accept your husband's poker nights, I guarantee you that in a few months or years, you'll be very full of resentment. But how can you learn to accept your spouse? It all starts with validation.

When your partner tells you how proud she was at the way you handled yourself at last night's town hall meeting or how she felt she was the luckiest gal at a party because you were with her, you are going to feel good. Much better than good, in fact! You feel valued, secure, and loved—all the qualities that validate your marriage.

The reverse holds true as well. When you tell your partner how much you appreciated her canceling an important business dinner because she knew you were exhausted from spending the day with your mother, she will feel good about her actions.

Love Letters

If you've been married for any length of time, you can usually tell when your partner says something that's genuine—or when she's faking it. Find the good in your partner and tell her. Because it's the truth, she will feel valued and accepted for who she is.

It might sound obvious, it might sound like Marriage 101, but it bears repeating: when your partner says something to make you feel valued and important, it strengthens your relationship. And the more valuable you feel, the more you'll value your partner. The more you value your partner, the more you'll accept her the way she is.

On the other hand, when you or your partner says something negative or hurtful, it can be a crack in the wall of a solid relationship.

The Flexibility Factor

Thanks to better medicine and research, we are living longer today—which means there's more time for goals and values to change. Acceptance may become more of a challenge as you grow old together, but flexibility accounts for a lot.

What is flexibility? It's a request, not a demand. It's a willingness—without resentment—to do what your partner wants because it's important to him or her. It means postponing or amending your desires or wishes and accepting that your spouse has needs, too. Flexibility also means accepting the fact that life changes, your life together changes, and you can change, too.

A flexible partner will go on a "horizontal" vacation in the Caribbean even though his heart was set on backpacking through Europe—knowing that the following year, he and his wife will visit Italy. A flexible partner is someone who will take dancing lessons because he knows his wife loves to dance. A flexible partner is someone who will watch Monday Night Football because her husband looks forward to it. A flexible partner is someone who will willingly compromise because he or she accepts—and loves—you.

Jack and Flexible Jill

To demonstrate flexibility, let's use an old nursery rhyme: Jack and Jill went up the hill—but only made it halfway. Jack got tired, so Jill told him to rest while she went to fetch the water. Or maybe Jill thought it would be better to get the water another day. Or maybe they decided together to hire a contractor and build a well in the valley. Either way, Jill was flexible and accepted Jack's feelings—and they just may live happily ever after.

Tolerance Builds Acceptance

Tolerance in marriage means accepting the things that make your mate happy or are really important to him or her. But sometimes being tolerant can be more easily said than done—especially when it comes to personality.

Some people have a more easygoing temperament than others. It takes a lot for something to get under their skin. Others are quick to jump at the slightest nudge. Chances are, if you got married, your temperaments were in sync—regardless if one of you was laid back and the other one was high-strung. But over the years, it's possible that things could start to bother the most easygoing person—and the nervous Nelly could be ready to file for divorce.

If this scenario sounds familiar, take a deep breath and try to remember what attracted you to your partner in the first place. Look for the "real person" underneath the behavior.

Laid Back and "In the Moment"?

Maybe your partner is so easygoing he forgets to mention he needed to work late all week. Or maybe he went to get a few items at the grocery store and came back hours later with more than you'll need for the next 2 months. You can be angry at him, but where would that get you?

Instead, learn from your significant other. By doing things more slowly, maybe he's more in the "now." He has a chance to breathe, to stop and smell the roses. Maybe you, too, could be more conscious of your surroundings and, if not, think of food shopping as quality time—just enjoy life a bit more.

You can always choose to stay the way you are, but you'll also need to accept the fact that your husband is on his own slow time. It's not a flaw—it's just different from you.

Can Drama Equal Excitement?

Drama queens can be draining, but a little drama can spice up your life. Maybe your spouse has complained about the way you make mountains out of molehills. He doesn't understand your hypersensitivity. But maybe your sensitivity makes you compassionate; you have the ability to understand how someone else feels. It makes you kind, and maybe your partner could learn from you.

For example, maybe your husband is a tried-and-true sports fan and goes ballistic when his team is in the playoffs. It's possible you could learn from his "drama" and use that sort of enthusiasm with your team at work.

The Art of Acceptance

It's not difficult to make your partner feel accepted—if you're sincere. But you do need to be conscious of yourself, your spouse, and your life together.

Remember, your partner is not a mind reader. You might think she looks great in that dress, but if you don't *tell* her, there's a chance she won't pick up on your approval.

With time, you may take your spouse for granted. Your relationship is settled. You have a routine. You know her like a book. What else is there to say? Plenty. Let's start with common courtesy. Why do we forget to give the most important person in the world the same simple "thank you" we give to strangers?

Beyond Please and Thank You

Misc.

Couples may forget the formal courtesies in life after a few years. Nods or half-smiles can take the place of "Thank you for getting me a cup of coffee" or "You're the best for going to the dry cleaners!" But mentioning a simple, "You're welcome" or "My pleasure" shows that the acknowledgment is there, the unsaid words saying "I appreciate all the little things you do."

Voicing criticism can be too easy to do—and make things worse. If you're really angry about always being the one to fold the laundry, choose your words carefully. Which sounds better: "Why do I always have to do this? I hate it!" or "If we do this together, it'll take half the time ...."?

First, Accept Yourself

It's possible you may be so busy trying to accept your spouse that you forget about yourself! Maybe you hate the way you need to control everything. Or maybe you hate that you can't be spontaneous. If you want your spouse to accept you as you are, you have to accept yourself first. Accept that you are human. Realize that you won't be the perfect mate all the time. Be as kind and understanding with yourself as you are with him or her.

Accepting yourself can be difficult if you have low self-esteem. Insecurity feeds imagination—and not always in a good way. You might be insecure, accusing your spouse of imaginary crimes, becoming jealous over nothing. Even if your spouse accepts your insecurity as part of who you are, his or her patience can run thin if it's unrelenting year after year.

Even worse, low self-esteem can make you feel unworthy of your partner's love. And if you can't accept love, you'll have difficulty returning it. If you need a confidence boost, talk to your spouse about it. But if this is something that's been a life-long struggle, you may want to seek professional help.

Marriage Trap

The desire to be accepted is one thing, but being needy is another. Seeking validation is good, but being clingy is not. It's important to give your partner room to breathe. If you're feeling insecure, your partner may not be giving you the acceptance you need. But like many other components to your relationship, timing is everything.

When Acceptance Is a Challenge

If you can accept the fact that you're a control freak, you can laugh about it—together. By both of you accepting your idiosyncrasies, you may find that you have more self-confidence; you like yourself. This not only makes it easier for your spouse to accept you, but it makes you more expansive when it comes to accepting him.

A relationship is particularly vulnerable when the two of you are fighting or having a disagreement. Whether from a difference in view point, forgetfulness on your partner's part, or actions that hurt, the fight itself takes on a dramatic life of its own.

The worst part of fighting? When you say something so hurtful that the other person can't forget it. It's hard to feel accepted after the words "You never do anything right!" or "You don't understand anything!" fly out of your mouth. Although there are times we would all love to eat our words, once they're out there, they're out there, reverberating in your partner's mind. You can't take them back.

As hard as it is during the heat of the moment, try counting to 10 before hurling any comments you know will leave a permanent scar. Even those few seconds can be the attitude adjustment you need and give you time to choose more appropriate words to express your feelings—and avoid hurting his. I tell my clients: take a deep breath, and focus on the situation at hand.

MISC.

Words Can Hurt

When used in a fight with someone you love, exaggerations can resonate—badly. Avoid "You were always a jerk—since the day I married you!" or "Why did I marry you? You are a total loser!" These words are hard to forget.

What if your marriage is about to break and you're so angry with each other that acceptance sounds like something from a country-western song? Accepting your spouse when you are furious with her is difficult—but not impossible.

It's difficult to keep emotions at bay when you're fighting. In the middle of yelling "You said you were going to take care of it and you didn't!" you probably aren't going to want to take a deep breath or call a time-out. But awareness is more than half the battle. Realizing that you can change your emotional barometer by taking a step back helps you remember to do so—if not now, then for the next time.

Circumstantial Acceptance

As if accepting who you are and who your spouse is weren't enough, there's also the need to accept external situations. Picture this scenario: when you wed, you both had high-paying jobs. You lived in a city apartment and ate out a few nights a week. You both belonged to a gym, and you both loved to shop. Sounds wonderful, doesn't it?

But it's 3 years down the road, and your spouse just lost his job. Money is getting tighter. You can't afford your apartment, let alone going out to dinner. You need to downsize. Suddenly, stress descends on you like an avalanche. You worry about paying your bills. You worry about supporting your children. You worry about getting sick and not being able to get the medical treatment you need. You worry about becoming homeless.

In short, life has changed. The stress can either make you grow closer or draw you apart. You can either resent your spouse for his part in creating this new situation, or you can accept your life and make the best of it. The good news—and the part we frequently forget—is that you have a partner with you to see it through.

At this point, you need to ask yourself some serious questions: Are you willing to make sacrifices to keep your marriage afloat? Do you still accept and love this person? If your answers are no, you may have to begin thinking of changing your life. But if the answers are yes, you can work to solve the problems at hand—together.

Disagreeing in an Agreeing Way

Fighting can be important to a lasting marriage. As one of my clients has said, "We fight all the time. We need to get our problems out in the open." But you have to be careful. Even if you are completely crazed at the way your spouse is spending money, you don't have to come out and say, "What's your problem? You spend money like we're made of it."

Instead, you can say, "I know you want to drive a nice car and have a nice home, but I'm concerned about the expense. I don't want us getting into debt." At least this way, your spouse isn't on the defensive and you've opened the way to a dialogue.

It may be a fight, but it can be a fair fight—focusing on the issues and not taking on the person. Neither of you should walk away bloodied. (Read more about fighting as a fact of life in Chapter 12.)

Marriage Trap	Beware the nag, the smirk, and the look. These actions are not only negative, but can shut down communication completely. You may think it's minor, but you could be sending an inadvertent message: "I think you're stupid, lazy, silly, or just plain annoying." Remember that things like this can leave your spouse hurt and withdrawn.

Take my clients Anne and Joe, for example. They always seemed to be fighting about the kids. Joe was constantly criticizing the way Anne handled them. "You coddle them, just like your parents did with you!" Not only did the fighting seem endless, but it was getting nasty: "You are making them spoiled brats—just like you!" And "You don't know anything about being a parent!"

When they came to see me, I instructed Joe to say something more along the lines of, "I know our parenting styles are different, and, between the two of us, I think we are doing a great job. But I don't always understand why you handle some situations the way you do." It didn't immediately end the debate, but it did turn down the volume. Anne got to explain her actions, and Joe got the opportunity to understand and accept them.

An Acceptance Inventory

I've been a marriage counselor for more than 35 years, but I'm still surprised when a couple comes to my office without knowing much about each other. They can be married 5 years, 10 years, even 25 years, and they still can't describe the perfect present their spouse would want. They can't remember the last time they said anything nice about each other. Sometimes they don't have a clue about each other's favorite movies or books, or even a favorite color! It can be difficult to demonstrate your acceptance of your spouse if you don't know what makes her tick—not when you first got married, but right now, in the present.

The following "Positive Partner Awareness Inventory" exercise may seem like a no-brainer, but you'd be surprised at how many of my clients don't know the answers. When they see the questions in black and white, they're shocked at what they actually don't know about each other!

Jot down your answers on a piece of paper, and ask your partner to do the same. You can even make it a game (the "Not-Newlywed Game"!) by guessing your husband's or wife's answer and seeing if you're correct.

Positive Partner Awareness Inventory

Finish each sentence:

1. My partner is happiest when …

2. My partner's favorite song is …

3. My partner's favorite type of movie is …

4. My partner's favorite article of clothes is …

5. My partner's favorite color is …

6. My partner likes to drive a …

7. My partner is most influenced by …

8. My partner likes it most when I …

9. The best present I ever gave my partner was ...

10. A positive memory my partner has of us together is ...

11. A special thing I did for my partner is ...

12. I tell my partner I am proud of him ... (daily, weekly, monthly, or can't remember)

13. I tell my partner I care for her ... (daily, weekly, monthly, or can't remember)

14. I touch my partner in an affectionate (nonsexual) way ... (daily, weekly, monthly, or can't remember)

15. I give my partner a positive sexual experience based on what he likes ... (often, occasionally, rarely, or never)

Becoming more aware of each other is the first step toward acceptance. And who knows? It may help you rediscover why you love your spouse all over again!

<table>
<tr><td>Marriage Trap</td><td>People say marriage is all about compromise—and that's true: couples who accept and respect each other willingly change plans to please each other. But compromise is not sacrifice—and it doesn't lead to acceptance. If you're only going along with your spouse because you don't want to rock the boat, it's only a matter of time until you feel resentment and anger.</td></tr>
</table>

Does Your Spouse Accept You?

Feeling accepted is not always something—an action or a word—you can pinpoint. But if you're feeling good about yourself, if you're happy in the relationship, chances are you're accepted for who you are.

But if you need proof, here are some signs you're being accepted:

- Your spouse can laugh with you about one of your habits, say, the way you chew your tongue when you're concentrating.

- Your spouse looks at you with a smile on her face.

- Your spouse finds the perfect gift—or words—for you every time.

- There is comfort in silence when you're together.

- Your spouse doesn't make plans that go against your grain.

- You don't want to be a slob, but you don't have to dress or wear your hair as if you are going on a date.

- It's not about sex. It's about touch. A kiss or a hug without being asked.

- You both lead busy lives, but you look forward to those nights when you can relax as a couple or a family.

- Whether it is a vacation or a 5-year retirement goal, you do your research together.

- You look forward to talking to your spouse about your day. There are no awkward silences; your conversations are natural.

- You know with certainty, deep down, that your spouse will be there for you when you need him.

In the end, acceptance is critical. It's a fundamental pillar for a lasting marriage. I'm not saying it's easy to come to accept your partner; it can take work and commitment, but it's well worth it in the years to come.

The more you accept your spouse, the more inclined she will be to accept you. Everyone is happy, and in the long run, everyone wins.

Essential Takeaways

- Acceptance takes work, but it can be learned.
- For a marriage to be successful, you both have to accept each other.
- To truly accept your partner, you need to be flexible and tolerate each other's needs.
- Don't accept your partner because you feel insecure, but because you love him.

chapter 9

Beyond Empathy

In your spouse's shoes

Drawing boundaries

Avoiding being judgmental

Influence is key

You've probably heard the old saying: you can't know what another person is going through until you walk a mile in his or her shoes. True, but you can imagine what it would be like.

For your marriage to last, you need to imagine life in your spouse's shoes. That doesn't mean you have to stalk him as he goes to work and hangs out with his friends. It's more about validating your spouse's feelings, and understanding what he's going through. It's showing respect. It's being kind. It's what you feel when someone you love is going through a difficult time.

Different Points of View

Ellen and Bill had been together for 22 years and knew each other inside and out. They finished each other's sentences, and on more than one occasion, one of them would say "I know what you're thinking" and they would be correct!

But over the years, they had begun to take each other for granted. They were caught up in their busy and increasingly separate lives. Ellen had her interior design firm, and Bill had his true passion, restoring vintage cars. Ellen was up and out of the house early every morning, and just about every night Bill was in the garage until very late. But if you had asked them at the time, they probably would have said, yes, they were busy people, but generally they were happy with their lives together.

Then Ellen's business took a downturn. None of her clients seemed interested in pursuing projects, and she was getting nowhere attracting new business. She had to let go of two of her employees, and suddenly she was doing the job of three people.

Ellen tried to talk to Bill about her concerns, but he wasn't around, or if he was, it seemed he was always on the phone trying to track down some bumper or engine or something. Ellen started to feel all alone, and after several months, she just gave up trying to talk to Bill.

Ironically, Bill was feeling isolated himself. What had begun as a hobby, buying vintage cars, restoring and then selling them, had turned into a nice little business for him, and he was like a kid in a candy shop—he loved it! He was so enthusiastic, and at every opportunity, he asked Ellen to come with him to a show or to look at a perspective car to buy, but she was too busy with her work. And besides, she just wasn't interested. She was annoyed that Bill had become so involved with his cars. While her resentment was building, so was Bill's. He asked her to try to see the beauty in these classics, but Ellen wasn't buying it.

They made an appointment to see me, and the first time we got together, I asked them to remember what they loved about each other. We then began to discuss the chasm that had grown between them.

I asked Bill, "Do you know that Ellen's having trouble with her business?"

"Of course I do! I tried to help her. I think she should just quit. She can retire, like me."

Ellen looked shocked. "You know I built that business from nothing. You know how I love what I do. Telling me to just walk away from it is not the help I need!"

When Bill explained that all the time Ellen had been working on building her business, he had been taking care of everything else in their lives, from paying the bills to doing the errands, the laundry, the food shopping—"and I was working at a full-time job, too," he said through clenched teeth.

Marriage Trap   It's great when you can understand what your partner's going through, and even better when you tell her so. But beware of talking too much about your similar situation. This is about her—not you.

Then it was Ellen's turn. "You never want to spend any time with me on the weekends. All you want to do is play with your toys and hang out at your club."

Bill said, "But I always ask you to come with me! I wish you would let me teach you a little about my world. Just try!"

Ellen thought about it and nodded her head. "You're right. It wouldn't hurt me to take more of an interest. The cars really are quite beautiful when you're finished with them."

Eventually, they reconciled. Together, after eight sessions, they compromised. Bill helped Ellen at her shop two days a week and went with her to prospective clients. And Ellen somehow got interested in the world of classic cars and actually used her wonderful eye for color when it came to the interiors and painted finishes.

The moral of this story? Step back, take a fresh look at the other person, and try to see what he sees. Everyone has a different point of view. The point is to respect the other person's view, even try it on for size. By doing that, you're validating the other person; you're showing her the respect she deserves. Relationships go well when partners respect each other—even if they don't agree with what the other is saying.

Respecting Each Other's Opinion

People get married because they're in love, but they stay married because their partners treat them with respect. Everything else flows from this core reality. When your partner gives you respect, it makes you feel good, plain and simple. And when you feel good, the relationship is strengthened.

In contrast, when your partner tears you down and says something that makes you feel bad, it hurts you and your relationship.

This doesn't mean you shouldn't get upset or disagree—that leads to other problems. But you need to communicate your feelings in a way that shows your partner respect.

Misc.

It's Not Sympathy

Sympathy is what you express when there's a death in a family. Empathy is what you offer when your partner is going through something. It shows you can identify with his feelings because you've gone through something similar. For example, if your husband has become immobilized because his sibling is ill, you might tell him, "I remember when my sister was sick. I was very close to her, and I was worried that she was going to die. I felt so bad I didn't feel like doing anything. I just sat around."

Keeping Judgmental Thinking to a Minimum

A key element in making relationships work is having nonjudgmental verbal exchanges. Often, when we were growing up, we heard judgmental messages from our parents: "Don't be lazy. Do your homework!" or "What's wrong with you? Why can't you listen to anything I say?" It's easy, even natural, to pick up these negative habits based on our childhood experiences—and we often don't even realize we're being judgmental.

The trouble is that we feel diminished and devalued when our partner negatively judges us. The result? Getting defensive or becoming passive-aggressive. Take, for example, this exchange between Adam and Susan during one of our sessions:

> *Adam:* "Why do you always tell that same joke when we meet new people?"
>
> *Susan:* "What are you talking about? Why not? It's funny!"
>
> *Adam:* "No, it's not. It's stupid."
>
> *Susan:* "Well, I think it's funny. And so does everyone else!"

Imagine a bell ringing in a boxing match and the two of them going to their corners. That's what this exchange felt like!

Another result of being the recipient of judgmental thinking is that you can stop listening. Instead of thinking, as in Susan's case, that Adam hates her jokes, she begins thinking, *I'm not funny. I always make a fool of myself when we go out.* Before anyone realizes it, things have spiraled out of control and you both are more distant than ever.

Marriage Trap	Judgmental thinking often leads to fights—and more judgmental thinking. The negative conversation can get even more heated, and before you know it, you're saying things that really hurt and can't be taken back, even with an apology.

Vive la Différence!

When an ego has been damaged by judgmental words, a lot of repair work needs to take place. The person who starts the ball rolling with a negative judgmental remark has to learn how to bite his tongue, while the recipient has to figure out a way to feel better about herself.

The best way to deal with judgmental thinking is not to do it. Instead of complaining about the way your spouse thinks or acts, celebrate it! Turn "she tells awful jokes" into "she's charming when she meets people." Of course, this is more easily said than done, but becoming aware that you're being judgmental goes a long way to repairing damage.

Establishing Boundaries

Have you ever been in a line and the person behind you is breathing down your neck? Or let's say you're in your cube at work and you're trying to take care of a request on your computer—and all while the person who asked you to do something is standing over your shoulder?

It's uncomfortable, isn't it? The same holds true in marriage. You can be as close as two peas in a pod, and normally you enjoy each other's company. But …

There will be times when you want to be alone. Or you don't want your spouse watching as you answer a text message, or, say, you want to take a bath in private. Like fences, boundaries make good neighbors—and spouses.

Everyone Needs Some Space

Setting boundaries is something we all do, either consciously or unconsciously. Maybe we don't talk about our personal lives at work. Or maybe we appreciate when our mother-in-law calls first before coming over. Or maybe it's as simple as what movie icon Greta Garbo used to say: "I want to be alone."

MISC.	**Deal-Breakers** Some boundaries cannot be crossed: any form of abuse cannot be tolerated. But other boundaries are subtler: repeating embarrassing stories in public may or may not be a deal-breaker, but if it bothers you, it's something you need to discuss with your spouse.

But when we get married, the logic of boundaries goes out the window. We need to feel like "one"—and if we don't, we fear our marriage is failing. After all, your vows made you one, right? Wrong. Marriage is a partnership. There's probably nothing in your wedding vows that said, "Two of us become one." In fact, a normal—and healthy—response when someone has gotten too close is to run away. We need to protect our egos, and that means the opposite of becoming one with someone.

I've had spouses sit in my office and tell me they didn't know what their own favorite color was—they were that involved with their spouse. Many couples, especially in relationships where one is very dominant and the other is very passive, lose their sense of self.

Your spouse may very well be your best friend, and that's a good thing. It means you are both truly connected. But no one person can be everything to everyone. Think of the pressure! It's important that you both have different interests and different friends so you're together as individuals, not as conjoined twins. Having a sense of self—and letting your spouse have a sense of self—shows respect for each other.

Emotional, Physical, and Financial Boundaries

They say one person's heaven is another person's hell. The boundaries you feel are important and shouldn't be crossed might be very different from someone else's—especially when that someone else is your spouse.

Do you know what boundaries are important to you? Take the following quiz to find out. On a scale of 1 (not important) to 5 (very important), see how you feel about these items:

1. Being alone when upset

2. Frequent reassurance

3. Privacy in the bathroom

4. Being well-groomed at all times

5. No talking in the morning

6. Having individual credit cards

7. Freedom to buy items without discussion

8. Cooking together

9. Going out with the girls or the guys without your spouse

10. Being coddled when sick

Now repeat this same exercise, but this time, rate the items from your spouse's point of view. Do you know how he feels? Do you know his boundaries? And most importantly, do you respect them?

Your Spouse's Needs or Moods

When counseling couples, the issue of "being happy" often comes up. Take my clients Carol and Armand, for example. When I asked Carol, "What do you want from your relationship?" Carol answered, "I just want to be happy." That's a wonderful goal, but Armand needs more feedback in order to do his part in working on the relationship. He needs to know what will make Carol happy, and that means knowing what she needs, whatever her mood.

Carol needs to specifically identify what being happy means to her. If she cannot articulate what she needs, how can her spouse anticipate them? How can she get what she needs if she doesn't even know what those needs are? Does feeling connected mean a phone call to her in the middle of the day? Does it mean doing the housework? Does it mean more romance?

Let's try an exercise designed to focus on what "being happy" means to your partner. List four things you believe would make your partner happy. Ask your spouse to do the same. It would be great if you can compare notes afterward.

But tread carefully. If you've gotten it wrong, your partner may become exasperated and say, "Haven't you been listening? I've been telling you this for years!"

Don't Cling

I've often wondered why being needy was a bad thing. People are so afraid to show that they need something; they don't want to appear weak.

I disagree, especially in marriage. I think you need to show each other what you need. However, you also need to love and let go. In other words, you need to know what your spouse wants in order to respect her wishes. You can be sure your spouse knows what you need. But you can't smother your spouse.

Marriage Trap

Whenever I hear the word *clingy,* I think of a child grabbing onto his mother's leg while she's trying to walk. No one wants to be clingy, especially as an adult. If you find that you can't bear to be apart from your spouse, you may need your own individual professional help to work out your insecurity issues.

You Can't Always Make It Better

Janet and Elliot were different from other couples. They both knew what each other needed, they could anticipate each other's needs, and they knew where their boundaries lay. Sounds like things should've been fine, right?

Wrong. Even though Janet knew Elliot liked to be alone when he was upset, she had to try to help. She couldn't stop herself. "When I see Elliot is upset, I just can't help myself," she told me. "I have to try to make him feel better. I hate to see the people I love sad."

After a few sessions, Janet realized that by ignoring what Elliot wanted, she wasn't showing him respect, she didn't understand what he needed, and she wasn't being empathetic. We worked out a strategy together: when Elliot was sad, she would occupy herself with something—go out of the house and do an errand, take an exercise class, or get on the computer. Even though every fiber of her being wanted to hug Elliot and tell him everything would be okay, she wasn't allowed to go near him for at least an hour. After that hour, she could ask him how he was. And Elliot, for his part, would need to talk to Janet because he needed to respect how she felt, too!

Respecting Each Other's Needs

While your ultimate goal is to make your marriage a lasting one, you can only get there by determining each other's needs. And to do that, you need to define, in black and white, what that means. Take a few minutes to think about which of your needs are important for your spouse to address.

MISC.	**Three Simple Rules** Here are three simple rules to a lasting marriage: listen to each other, respect what each other feels and thinks, and make decisions together.

The following Qualities of a Good Relationship exercise identifies specific qualities I believe make up a good relationship. Take a look at them and compare them to your "needs" list. Are you getting what you need? Are these qualities components of your married life?

Rate how important each quality—including any on your list not listed here—is to you on a scale of 1 (not at all important) to 5 (very important). Don't rate the satisfaction you're feeling in each area, only how important each quality is to you.

Qualities of a Good Relationship

1. Being able to speak my mind

2. Feeling supported

3. Making a contribution to the marriage

4. Resiliency in my partner

5. Flexibility in my partner

6. Optimism

7. Balance between being together and having individual lives

After you've completed it for yourself, go back and fill it out as you think your partner would respond.

The Importance of Influence

Over the years, the roles and relationships between men and women have changed for the better. Years ago, men had to be macho and women had to be meek. Men went out to earn a living, and women stayed home, cooked and cleaned, and raised the kids.

Happily, those rules have changed. Even better, there are no rules anymore! Women are bread winners. Men raise children. Husbands and wives share chores. But remnants of the past still exist:

> "You have to check with your wife before you can go out with the guys?"

> "I am listening, dear. Please tell me again. Please."

> "We're not lost! I'm not asking for directions."

> "Whatever you say, dear."

It's easy to determine which phrases come from the mouths of men and which come from the mouths of women. The sad truth is that even in today's modern world, men still influence women far more than women influence men. Women are more prone to avoid fights; they are peace-makers. Men, on the other hand, still expect to have the right-of-way—and aren't always aware of it.

Love Letters

A long-term study of 130 newlyweds through 8 years of marriage done by Dr. John Gottman found that the happiest marriages were ones where husbands allowed their wives to have influence over them.

A case in point is Lois and Geoff. For all intents and purposes, theirs was a marriage in which influence was equal. They both worked and liked their jobs. They discussed big-purchase items and compromised where necessary. They didn't always agree, but they respected each other's opinion—until it came to buying a house.

They both wanted an old Victorian, and neither of them wanted a huge mortgage. Sounds like all was well, right? It was—until Geoff saw the Victorian home of his dreams. It had gables and window seats and gingerbread finishing. And it was also far beyond their means.

Lois loved the house, too, but she knew they couldn't afford it. She figured Geoff felt the same way. Wrong. Geoff wanted that house, and that was that. They had arguments about it, and Lois couldn't believe that Geoff was being so irrational. But Geoff was adamant. Eventually, Lois let herself be influenced by Geoff, but their marriage was, unfortunately, headed for disaster. The financial strain of the new house ended up being too much.

Ironically, in their divorce settlement, they had to sell the house that started them down the road to divorce.

Influence Between Spouses

Do you listen to your spouse? Do you let him influence your decisions? And conversely, do you have influence over your spouse? Do you both treat each other with respect? To see where you stand on the influence scale, rate the following statements true or false:

1. I have a lot of respect for my spouse.

2. I frequently tell my spouse how much respect I have for her.

3. My spouse listens to me.

4. I listen to my spouse.

5. We always discuss big-item decisions.

6. We have learned to compromise.

7. I value my spouse's opinions and really want to know what he thinks.

8. I don't cut off my spouse, even when she is saying something I don't agree with.

9. My spouse gets very emotional, and I've learned to wait until we cool off to discuss things.

10. I don't think in terms of "winning" or "losing" when it comes to making decisions.

11. I seek out my spouse's opinions.

If you answered "true" to most of these statements, chances are you have a happy marriage. You respect each other, and you each equally influence the other.

If you had a lot of "false" in your answers, it doesn't mean your marriage is in trouble. But it does mean you need to have a conversation with your partner, and you both need to become more respectful of each other.

Marriage Trap

Influence is different from control. When a partner thinks her feelings and ideas are dismissed and not taken seriously, she'll get angry and eventually remove herself from the relationship.

Empathy Helps Foster Influence

Once you've walked a mile in someone else's shoes, it's hard not to understand how he feels. And it's impossible not to have a newfound respect. Truly understanding what the other person is going through helps you know where she is coming from.

And the better you understand each other, the more you'll listen and the more you'll allow each other to influence the other.

Dealing with Contempt

Contempt is the opposite of respect. Love and the positive feelings that come with it are severely injured when one partner believes the other is being patronizing and disrespectful. And how do they come to this conclusion? The partner ignores the other's opinions. What's worse, if one partner starts feeling contempt for his spouse, he also starts developing amnesia about the positive, good qualities she had when they first got married.

The best way to counteract contempt is easy: just listen to your spouse, respect what he or she is saying, and talk about it. Simple, right?

A good exercise to start the influence ball rolling and dampen any contemptible flames is a team-building exercise used by many corporations:

Imagine the two of you were in a shipwreck and made it to a deserted island. You need to escape the island, but you can only take with you five items from the boat that were drifting toward shore. Here are your choices:

> One battery
>
> Yards of rope
>
> One inflatable raft
>
> Three flares
>
> One white flag
>
> Matches (kept dry in a plastic bag)
>
> Candles
>
> One gun with ammunition
>
> One tent
>
> Cans of soup
>
> One net
>
> Two spears

Each of you makes your own list of five items. Then, go over your lists together, explaining to the other why those five items will help you survive and escape the island. Once you've listened to each other, combine your lists so you both have five items you agree on. Rescue will be imminent!

The point of this exercise is to see how much influence you each have over the other. It's also a way of showing respect to each other and coming to a mutual decision. It's hard to have contempt for your spouse when you're trying to escape the deserted island. Similarly, it should be just as hard to show contempt in real life. Your current situation might not be your own unique version of *Survival: Timbuktu,* but survival is still at stake—your lasting marriage.

Essential Takeaways

- Boundaries are important to set for a happy marriage.
- Respect each other's different points of view.
- Try to keep judgmental thinking at a minimum.
- Having empathy for your spouse means understanding how he feels and what he thinks.
- Feeling you have influence over your spouse is an important element of a lasting marriage.

chapter 10

In You I Trust

The importance of trust

Different types of trust

Building trust

When trust is broken

For many couples, *trust* is synonymous with *love* and *marriage*. After all, how can you share your life with someone you don't trust? But trust issues are more complicated than that. You don't automatically trust someone, even if you love them. Just ask anyone who has ever been jealous.

Trust is complicated. There's personal trust, situational trust, even irrational, blind trust. In this chapter, I examine the different types of trust couples have between each other. I also explore how trust develops and why it has to evolve.

Trust is a key to lasting marriage, but it has to be heartfelt. Read on ....

A Cornerstone of Marriage

Couples must be able to trust and feel safe with one another. This is a basic building block of any relationship. One aspect of trust is being confident that your partner will be there when you need him.

Crises such as illness or death offer a tremendous opportunity for a relationship to grow. When one partner sticks by the other through a crisis, when she is being emotionally supportive, the experience creates a profoundly positive impact: "I feel safe and protected because my spouse was there with me when the chips were down."

Trust Has Many Layers

Trust is not just about "being there." Nor is it all about being faithful. Trust is a powerful connection between a husband and wife—but it doesn't happen overnight. And it cannot be false.

I remember Ann and Carlos. When they came to see me, their marriage was breaking up because Ann was convinced that Carlos had been unfaithful. The more he denied it, the more she believed he had cheated.

"I don't trust you, and I never will," Ann told him.

In Carlos's mind it was becoming, "If that's the case, I might as well do the crime."

> **Marriage Trap**
>
> Rejection is only one result of infidelity. When one of you cheats on the other, trust is torn apart—and it takes a lot of work to repair it.

When Carlos was younger, he was a ladies' man. He was a dark-eyed Latino with movie-star good looks. Ann was pretty, but she was more average-looking. She hadn't dated a lot when she met Carlos.

They fell in love after a few dates. Carlos loved Ann's sense of humor and her kindness. He thought she was beautiful. Ann fell in love with Carlos's good looks and also his kindness and consideration. They clicked.

The problem came from the outside world. Just because Carlos wasn't interested in any other women didn't mean they didn't look at him. He couldn't hide his good looks, and whenever they went out to dinner or just took a walk around their neighborhood, women did an about-face. Some of these women were also beautiful—and Carlos looked at them, too.

"I wasn't interested in meeting them," Carlos told me. "I just appreciated their beauty. That's all."

But it made Ann crazy. She was convinced Carlos wanted to have an affair. After all, she didn't have guys turning heads for her!

By the time they'd come to see me, Carlos was ready to cheat. He was tired of trying to convince Ann he loved her and he wasn't interested in anyone else.

It took several sessions for Ann to realize it was her own low self-esteem that made her feel insecure. The more she mistrusted Carlos, the more he resented it. In his mind, it wasn't fair. He trusted Ann—and it was about time she trusted him.

Eventually, Ann and Carlos reconciled their differences. Carlos gave Ann more reassurance, telling her how much he loved her and being more affectionate. This helped Ann feel more confident and trust Carlos more.

Trusting Yourself

Trust is not just about whether or not your spouse cheats on you. Trust is something you learn. If you grew up in a household where your father lied to your mother, or your parents lied to you, trust isn't going to come easy to you. In order to trust someone else, you must first learn to trust yourself, your feelings, and your judgment.

This is more easily said than done. Add a little insecurity to the brew, and it becomes seemingly impossible. But it isn't. Here are some things I tell my clients:

Listen to your inner voice. We have become so used to listening to other people's opinions that we forget we have our own. Dig deep. How do you really feel?

Say it out loud. Maybe you have your own opinion, but your insecurity stops you from declaring it. What if you're laughed at? What if someone judges you unfavorably? Tell yourself the worst that can happen is that someone won't agree with you. The world won't end. There will still be people who like you—and, yes, people who won't like you. But one opinion won't change that equation.

Keep a journal. Writing down your fears can help diminish them. Self-enlightenment can go far in making you see that your mistrust of your spouse is based on something that happened in your past—and has nothing to do with reality or even him.

Seek professional help. Sometimes your insecurity and lack of self-confidence so undermines your trust in others that you need a one-on-one therapist to help you. Before you can heal your marriage, you need to learn how to heal yourself.

Repeating the Past

If you were neglected as a child, those same feelings you experienced can occur when you're an adult. Say your mother would get angry and leave the house without saying where she was going. You and your older sibling were in the house by yourselves for hours, and you were terrified she wasn't coming back.

Now think of yourself today—when your spouse gets angry and slams the door without telling you where he's going. That same feeling of terror you felt as a kid puts the present situation completely out of perspective. You become terrified of abandonment, when in reality, your spouse was just taking a walk around the block to cool off.

I call these "memory windows." Becoming aware of them can help you close and lock them for good.

Between the Two of You

Trust is a pact, an unstated agreement that not only do you love each other, but you have faith in each other. Trust in a relationship involves a few other things, too:

Respect. When you listen to your spouse and take her opinion seriously, she'll know you trust her.

Honoring personal feelings and opinions. If your spouse loves a movie you absolutely hate, it doesn't mean he's a jerk. He's allowed to have his own feelings—and they count just as much to him as your feelings do to you. Validating his feelings helps build his trust.

Giving in. When you defer to your partner, it doesn't mean you're weak. Sometimes you need to weigh the value of something she wants—and whether or not it's that important to you. Backing down shows you trust your partner, as does your willingness to go along with her even though you don't agree.

Belief. If you find it difficult to trust anyone, you won't automatically trust your spouse. But it's important to give him the benefit of the doubt. After all, if you don't believe what your spouse is saying, it's hard to believe you really love him.

Love Letters	Trust takes courage. It's a leap of faith. But then again, so is love. The saying, "'tis better to have loved and lost than not to have loved at all," emphasizes the importance of taking that leap. Trust the person you love—it's bravery that will make you feel like a hero.

Developing Trust

Trust is a key component to a lasting marriage because when no trust exists between partners, the relationship will fall apart, pure and simple. If trust has deteriorated on some level in your relationship, there are ways to re-establishing it.

But trust is tricky. It can mean different things to different people. The first step to developing trust in your relationship is to define it.

Think about what trust means to you and then what you think it means to your partner. Now ask your spouse to define trust. Discuss your answers together, over dinner or during a quiet time. You might be surprised at the answers!

How Much Trust Exists Between You?

I've got you thinking about trust, and I want you to roll it around in your mind a little more. What can you trust your spouse about? What are your concerns? Take the following quiz to see where your trust issues lie and where you think your spouse's lie.

Rate each of the following statements on a scale of 1 to 5, where 1 means "strongly agree," 2 means "somewhat agree," 3 means "don't know," 4 means "somewhat disagree," and 5 means "strongly disagree."

I trust that my partner will …

1. Be there when I need her.

2. Be honest with me.

3. Be sensitive to my emotional needs.

4. Make good decisions on what I consider small issues.

5. Make good decisions on what I consider medium issues.

6. Make good decisions on big issues.

7. Make good decisions about our money.

8. Be helpful.

9. Follow through on things.

Tack onto this list any other trust-related issues you can count on in your spouse not mentioned here.

I trust that my partner will not …

1. Overreact.

2. Tell my secrets to anyone else.

3. Abandon me if the going gets tough.

4. Abandon me if he gets angry with me.

5. Embarrass me.

Add any other trust issues you don't think you can count on in your spouse not mentioned here.

Now, go through the exercise again, this time rating the items how you think your partner would respond if he were evaluating you.

Finally, think about a trust issue you believe is of concern between you and your spouse, and be prepared to talk about it.

Set aside time for both of you to go over your answers. Remember, the more time you're able to give to these trust issues, the more you'll trust each other—and the more your marriage will stay strong.

What's Yours Is Mine

Part of trust is sharing—but that doesn't always mean sharing something physical. If you trust your spouse, you still might not want her wearing your favorite scarf. You still might get angry if he takes the last piece of cake.

Trust and sharing have many levels of meaning. They can be ...

- *Physical.* Making love when you trust your spouse can be very hot! You won't be afraid to experiment.

- *Emotional.* Telling your spouse about your past can offer a great deal of relief.

- *Mental.* When you trust someone, you know she understands you and what makes you tick.

- *Vocal.* When you trust your spouse, you won't be afraid to voice your true opinions.

Marriage Trap

There's sharing—and then there's sharing. Sometimes too much trust can go into too-much-information territory. Dirty habits, slovenly dress, open-door policies—sometimes these can be real turn-offs. It's hard to feel sexy about someone after she's been bleaching her mustache or he's been tweezing his nose hairs. You can feel safe when you trust someone, but that's no excuse to always scratch where it itches.

Money Matters

Money can be an explosive topic. And the way you and your partner handle it may look strange to another couple but be just fine between the two of you. You and your spouse may have joint bank accounts, for example, and be perfectly comfortable with the setup, while another couple may keep bank accounts separate—and still trust each other.

If you do have joint accounts, it's possible that you can look at the couple who keeps separate ones as a couple who doesn't trust each other enough to share their money. Instead, they might feel responsible for different money matters, and they don't want to fight about money. Keeping independent accounts prevents that—and they still trust each other explicitly.

Sharing Spaces

The more trust you and your spouse build between each other, the safer you'll feel in each other's company. And a safe emotional space is imperative to a lasting—and happy—marriage.

In fact, an emotionally safe environment is so important to a marriage that without it, you can be in danger of abuse. Abuse is more than a physical blow to the face or a despicable sexual act. When you neglect a loved one, you are showing him emotional abuse. When you create an unsafe environment, that, too, is abuse. Being afraid to say or do something is a type of abuse—which is the opposite of trust.

> **Marriage Trap**
>
> When you don't trust your spouse, it can be awful not only for your marriage—but for yourself. Being anxious, worrying about something that will probably not happen, feeling jealous—all these mistrustful feelings are emotional torture. Put yourself out of your misery by sitting down with your spouse and talking about your feelings.

Being There

One big aspect of trust is knowing that your partner will be there when he or she is needed. This can be extremely positive for a relationship. In fact, crises such as illness or death offer a tremendous opportunity for a relationship to grow.

When the partner who is not directly affected sticks by the partner who is going through the crisis and is emotionally supportive, the experience provides a profoundly positive memory.

Essential Takeaways

- Developing trust takes time and effort. But it's worth it!
- Everyone has a different definition of trust. Talk to your partner to discover what it means to each of you.
- Trust is a basic foundation for a lasting marriage.
- You have to trust in yourself first before you can trust anyone else.

chapter 11

The Importance of Good Communication

The rules of effective communication

But versus *yet*

He said/you heard

Effective negotiation

How many times have you heard couples say, or said yourself, "He finishes my sentences"? Or "She knows exactly what I want"? Or the best of all, "We talk about everything. We have no secrets"? All of these are important in a good marriage, and they all involve communicating with your spouse in one way or another.

Communication is a buzzword for just about everything today—getting a good job, keeping the peace, and, yes, making a marriage work. But communication is more than just "talk." It's the way you use your body, the words you use and the way you say them, and most importantly, the way you listen when your spouse is speaking.

Communication: More Than Talk

I often ask my clients what they know about each other—not the obvious things, like faith or education or hobbies, but the actual culture they both share. Are your families similar? Do your needs mesh? Do you have the same perspective on life?

Many of my clients don't know what I'm talking about. They've never sat down and dug deep into each other's psyche. It wasn't their style. But the fact that they were sitting in my office meant there was a problem in that silence. They needed to communicate who they were to each other. And they needed to communicate what they found in each other that made them feel loved.

> **Communication Art**
>
> misc.
>
> The idea of effective communication isn't new. In Milton Wright's 1936 book called *The Art of Conversation,* he wrote (and I paraphrase) that conversation is not made up of monologues, and silence is as important in conversation as notes are to music.

One thing I've learned in my more than 35 years as a marriage counselor is that communication can be learned, and it's never too late to start a conversation going.

The Difference Between *But* and *Yet*

It's important for you to be aware of two very simple three-letter words with a lot of meaning: *but* and *yet*. Short but powerful, these words strongly influence the communications you and your partner share. One is good; the other is bad. *But* is bad. Any time you say something to your partner that's followed by a *but,* you've just negated what you previously said.

For example, if you say, "I love you, but you are really sloppy," your partner only hears, "You are sloppy," and the "I love you" gets lost in the vapors.

If he says, "I'm looking forward to going out tonight, but I'm really tired," you only hear, "I'm really tired," which, translated in your mind, means he doesn't want to go out with you.

If you say, "I think it's great you bought a motorcycle, but I'm afraid to try it out," he only hears, "I don't want to share your motorcycle rides" and, taking it another step, "How could you waste money on that?"

MISC.

Communication Can Be Hard Work

Thousands of books, articles, and even tweets have been written about communication. With all this attention, you'd think it would be easy to speak to each other! To communicate in a marriage, you have to be honest with yourself and your spouse—hard work that leaves you vulnerable.

Yet, on the other hand, is good. If you use this word and really mean it, *yet* can be a powerful, positive force when communicating with your partner. Look at the difference in impact in these two dialogues:

A bad dialogue:

> *Harry:* "I'm really overwhelmed with work right now and can't talk."
>
> *Sally:* "You never have time to talk to me!"
>
> *Harry (raising his voice):* "Why do you always have to be so defensive?"
>
> *Sally (raising her voice):* "I'm not defensive. You just don't want to talk to me—ever!"
>
> A fight ensues ….

A good dialogue:

> *Harry:* "I'm really overwhelmed with work right now and can't listen to you yet."
>
> *Sally:* "Oh, okay. That's fine. We can talk later."
>
> And they go about their business without a fight.

Why is *yet* so much better? Because it implies that there will be a time in the future when you will be able to speak to each other. In the first example, Harry was most likely irritated that Sally interrupted him, and it showed. But in the second example, Harry makes certain Sally doesn't think he's brushing her off; he demonstrates the importance of their communicating later by implying that he can give her more time later, when he can really be there emotionally.

Yet is interchangeable with *right now* or *at this moment.* They all mean the same thing: now isn't a good time, but we will talk later.

A word of caution: if you do postpone a conversation, event, or issue, you need to follow up. If you don't, your spouse will hear the *but* anyway—and your relationship erodes that much more.

If you aren't *yet* ready to talk to your spouse after a short period of time, be sure you tell her you haven't forgotten, but the task at hand has taken longer than expected. You might not be able to remember to do this right off the communication bat, but eventually your spouse will realize, yes, you are sincere because you're not forgetting about it; you're demonstrating that she is important, too.

Don't say *yet* if you don't mean it in the hopes your spouse will forget about it. I guarantee you she won't. If it won't be a good time until the next day, it's okay. Just be honest about it to reinforce your good intentions.

The only time *yet* isn't a good strategy is if, say, Sally was really upset with Harry and she just can't wait to talk. Hopefully, Sally can learn to be patient, but if it's really important to her that you talk now, you'll have to be flexible and put aside what you're doing.

The *yet* message is extremely important for two reasons. Critical issues that aren't addressed do not go away. If anything, they get worse with time—and come up as ammunition in a fight down the road. And by not giving your partner a timetable, even a vague one, she'll feel dismissed, unloved, and left with the message that her feelings don't matter to you.

The Do's and Don'ts of Communication

One of the biggest complaints I hear from the couples is, "We just don't communicate well." That sentence is both very telling and vague at the same time. What does it really mean? In which way don't they communicate well?

It's How You Play the Game

When you're talking to your spouse, remember: this is the person you love—not, say, a competitor at work. Winning is beside the point. Partners in a solid relationship communicate in such a way that both people feel listened to, accepted, and understood.

Here are some don'ts when talking to your partner:

- Don't interrupt.

- Don't be hurtful.

- Don't always have to be right.

- Don't be coy.

- Don't lie.

- Don't assume your spouse should know what you're talking about.

- Don't be accusatory.

- Don't put your spouse in a position where he feels it necessary to defend himself.

- Don't start a conversation when you're angry.

- Don't threaten.

Avoiding this list of don'ts is more easily said than done. But with a little guidance, you can make communication a cornerstone of your marriage.

Rules sound very inflexible—and apt to be broken. And each happy couple has their own set of rules that make their marriage work. Rather than offer you hard-and-fast rules, I'd like to address some strategies that can be useful when working on better communication with your spouse. I call these "do" strategies "The Ten Communication Commandments." See how many you already follow, as well as which one or two you can implement right now for better communication with your partner:

Commandment 1—Listen. Hear the emotions behind the words; they say a lot more.

Commandment 2—Focus. Pay attention to what your partner's saying instead of thinking about your answer.

Commandment 3—Look. Many people don't feel listened to unless they're being looked at.

Commandment 4—Use I. You sounds accusatory, whereas *I* gives the speaker ownership of his or her feeling; rather than "You always yell at me," say "I feel like I'm always being yelled at."

Commandment 5—Timing. When you need to discuss an important and/ or difficult issue, be sensitive in choosing an appropriate time for the conversation.

Commandment 6—Clarity. State things simply, and ask your spouse for more detail if you need it.

Commandment 7—Perception. The real meaning of every communication is how it's heard, not what's intended.

Commandment 8—Awareness. Notice your partner's reaction when you speak. Is he withdrawing? Does he look like he's being attacked? Is he paying attention?

Commandment 9—Ask. Questions help you better understand what your partner's saying. Curiosity helps you learn what's important to her.

Commandment 10—Recognition. Be attentive to your partner's response. If your partner looks distracted, stop and ask him for feedback, or continue the conversation later.

Silence Isn't Always Golden

MISC.

Listening to your partner is good. Saying nothing is bad. Silence is often perceived as a negative communication, and your partner will either think you don't care or you're shutting him out.

Obviously, you can't tackle these "Ten Commandments" all at once. Remember that Rome wasn't built in a day, and neither is a lasting marriage.

One more word of advice: avoid telling your partner "You need to follow this list." That will put him on the defensive, and he won't want to participate. Instead, ask him if he's interested in communicating better, or simply make a copy of the list and leave it on the table or nightstand. The list shouldn't be yet another issue.

Recognize the Mars/Venus Aspect of Your Marriage

According to John Gray, Ph.D., in his best-selling book *Men Are from Mars, Women Are from Venus,* men and women speak different languages and communicate in different ways. And this is, of course, valid: men and women are different physiologically and emotionally. Dr. Gray believes that until men and women acknowledge and accept these differences, they'll never be able to communicate effectively and be happy together.

Dr. Gray's theories include the way men and women communicate when there's a problem or issue at stake. When women communicate a problem, they're looking to have their feelings acknowledged. When men communicate that they're having a problem, they're looking for solutions.

> Misc.
>
> **Defying Convention**
>
> Social psychologist and best-selling author Susan K. Perry, Ph.D., has found that the more men and women switch roles, or become androgynous, the happier the marriage, because each is free to take the role he or she is suited for, not the roles expected of them.

On the other hand, Dr. John Gottman, the famed marriage researcher whose Seattle's Love Laboratory findings many marriage counselors—myself including—are influenced by, believes that although gender may influence the way problems are handled, they don't cause them.

What You Say Might Not Be What He Hears

No one would ever think Bill and Sandy had problems. Married for 21 years, they seemed the perfect couple. They enjoyed each other's company; they laughed a lot; they were good parents. But below the surface a cold war was raging. Resentment had been building for years because they weren't communicating with each other. Instead, they were talking *around* each other, not paying attention, or denying there were any problems at all.

Things got really sticky when money became a little tight. Bill, an accountant, had lost his job in the recession, and Sandy suddenly had the pressure of being the sole breadwinner. She made decent money as a pharmaceutical sales rep, but she needed to work harder and longer in order to receive a bigger paycheck. She didn't feel it was fair; she resented Bill. And Bill? He felt guilty that he wasn't working, but he was also feeling angry at Sandy because she had no compassion for his situation.

When Sandy asked Bill what he did that day, he heard it as "You aren't doing anything. You aren't looking for a job. What's wrong with you?" In actuality, Sandy was genuinely asking because she wanted them to share.

When Bill didn't get to an errand at the drugstore because "he didn't have time," Sandy became furious. "What do you mean you didn't have time? What else are you doing?"

Ouch. Sandy and Bill needed a communication lesson quickly.

In one of his studies, Dr. Gottman found that 70 percent of women feel the friendship they share with their husbands was the reason why their marriage worked. He also found that 70 percent of men felt the same way—proving men and women are more alike than we thought.

Your Intention Might Not Get the Right Reception

I never quite understood the meaning of the old proverb, "The road to hell is paved with good intentions," but I do know that the best of intentions cannot always salvage a marital problem, especially when it comes to communication.

Let's look at Bill and Sandy again. Bill genuinely regretted that he didn't get a chance to go to the drugstore and is genuinely concerned about that he upset his wife. His intentions were good.

However, Sandy received his news with the anger that had been brewing inside her for a long time. She blew the oversight way out of proportion. She was fed up with having to take care of all their finances and, to top it off, Bill didn't even have care enough to go to the drugstore and pick up a prescription for her!

In this case, the "receiver," Sandy, catches a totally different ball from what the "sender," Bill, has thrown.

The Receiver Determines the Real Meaning

It's a fact of communication life: the real meaning of anything said is determined by the receiver, not the sender. In the case of Bill and Sandy, the receiver is Sandy. Sandy's perception of Bill's comment will drive the way she responds to his conversation. Conflict is likely to arise if she misinterprets his intent—which she did.

In turn, if Bill were to respond with comments designed to convince Sandy she was wrong, he could conceivably make her angrier. If he focuses on being offended, hurt, unappreciated, or misunderstood, the outcome will be even worse. Bill's goal was to try to connect with Sandy—not drive her away.

How can Bill change the way Sandy, the receiver, took his words? By using one of these strategies:

- Acknowledging fault and apologizing. Bill might say something like, "Yes, you're right, Sandy. I really should have remembered to stop at the drugstore. It was a little passive-aggressive of me, and I'm sorry."

- Offering a solution. Bill could say, "Next time I will write myself a note to stop at the drugstore." (Obviously, it's important that Bill remember to follow through the next time!)

- Showing immediate remorse. Maybe it will cost Bill, but he can apologize and suggest that "I make dinner tonight and clean up."

- Adding consequences that can benefit Sandy. Bill might add that "The next time I don't follow through on errands while I'm still at home, I promise to take you out to dinner."

You'll notice that each strategy is designed to show that Bill hears what Sandy's saying and understands why she's upset. Even if Bill feels offended, he's diffused the situation because he had to placate Sandy. If he'd tried to show Sandy his point of view, she wouldn't have heard him and their brief communication would have ended up in a fight.

Plan Effective 30-Minute Meetings

When you think about meetings, it might conjure up boardrooms or assembly halls—official, serious gatherings to discuss big, important things. In reality, a meeting can be as casual as a discussion over dinner or talking while riding in the car. When it comes to couples, meetings are very important to sustain long-lasting marriages, but they can be enjoyable, too.

I believe meetings can help with communication because they're an opportunity to understand each other better. That means they have to be constructive—not more opportunity to yell and scream at each other.

Love Letters	Yogi Berra once said, "You got to be very careful if you don't know where you're going because you might not get there." In other words, think about your meeting before it begins. And don't call it when you're still flush with anger.

Preparing for the Conversation

Attitude is everything. Start meetings by discussing some positive things that have been happening or recent accomplishments you or your spouse have had. In other words, you are both calm, positive, and ready to talk—not argue.

If you know you're going to enter a potentially explosive situation, take some time before you sit down to put yourself in your spouse's shoes. Put his or her perspective in your mind.

I always suggest that my clients take 5 to 10 minutes prior to a meeting to write down some of the things they think their partner will say. Be careful to stay descriptive, not judgmental. The more you focus on, listen to, and understand the other person's point of view, the more open you'll be to finding new ways to create a positive situation.

"Most wars are won or lost within our mind before we even step out on the battlefield." This was said centuries ago by Lao Tsu in *The Art of War,* but it's just as true today. Don't plan a meeting unless you can understand on a gut level your partner's point of view, or you will lose your cool.

During the Meeting

I've made a list of things to keep in mind when you're meeting with your spouse. These work whether you're communicating in a spontaneous way or if you've planned ahead for a sit-down:

- Look for areas of similar perspectives and agreement.

- Discuss the smaller issues first.

- Make small concessions on issues without trying to get something back immediately. This not only shows that you're reasonable, but it also instigates the psychological *law of reciprocity.*

The **law of reciprocity** is basically a behavior in which you give freely, with no strings, which makes the recipient want to do the same, also freely and without strings.

- When your spouse makes a compromise, reciprocate by compromising on a different issue.

- Be respectful of your spouse.

- Eat! Having a snack ready shows you went out of your way. It's a kind gesture. And it makes talking more entertaining (as long as you don't talk with your mouth full).

- Keep to the 30-minute time limit.

- Try to schedule meetings twice a month.

- Consider alternate solutions. Don't just look to justify your own point of view.

- Think win-win. There are no losers when you meet. Both of you have to communicate your different points of view in order for the discussion to be a success. Both of you have to feel good about what you talked about.

- Don't pretend things aren't bad if they really are. Your spouse won't believe you, and it'll make anything you say later suspicious.

- If a meeting is starting to heat up, take a break!

Too often our conversations end up sounding negative and focusing only on all the things that are going wrong. Remember bull sessions, when friends were supposed to open up to each other and be honest? About 98 percent of the time, one or more of your friends ended up crying. Being negative accomplishes nothing. Constructive criticism belongs on the job or at school. When you meet with your spouse, the goal is to communicate: your desires, your fears, and why you feel the way you do.

MISC.

The Body Speaks

There are other ways to communicate besides using words. If you're looking at your spouse, smiling, and perhaps touching her hand once in a while, you're saying, "I am open to you. I want to understand you." On the other hand, if you sit down with your arms crossed in front of your chest, your head down, you don't even have to say a word for your spouse to know you're upset and most likely won't listen to what she has to say.

Keeping Lines of Communication Open

Good communication is one of the building blocks of a successful marriage. If you find it difficult to talk to your spouse, try to figure out why. Speak to a close friend. Maybe she can help give you some insights into your other half. Spend time reflecting on your partnership.

If you find your communication lines wearing thin, talk about it! Discuss why you think you two haven't been talking to each other. Find out what the other person is feeling and thinking. Be objective and calm. The most important thing is that you're talking.

Opening the Curtain on Denial

Shirley and Carl had been married for more than 25 years. Shirley was the eternal optimist: everything will be fine as soon as the kids leave the house, or you get the promotion, or our portfolio grows, or ….

Carl, on the other hand, had been quietly desperate for a few years now. He was scared about their future. They never talked about their feelings, and, consequently, their marriage almost broke up. Carl had felt so repressed that he had a short-lived affair.

When they came to see me, Shirley and Carl wanted to save their marriage. It would be a difficult road because of the infidelity but not an impossible one. But the first thing Shirley and Carl needed to do was communicate. Carl needed to tell Shirley that he was scared, that he felt all alone. Shirley needed to tell Carl that she sometimes felt like a cheerleader. In reality, she felt scared, too. She was afraid that if she admitted it, Carl would leave her. And look what happened!

The moral of this story? Talk and talk some more. Instead of rationalizing your feelings about critical issues, talk about them.

Enhancing Your Conversations

An effective tool to keep communications alive is to think of a scale from 1 to 100. Ask yourself how satisfied you are in your marriage and how you can make it 5 points higher. Could you give your husband more compliments? Can you tell your wife how much you appreciate her? What small things can you do to increase your marriage scale another 5 points? What can you do to make your marriage a 75 or a 90? You can think about these improvements anywhere—when you're taking a walk or driving in your car.

The next time you get together with your spouse, talk about your points. Discuss how you can both improve your marriage an extra 5 points. Not only will you be keeping your lines of communication open, but you'll be improving your marriage at the same time!

Essential Takeaways

- Communicating with your spouse is a cornerstone of a healthy marriage.
- Understanding the positive feelings conjured up by *yet* and the negative ones that crop up with *but* is key to positive communication.
- Understand and respect your gender differences, but also realize that even though "men are from Mars" and "women are from Venus," they sometimes see things more alike than not.
- Keep the lines of communication open with 30-minute meetings twice a month.

chapter 12

Fighting Is a Fact of Life

Why we fight

Anger busters

Fighting better

Avoiding hurtful words

Anger is as primal an emotion as happiness or joy. When I hear a couple say they never fight, I don't believe them. Either they're not telling the truth, or their definition of fighting is different from the typical "shouting match."

Your very first fight was most likely devastating, but let's face it, making up was a lot of fun. The emotional adrenaline released when you're fighting can turn on many couples. But when one fight leads to another and yet another, and when it seems like the past 10 years have been one big fight, it's no longer fun. It's hurtful and scary and a definite sign that something is amiss in your marriage.

In this chapter, you learn how to get at the real reasons why you fight—and how to deal with those reasons. The strategies you find in the following pages can help stop an argument about the dishes from turning into a full-blown "I want a divorce!" fight.

Anger Has Many Faces

In my more than 35 years as a marriage counselor, I've seen hundreds of angry people in my office. Sometimes they sit there, arms crossed, not looking at each other. Other times they scream at each other, totally ignoring the fact I'm even in the room.

I've also learned in my years as a therapist that anger is very rarely what it appears to be. A fight might start because of the TV remote or an errand not done, but the reason behind it is very different.

Not Feeling Loved or Necessary

Janice and Tom came to see me because they'd been fighting on and off for years, and each had reached an impasse. Neither one could understand each other's point of view.

The proverbial mess hit the fan when Tom started to come home late from work. At first, Janice was appreciative that Tom called her to say he'd be late. And to be honest, it gave her some free time to have a drink with a friend she hadn't seen in a while or to watch a chick flick on DVD. But the home-alone glow soon dissipated when Tom started staying out three and four nights a week.

What was going on?

Janice was always proud of the open way she and Tom communicated. Whether it was as important as disciplining the kids before they became adults or as simple as where to go on vacation, they were always able to reach some sort of compromise, even if they didn't always agree.

This time, however, was different. When Janice asked Tom point-blank if he was staying away from home on purpose, he looked at her as if she'd grown three heads. "What are you talking about?" he said, his voice getting louder.

"What do you mean, what am I talking about?" Janice countered, her voice also getting sharper.

Tom became angrier and angrier. Did Janice think he was having an affair or something? Didn't she trust him? Did she think it was fun having to work 16-plus-hour days?

It was a short jump from Tom's outbursts to Janice's tearful responses. "You don't care about me anymore." "You never worked like this before." "Why are you so angry?!"

Anger Monitoring

Misc.

Research done in Dr. John Gottman's Love Laboratory in Seattle, Washington, found a definite link between our physical and mental states when we fight. When people get angry, their resting heart rate jumps and their adrenaline kicks in—adding fuel to their stressful mind-set. The more stress, the angrier a couple becomes. With their adrenaline pumping and hearts racing, it's nearly impossible for each spouse to be rational and hear what the other is saying.

The fight between Janice and Tom escalated. The focus of the fight moved from his working late too many nights, to an issue about trust. Tom became angry that Janice didn't trust him. Janice became angry because Tom didn't convince her she should trust him.

The entire fight might have been avoided if Janice had understood that she was feeling left out, that she didn't feel needed or loved. If she had been able to articulate her real feelings, Tom would have immediately understood, and he would have reassured her he loved her and he really was just working late.

Instead, the fight lasted well into the night with no real resolution. Janice felt placated for the moment, but she would need more reassurance in the future. And Tom was well on his way to feeling more and more resentful.

The Aggressive Shape of Feeling Helpless

Anger is also associated with a feeling of helplessness and loss of control. In my experience, the more helpless a partner feels, the more he or she will show it in an aggressive way: anger. And if we continue to feel more and more helpless, that anger can turn into rage.

Think of the last time you were angry at your spouse. What was the scenario? Was he refusing to listen to you about a problem you were having with your mother? Was she refusing to see your point of view about spending your yearly bonus? Did you find yourself getting angrier and angrier the more your spouse kept up his or her end?

Now, imagine that same scenario but with you feeling in control, with your thoughts and perceptions being heard, respected, and having influence. Maybe your partner offers suggestions on how to cope with the problem you're having with your mother; he's empathetic to the situation. Or perhaps your partner nods his head when you talk about spending his bonus money. Maybe he tells you he understands your point of view and suggests a compromise. How angry are you feeling when you think about being in control of the situation?

My clients' expressions always soften and, in a more gentle voice, they say, "I'm not angry at all."

Depression Turns Anger Inward

People don't always express their feelings of helplessness in anger. Instead of acting aggressive toward their partners, they turn their feelings of helplessness inward and become depressed. Instead of thinking, *How dare he?!* they think, *What's the matter with me? I should have said something to him. … It's all my fault.*

Blaming yourself leads to a whole host of complicated feelings:

- *Loss of empowerment.* You feel your role in this relationship is insignificant.

- *Inadequacy.* You begin to believe you have a defect that causes your spouse to get angry.

- *Insecurity.* With all these defects, who could love you?

- *Neediness.* Insecurity leads to feelings of anxiety; you may start ruminating on what's wrong with you or worrying your spouse will leave you.

- *Depression.* Ultimately, all these things lead to feelings of hopelessness and helplessness—which gets worse and worse if not addressed.

The best way to avoid getting depressed is to first recognize what's going on. Once you realize your depression is an expression of your anger toward your spouse, you can address the root causes. (See "Strategies for Fighting" later in this chapter.)

Resentment and Passive-Aggressive Behavior

Each disagreement should be seen as a separate unit. Unfortunately, in the heat of the moment, situations from the past may crop up. Old resentments can become new. Instead of arguing about something specific and immediate, you end up fighting about something that happened a month ago, two months ago, even "way back when."

As we saw in Chapter 11, communication is a key ingredient of a lasting marriage. But talking about something that bothers you is more easily said than done. Often, instead of communicating, we keep quiet and seethe. We file away whatever's bothering us, and it can come out later as *passive-aggressive behavior*—without our even being aware of it!

Definition	**Passive-aggressive behavior** is when you do something that's not overtly aggressive but still meant to make a point. Instead of provoking a fight, for example, you fill the house with flowers—knowing your spouse is allergic to pollen.

Take the case of Marge and Michael. About a month ago, Marge saw a great deal on a digital camera on QVC. Michael had been laid off a few months ago, and they were trying to tighten their belts. But QVC offered "four easy payments," and they'd both been wanting a new camera for a long time. Marge bought the camera without discussing it with Michael. When the package came in the mail, he went ballistic. "What are you doing? We can hardly pay the mortgage, let alone buy a camera!"

Marge started to cry. She got defensive. "It's not my fault we can't afford a camera! I'm bringing in money. I'm tired of doing without because of you!"

Let the fighting begin ... and begin ... and begin again. Reading this scenario, it's easy to see that Marge has been angry at Michael for months. She's been feeling very resentful that he hasn't been working. A camera wasn't something they needed, but it was the perfect passive-aggressive tool to use against Michael. She'd show him!

Marge really believed she was being smart when she bought the camera in the four easy payments. She'd even believed she'd been very supportive of Michael—helping him with his resumé and searching for jobs online.

And Michael? He'd spent the past few months feeling demoralized. He felt guilty that he wasn't being a good provider. He hated himself, and he was getting depressed. He didn't think he was angry at Marge. How could he be?

When they came to see me, Marge and Michael were on the brink of divorce. After several sessions, they were able to peel back their surface feelings and see what was really going on: Marge had been angry at Michael for losing his job, and the resentment had piled up until she did something passive-aggressive: buy the digital camera. Michael, on the other hand, was resentful Marge was being so helpful to him; he saw it as her feeling superior. His passive-aggressive behavior was taking his time to find a job. When they fought about the camera, they were really fighting about a completely different situation. Instead of fighting about the camera purchase, they were fighting about the past.

Marriage Trap	I found myself asking a client, "Would you rather be right, or would you rather be effective?" It made him pause and think, and the fight he'd been having with wife was diluted.

Anger Uses a Lot of Energy

Anger robs us of a great deal of energy, and it distances us from other people. If we overdo it, we can lose our friends, our spouses, our children, and even our jobs. When we're angry, we don't have peace of mind.

Fights can be a particularly vulnerable time for relationships. One of my "Dr. Marty Rules" for couples is never to negotiate when you're upset. Attempts to compromise can escalate into a bigger fight—and even more wasted energy. Instead …

1. Become aware you're upset.

2. Cool down, and take a deep breath.

3. Realize the fight is not such a big deal—your relationship is a bigger deal.

4. Don't push the argument under the rug. Make a plan to talk later, when you can both come up with a creative solution.

Try these steps on your own so you can see how they work. Then offer to show your spouse how you can both handle the next argument that comes up.

The Anger Diluter

In working toward rebuilding a relationship, it's necessary to deal with this potentially destructive emotion. To start understanding your anger, take this simple test:

Which of these do you think is the best way to handle anger?

> Get even with that son-of-a-gun.
>
> Forgive the person you're angry with.
>
> Ignore the situation—and the fact that you're angry.

The correct answer is none of these. Anger consumes an inordinate amount of time, energy, and space in our brain that could be put to much better use. Instead, try diluting your anger. Here's how:

Anger diluter 1: When you're fighting with your spouse, rate yourself using my "Dr. Marty Anger Scale": a scale of 1 (mildly annoyed, such as when your spouse is 10 minutes late for a dinner reservation) to 5 (very annoyed, such as when your spouse has brought the boss and her husband home for dinner without advance warning and you're wearing a robe and facial mask when he ushers them in).

Anger diluter 2: Now think about a different situation when you and your spouse were fighting, and imagine walking away from it to calm yourself. Too often we want to go after the person who's angering us. While we may feel completely justified at the time, this aggressive behavior really only reinforces the negative feelings.

Anger diluter 3: Examine the origin of your anger. What made you feel out of control and angry in the first place? Now imagine the same situation without the out-of-control anger. This should significantly diminish your desire to fight.

Anger diluter 4: Develop a plan that enables you to regain control the next time you and your partner get into a battle. I suggest doing this 20 to 30 minutes after completing the first two anger diluters, when you have a clearer head.

> **Misc.**
>
> **The Anger Theme**
>
> All arguments are based on the same theme: Do you respect me? Do you think my opinion has value?

These four basic steps are straightforward, but they're not easy to do. Here are some suggestions to help you through these four steps:

- Ask a friend for help with Anger Diluters 3 and 4.

- Write down your thoughts when working on Anger Diluters 3 and 4.

- If you weren't able to reduce some of your anger or come up with a new plan to regain control, let some time go by and try this exercise again in a day or two, when the anger may be more diluted.

Listen, Don't React

When your heart's pounding and the words are flying out of your mouth, it's difficult to "stop, look, and listen." Right now, all you want to do is kill her with your weapon of choice.

Although you can't believe it in the heat of the moment, your partner might have a legitimate point of view—even if you don't understand it. By listening to what she is saying, you can be able to relate to it while still keeping your own integrity.

When I say "relate to," I don't mean the surface fight about walking the dog or picking up the dry cleaning. I'm talking about the underlying causes of your partner's anger. Identifying the emotional reasons below the surface of her anger enables you to understand why she seems angry at everything you do!

Here are some examples of underlying feelings that can make your partner lash out. Do you recognize any of them as possibly causing her anger?

- Not feeling loved or nurtured

- Not being listened to

- Feeling ignored and taken for granted

- Feeling bullied

Take a moment to listen to your partner. Then jot down what you think is the real reason she's fighting with you.

Meaningful Input in a Situation

As a marriage counselor, I often hear, "She's going to do what she wants no matter what I say." All of us want to feel that we have influence over our partner, that we provide solid input when it comes to making a decision.

However, this doesn't mean our partner has to do everything we want or agree with us on everything. But it does mean we need to believe our point of view is respected and heard. It's amazing how anger can dissipate when you realize your spouse finds what you say valuable. Or that you can take a step back from your own emotions and see your partner's point of view.

Marriage Trap	Four hateful words can escalate any fight: "It's all your fault!" Yes, bad things happen. And yes, sometimes they're more your partner's fault than yours. But the blame game doesn't help anyone. If true, it can be like adding salt to a wound. If false, it's completely unfair. It's a no-win situation for both of you.

Strive for Clarity

Before you can resolve an argument, you need to know what you're fighting about. Here are some signs your marriage needs more clarity—which can bring about fewer fights.

Lately, you've been fighting less and less, but you feel more distant than ever. Beware of "emotional checkouts." Address the distance in the same way you'd address a situation that makes you angry.

Everything is negative. Instead of focusing on what you like in your partner, you focus on what you hate—spontaneous combustion for any fight!

You feel like your spouse is deliberately trying to hurt you. Be sure you understand both your own and your spouse's underlying emotions beneath the angry words.

Your fights never seem to end; they just get pushed aside. There are only two ways to settle a dispute: either you figure out a compromise you both can live with or you agree to disagree—in a respectful way.

One of you always overreacts. It's not a good sign when everything you do is taken the wrong way or ends up in an angry fight.

You don't take time-outs. If all you seem to do is fight with each other, it's a warning sign your marriage is in trouble. Work with the advice in this book, or seek out a professional counselor.

Neither one of you feels you have influence over each other. Influence is not control; it's more about respect. If your spouse thinks you're not taking him seriously, he'll either instigate a fight or emotionally withdraw from the marriage.

After working on some of these points and clearing the air, you might find you spend less time fighting.

Try Laughter

There's nothing like laughter to stop a fight in its tracks. Have you ever been in the middle of a huge fight with your partner, only to look at each other and crack up? Maybe it's the way your partner raised her eyebrow in that particular way of hers—which you mimic and makes both of you laugh. Or maybe it's the phrase you use (over and over again) that stops both of you in the middle of a shouting match and start laughing instead. Laughter puts a fight into perspective; it helps you see how ridiculous it is for both of you to be fighting.

Of course, laughter cannot be forced. You can't pretend to laugh just to stop a fight. Nor can you be so angry with each other that you're not even listening—let alone looking at each other!

> **A Quick Laugh**
>
> Misc.
>
> Rodney Dangerfield once said, "My wife and I were happy for 20 years. Then we met." He also said, "I haven't spoken to my wife in years. I don't want to interrupt her." Ba-dum-dum!

It's Not the Fight, but *How* You Fight

People have different ways of fighting—and one is not necessarily better than the other. When couples come to see me, it's because the fighting has divided them and the conflict is too deep to handle on their own. They're trying to save their marriage, but they need help.

A lot of couples argue and fight all the time but never feel the need to see a marriage counselor. Nor do they think their marriage is in trouble. Some people just relate at a higher decibel level. They don't talk; they yell. But in most cases, you'll find that the fundamental values and beliefs are the same—they're just demonstrated in different ways.

Do you remember the old TV sitcom *The Odd Couple?* One roommate was neat; the other was a slob. They fought all the time. But at the end of every show, one of them or both of them had made a compromise based on the values they held important.

I know a couple, Alex and Christine, who never raise their voices—and they, too, have a happy marriage. When they start to get angry with each other, Alex just nods his head and turns on the TV. Christine grabs her pocketbook and goes for a drive—usually to the closest mall. A few hours later, it's like nothing happened. Christine comes home. Alex turns off the TV. They have dinner and chat. This may sound as if they're avoiding a fight and doing the opposite of what I counsel my clients: sweeping their anger and resentments under the rug. But in reality, Alex and Christine have figured out a way to handle their disagreements. Different? Yes. Not common? True. But it works for them.

The way a couple deals with anger and conflict significantly impacts their relationship. Usually they don't know how to successfully disagree or even argue, and, unlike Alex and Christine, the results are disastrous.

Talking Through Problems

It's not always easy to discuss what's going on underneath a fight. And as we saw earlier in this chapter, it's not wise to try to figure it out while you're in the heat of the moment. But after some time has passed, you'll need to discuss what happened to ensure it won't happen again. Here are some suggestions:

- Talk about what you want from your partner: "I would like you to …."

- Think about what you need and then make it concrete for your partner: "I need more intimacy" is not as clear as "I need you to tell me more about how you're feeling about me."

- Avoid focusing on what the other person has done wrong.

- Accenuating the positive in requests makes things clearer for your partner: "I don't want you to yell at me when you're angry" is not as clear as "Let's stay calm while we talk."

Marriage Trap

A word of caution: when you revisit a fight to work out your differences, avoid talking about what you don't like about your spouse. It will be heard as criticism and is more likely to trigger a defensive response.

Taking Time-Outs

When you're in the midst of an argument, don't get into a screaming match. If your partner becomes "overheated," explain to him that you're willing to talk, but right now both of your tempers are too high for things to get settled.

Promise to discuss the issue after the time-out. Pick a specific time to check in with each other, and suggest it in a nonthreatening way: "How about talking tonight when we're both in a calmer place?" or "When you feel you're ready to talk about it, let's be sure we make time." I call this withdrawing with reassurance.

Be sure to follow up on your promise. If your spouse is still upset when you check with him, set up a new time. If this keeps happening, you may need to speak to a third party to help you get back on track and communicate properly again.

Avoiding Words and Behaviors That Hurt

It's true that fighting is a necessary component in a lasting marriage, but it can also be dangerous. When you fight, there's a strong possibility of saying hurtful things, which can make the other person feel devalued.

Love Letters

Did you say something you can't take back? All is not lost. Diffuse the situation by doing something nice—and not necessarily an expensive present from Tiffany's. Do something that takes effort and shows remorse, such as making your wife's lunch for the next day at work and writing a note on the brown bag about "how much your grouchy husband loves you."

To avoid saying something that will hurt your partner, try to keep the fight on the specific issue at hand. A good way to ensure you don't say something you'll regret is to say something positive about your partner first. Even if you're really angry, saying something positive will stop you from saying something deadly. The following examples don't negate the disagreement at hand, but they also acknowledge your partner in some way:

- "I know you want our home to look nice, but I'm concerned about the expense."

- "I know how important it is to you to have a nice car, but I'm worried that it will put us in too much debt."

- "I know you love and respect your family—I love them, too—but I'm anxious that we won't be able to do the other things we wanted this holiday if we spend the whole week with them."

Strategies for Fighting

People are different, and no matter how much you love and respect each other, you are individuals, too. Your priorities will vary from time to time. When you fight, your goal is to discuss your differences—but to also be clear that although you don't agree with your partner's priority, you respect him.

A friend of mine in a strong, lasting marriage summed it up this way: "We fight all the time. We need to express ourselves and get our problems out in the open." The success of this couple's marriage is most likely due to the way they fight.

Take a Deep Breath

Max and Rose had been married for more than 25 years when they came to see me. They had had plenty of fights over the years, but lately, they'd become more bitter and angry—or they may have just gotten tired of their usual routine.

Usually, after a good 10 minutes into the fight, Max would storm off and go into the garage to tinker. Rose would immediately begin to get anxious. She would go from, "Why did you do that?!" to "I'm sorry! You're right! Don't fight anymore!" She would come into the garage, pleading and crying. Lately, Max had taken to locking the door to the garage and turning up the radio while Rose knocked and knocked on the door. "Let me in!" An impossible situation, yes. It was no wonder they felt they needed help.

I realized that Rose and Max's problems went back a long way; they had patterns of acting in very passive-aggressive ways and several problems were at work: Rose's need for reassurance, Max's need for Rose to respect his boundaries, and the need for both of them to communicate what they felt and what they needed from each other.

But before anything else, Rose and Max needed to calm down. Although both are very common, panic and its counterpart, emotional withdrawal, can be a couple's worst enemy when they fight. In fact, the first thing I tell couples like Rose and Max is to take a deep breath and count to 10.

Here are some strategies I use to help my clients calm down and be more rational:

- Think of someone who cares about you and imagine what he or she would say. It's comforting to "hear" a reassuring voice, even if the person isn't really there.

- Exercise. Even if it's just stomping in place for 10 minutes, doing something physical (other than punching your spouse!) is a great stress-reducer.

- Remember a difficult time you both successfully went through. Remember how you worked as a team to ease any conflict during that period.

Choosing Words That Taunt, Not Haunt

Do you remember the childhood rhyme, "Sticks and stones may break my bones, but words will never harm me"? If only it were true! Unfortunately, words can fade quickly, but the hurt they cause can take much longer to disappear.

One couple, Carl and Jennifer, who had come to see me were still being tormented by words said rashly in the moment. Three years before they'd even made an appointment with me, Carl and Jennifer were fighting. Carl got so mad, he told Jennifer he thought she was fat. Ouch!

Jennifer never forgot what he said, even when he apologized profusely, told her how much he loved her, and asked how he could make it up. Over the years, they had good times and shared many happy occasions, including their daughter's wedding and their son's graduation from college. But invariably, whenever they started to fight, Jennifer would bring up the fact that Carl thought she was fat.

Over the course of several sessions, Jennifer was able to tell Carl how much he had hurt her, and Carl was finally able to convince Jennifer he didn't mean what he'd said. Ten years after they'd had their last session, their marriage remains strong, but they also count to 10 before they say anything hurtful to each other—even if they're in the midst of a heated argument.

Marriage
Trap
Avoid exaggeration and hyperbole that demean your spouse when you fight. You can say, "I hate when you leave tissues around the house," but avoid "You're a hopeless slob!" You can say, "I wish you wouldn't start talking to me when I'm taking a shower!" but avoid, "Stop bothering me! You never leave me alone!"

Postmortem Analysis

I've discussed the importance of letting time pass before discussing the reasons why you had a fight. But just as important as understanding why you had a particular fight is to avoid the same fight in the future. To accomplish this, one of the tools I use with my clients is the "Complaint Compass."

One at a time, list your partner's three main complaints and explain why you think she feels that way. When both of you have finished the exercise, discuss your answers. This simple exercise helps you both better understand each other so you can be more sensitive to each other's needs—and more able to ward off a potential fight. Use this exercise as a method for figuring out how you can respond to your spouse's complaints in a positive way the next time you find the temperature rising.

Essential Takeaways

- Anger doesn't always look like a shouting match. It can be turned inward in the guise of depression, or it can come out in passive-aggressive ways.
- Never try to resolve an argument in the heat of the moment. Allow at least 20 minutes to pass before trying to calmly and rationally discuss the issue at hand.
- Avoid using words that can hurt your partner. They're not always easily forgiven and can haunt a marriage for years.
- Try to understand the underlying reasons why your spouse is angry. Knowing the "whys" can help diffuse a potentially explosive situation because it helps you be more in control of your emotions.

chapter 13

Playfulness Is Key

Laughter and your health

Dating your spouse

Having fun together

Spending quality time together

What do you think of when you hear the word *play?* Do you think of sandboxes and hopscotch? Do you think of playing Life or Monopoly on family night? Or do you think of snowball fights on a cold afternoon? Whatever visions play conjures up for you, I doubt it conjures up playtime with your spouse.

We aren't wired to think of play as something we do with our spouse. We can be relaxed with our spouse; we can "get away" with our spouse; we can hang out with our spouse; we can go to the movies with our spouse. But play? Maybe an occasional game of Scrabble or chess, sure, but that's about it.

But playing with your spouse—having fun for the pure sake of having fun—is a key ingredient for making your marriage last. This chapter puts to rest the idea that play is just for kids.

Laughter Helps You Cope

I remember a tense moment I had with my partner one night. We'd been having a discussion about where to go on vacation. It should be fun, yes. But we were disagreeing about where to go. I wanted to go to Europe, and my partner wanted to go to Cancun. Suddenly we looked at each other and burst out laughing. How ridiculous to fight about a vacation! We were lucky to even be able to go on a vacation!

The laughter diffused the situation, and we were able to come up with a great solution: we went to Cancun but spent a couple days in Mexico City and at the Mayan ruins. It was one of the best trips we ever had.

Laughing Can Be Erotic

The main element of play is fun—and one of the least expensive and most joyous kind of play is making love. The lines between play and sex are hazy, and when you're in the midst of making love, who cares?

In fact, play is a component of foreplay. Having fun in a nonsexual way can make you feel safe, happy, and loving toward your mate. When you laugh together, you're in sync; you're a unit; you're a team. If it leads to sex, so much the better!

Laughing together as a couple also releases *pheromones,* subtle chemicals that make us attractive to the other sex. In other words, laughter can be a powerful aphrodisiac!

Definition

Pheromones are chemicals triggered by a powerful response—such as sexual attraction and a belly laugh with someone you're attracted to. The more pheromones released, the more attracted you become to the opposite sex.

Thanks to movies, books, and television, many couples have an exaggerated, sometimes stressful image of sex. Not only do you have to perform, but you have to look great, too. Play doesn't even enter the picture—just lust.

There's a simple solution to having more fun and still feeling sexy: just focus on having fun instead of meeting some preprogrammed goal. Some sex encounters go well and some don't, so have a sense of humor about it! Spend more time giggling, talking, and being silly—and less time under pressure to perform. A lighter attitude makes sex more fun.

Laughter Brings You Closer

Someone once said, "At the end, when you think over your life, you don't remember work. You remember the laughter." When you think about the great times in your life—be it as a little kid making up a silly game with your siblings, giggling uncontrollably during assembly at school, or laughing with your compatriots in that first job in the real world—it puts a smile on your face. The "good times" were full of laughter, of letting loose in a spontaneous moment. These are the things we cherish, and these are the times that bind us together as schoolmates, families, and yes, as husband and wife.

As a couple, you and your spouse can have private jokes that are just funny to the two of you. It might be something as silly as talking about the "legendary mashed potato dish" or "Aunt Martha's dress"—something triggers a laugh between you, as incomprehensible as it may seem to the outside world. These private jokes represent a bond so deep it's spoken in a language only understood by the two of you and no one else. You're the only two people on the planet who get it.

A Smile Brightens Anyone's Day

Do you know the enormous power you possess? Do you realize that just by turning up the corners of your mouth, you can influence the people you love? How wonderful to send your husband or wife off to work armed with the positive energy that came from the last thing he or she saw: a great big smile on your face, a smile that said so much more than "Have a good day!"

MISC.

The Best Medicine

It might be a cliché, but like any cliché, it comes from truth—there's even clinical evidence to back up the claim. When you laugh, you release mood-enhancing hormones like endorphins in your brain and, at the same time, reduce the hormones released during stress, like cortisol and epinephrine. Laughter really is good for your health—and your soul!

"Smile and the whole world smiles with you"—wise words. When you smile and laugh together as a couple, it makes your bond stronger. It's a pleasure you both share, and it creates a happy memory.

Making Dates and Keeping Them

Dating. The meaning of the word has changed over the last few decades. Originally, making a date meant setting a time and place to rendezvous and share what would hopefully be a pleasant experience (as long as the man called a few days before Saturday night). These days, dating is much more casual. It's hanging out. It can include being with friends. It's not so much about boyfriend and girlfriend as it is spending time with the person you like.

But whether 50 years ago or today, dating has always been synonymous with "adventure" and "fun." A date should be fun—but why should this fun have to be limited to those newly matched, preengaged, not-yet-committed-and-having-too-good-a-time?

Plan Fun Events

If you or your spouse are in the type of business where you have to entertain clients, if you have a wide circle of friends you see regularly, or if you're members of various clubs and organizations, you might spend a lot of your time—too much of your time—socializing with others.

You might think it isn't important that just you and your mate have a night out alone. Well, I'm here to tell you it is!

> **Love Letters**
>
> Have trouble making time for a date? Try this: on separate calendars, each of you pick four nights and four separate activities—say, a movie, a concert, a hockey game, and a dinner out. Look at each other's calendars and pick one event that sounds like fun for both of you—and make a date to do it! Save the other activities for other date nights.

Schedule Date Nights

Dating can and should be a lifelong pursuit in any healthy, enduring marriage. How wonderful to get out of the house, away from the kids and worries, just you and your spouse out for the express purpose of having a good time! These dates, whether once a week, twice a month, or once every few weeks, can keep life fun and interesting.

But you should have some ground rules for a successful date:

- Keep your date no matter what. Treat it like a business meeting or a parent-teacher night at school.

- Don't invite anyone else on your date. If, as you're bragging about your upcoming date while at a neighbor's barbecue and the hosts hint they've not been out for a while, do not ask them to join you. This is your night as a couple—only you two.

- Change it up. Don't do the same thing every date night. If you went out to dinner last time, go bowling or to a movie the next.

- Keep it light. The whole idea of your date night is to have fun—not necessarily end up in bed. Don't use this time to see a Eugene O'Neill play or a documentary about global warming.

- Enjoy yourself! Remember, this is your play time. Push away the thoughts of the kids, the bills, and the project due at work. Focus on you and your spouse. The minute you start thinking about something else, ask your spouse to tell you to stop—immediately!

You don't have to break a bank for your date nights. If theater tickets or sporting events are too steep, make a date to go to a neighborhood bistro, take an afternoon stroll through your town's main shopping center, or walk through the woods on a crisp fall day.

Share Hobbies and Sports

Any leisure interests you share as a couple are great. You can relax, de-stress, and spend quality time together. Sports like tennis or golf are great. Not only do you get to bond and have some fun, but the exercise is great for both your body and your soul.

Take a Class Together

Taking a class is a wonderful thing to do as a couple. These days, adult courses are offered in a variety of places—universities, evening adult classes at high schools, libraries, and organizations in a field that interests you both.

How about a class like selling real estate or investing for retirement, something that can bring you together to discuss the future and build your nest egg? What about something that's pure fun and something you have never done, like Chinese cooking or understanding opera? By doing something that's new for both of you as a couple, you're starting at the same level, together. There's no competition.

Where can you find classes? A local high school is a good place to start. Most of the courses offered are inexpensive, so if it turns out it's not what you both expected, you haven't made a big investment.

Take a Hike

There's nothing like being outside on a beautiful day, breathing in fresh air, and going off into the woods for some quiet time together. Nature can be exhilarating and, for many, a true spiritual experience. And to share it with your loved one can be a time of profound bonding.

Being in nature doesn't have to mean going on a serious hike in the wild. If you're more of a homebody or less athletic, take a car ride instead and find a pretty solitary lake or park where you and your mate can commune with the beauty of nature and each other.

Marriage Trap

If you decide to go out hiking, think safety first. Know what you're doing before you venture out. Use a familiar trail, or hire a guide. Be sure you get the right experiment, and know your limits. Let your family know where you will be going.

Learn to Play Your Spouse's Game

If your husband thinks heaven is a rolling green, and you think an iron is only something to press shirts with, it's obvious you don't share his passion for golf. But have you tried to like it?

Maybe you think golf is "his" and you feel intimidated; you don't want to step on his turf. Or maybe the idea of smacking a little white ball all afternoon simply isn't your version of fun.

But maybe golf is one of those things you don't know you'll like or dislike unless you try. Even if you never advance enough in the sport to be at the same level of competition as your spouse, you can at least share in something your spouse loves and vice versa. You can learn the game and understand the lingo, which can be another dimension of sharing between the two of you.

A couple who'd seen me a few times was having difficulty because their marriage lacked fun. They didn't know how to play together—and, worse, they didn't know where to start. Craig, an impassioned scuba diver, wanted to teach his wife, Isabelle, how to dive, but she was scared to death. When they went away on vacation, all she ever wanted to do was sit under an umbrella, drink piña coladas, and read a sizzling book. I encouraged Isabelle to try scuba diving with Craig. She could take a few lessons in a local pool, where she didn't have to worry about being stranded or losing air.

Isabelle was game. She put on a wet suit and the rest of the gear and jumped into the water. And she tried. She really did. But it just wasn't her thing. The good news was that the next time they went to the beach, Isabelle and Craig went snorkeling—and got to enjoy the amazing underworld of the sea together.

The important lesson here was not that Isabelle liked scuba diving, but that Craig was thrilled she'd tried for him.

Play Does Not Have to End in Sex

Sometimes having fun is just about having fun. I suggest you don't even think about sex; it can add pressure. Instead, laugh, enjoy each other's company, and let things happen—or not happen—naturally.

Essential Takeaways

- Sharing a good laugh can make your bond as a couple even stronger.
- Playing games is something we forget as adults—but we really shouldn't.

- You don't have to spend a lot of money to have a fun date; going to a local bistro, taking a stroll in the cool night air—all sorts of activities can make a lovely evening out.

- Make an effort to try to learn your spouse's hobby or sport. Even if it's not for you, you'll have more to talk about.

chapter 14

Lasting Romance and Sex

Adding spice to your love life

Communicating what you want

Staying sexy

Appreciating each other

Candlelit bedrooms filled with the scent of flowers. On the beach at night, the sounds of the waves in your ears. Dancing cheek-to-cheek at a friend's wedding or fogging up your father's car. Whatever your scenario, chances are, when you and your spouse were dating, all you wanted to do was have sex.

But now you're married maybe 10, 20, or 40 years, and those hot nights and languid afternoons are only beautiful memories. You fall asleep after a long day of work as soon as your head hits the pillow. The sand scratches. Having champagne is more important than dancing. And the car? It's now filled with kids and groceries.

What can you do to bring romance and sex back into your life? Read on.

Keeping Lust Alive

Our views of romance have been skewed, thanks to steamy romance novels and dramatic, tear-jerker romantic movies. Romance is wonderful, but it doesn't have to be grandiose. As a matter of fact, without little bits of romance all along, the grandiose gesture won't work.

Judy and Bill had been married 10 years when they came to see me. They told me the spark was gone from their marriage, and they were bored with each other. I listened and took notes. Then I asked both of them what they considered romantic, a gesture that would bring back the spark.

Bill thought for a moment and said, "Showing me that she understood when I had a bad day."

"What would that entail?" I asked.

"Not much. Maybe a hug. Maybe a back massage. An e-mail telling me to hang in there. No demands."

I asked Judy the same question. She replied, "Maybe going food-shopping together. Checking the fridge and the pantry so I wouldn't have to do it. A hug. A compliment. Writing me a quick text during the day."

Bill and Judy taught me something that day: romance doesn't have to be all flowers and champagne and weekends away. It can and should be as simple as writing a short text message, taking on a responsibility the other spouse usually does, and showing that, yes, I understand, I love you, and I am here.

When they realized the romance had not gone out of their marriage but that it had just evolved over the years, Bill and Judy felt loving toward each other again. They felt the spark that had always been there—just not recognized for what it was.

> **Love Letters**
>
> Sometimes life is too busy or too crazy to even think about sex. That's okay. A simple sign of affection—a hug, a kiss, a touch—can keep the lust alive.

Communicating Sexual Needs

Sex can be as complex or as simple as you want to make it. It can be three times a week or three times a year. It can be "down and dirty" or comfortable. What matters is how the both of you mesh and how much your sexual needs are being fulfilled.

In short, *sex* can be defined however you as a couple define it—as long as you're both getting what you need.

Sex Is Good for You

We've all heard the old adages about sex: it makes your skin glow, it keeps breakouts at bay, it improves the way you walk, and it helps keep you thin. Certainly, quality sex with your spouse can give you an inner beauty, better health, and make you happy.

In addition, sex can …

- Be a wonderful way to share. When you and your mate are being intimate, you're in sync. As corny as it sounds, you are two joined together as one and are as close as a couple can be.

- Be fun! We all need time out to enjoy life—and what better way to do so than with some light-hearted sex?

- Provide the security and affection you need. Some people have difficulty expressing their love; they are not touchy-feely. But when they're having sex, their love is in full bloom and there's no doubt where their affection lies.

Familiarity Means Safety

The brain is the most important sex organ. Without the brain, none of the other parts work. The brain receives stimuli and responds by releasing *hormones* throughout your body. The brain is where that stimulus is translated—the things that turn us on, that are erotic to us—and everything follows from there.

> **Definition**
>
> Mood-affecting **hormones** are chemicals released in the brain when triggered by outside stimuli, such as a kiss. Hormones are also automatically released when triggered by the body, such as hormones that dictate monthly menstruation.

The brain also relays the release of pleasurable hormones, such as endorphins, when you're happy. Research shows that when men and women are enjoying a sexual encounter, their levels of the stress hormone cortisol drop, while levels of oxytocin, a pleasure hormone, goes up. This doesn't necessarily mean while you're in the midst of an orgasm; it could be as simple as feeling close, connected, and happy to your spouse.

Free to Be Uninhibited

Men and women often have the same type of fantasies, including those involving more than one partner, same-sex partners, and one-night stands. But women's fantasies tend toward taking a passive role while men's fantasies usually have them taking a dominant one. But no matter what the subject, according to the Kinsey Institute for Research in Sex, Gender, and Reproduction, sexual fantasies are healthy. People who have sexual fantasies usually have fewer sexual problems and enjoy more sexual satisfaction.

Although we all have sexual fantasies, we don't usually act them out. But one of the nice things about being married for a long time is the safety aspect—you can be free to explore your sexual fantasies together.

Exploring the darker, erotic side of your sexuality with your spouse combines physical pleasure, emotional needs, and play. It's a safe way for you to share with each other and grow more intimate. This darker side doesn't have to involve silhouettes, cheerleader outfits, or black leather. It can be something as simple as talking dirty to each other or having a "quickie" at a party in an empty room.

Tom and Grace came to see me years ago because they were having sexual problems. Grace was worried that because she didn't want to have sex as much as Tom did, he would have an affair. She felt Tom was insatiable, even after 12 years of marriage, whereas her desire had ebbed. Tom, on the other hand, unconsciously equated sex with love. If Grace said no, she rejected him. If she said yes, she loved him.

Obviously, Tom and Grace needed to discuss their intimacy with each other. Over a few months, Tom learned that being intimate didn't have to always end in sex, and that Grace loved him whether or not she was in the mood.

Grace, on the other hand, needed some "spice" to make her feel more erotic. She'd always been too embarrassed to tell Tom what aroused her. But when she and Tom began to speak honestly to each other, the spark was rekindled. They experimented with some harmless role-playing and some x-rated movies, and Grace soon was initiating sex more often.

Love
Letters

Just as couples have different sexual fantasies, they also have different ideas of what's "sexy." One man may love to see his wife in Victoria's Secret lingerie while another one may be turned on when she wears one of his shirts. Women, too, have different preferences. Some may like tiny bathing suits on men whereas others will be completely turned off. Talk to each other, and learn what turns on each of you.

Keeping the Flame Alive

Sex changes over the years. That's natural. You're not going to be hot and heavy 10 years after your honeymoon. Your stamina changes over the years, as do your bodies. The familiarity that enables you to feel safe can also make you feel like roommates instead of husband and wife.

Your needs change over the years as well. Some couples are comfortable with having sex only a few times a year, while others have sex several times a month. Problems only arise if one of you wants more or less sex than the other.

The Kinsey Institute for Research in Sex, Gender, and Reproduction, the first research laboratory to study sex in men and women, reported that …

- 1 percent of married men and 3 percent of married women haven't had sex in the past year.

- 13 percent of married men and 12 percent of married women only have sex a few times a year.

- 43 percent of married men and 47 percent of married women have sex a few times a month.

- 36 percent of married men and 32 percent of married women have sex a few times a week.

- 7 percent of married men and 7 percent of married women have sex four or more times a week.

These findings indicate that married men and women are fairly equal when it comes to frequency of sex. They also show that there's a wide variety of sexual activity—which, translated, means there's no "right" or "wrong" number of times men and women should have sex.

Reminisce About the Early Years

One of the ways married couples can rekindle the flame is to talk about the past—not the past that included the difficult times, but the times when you first fell in love, when you first had sex, when you went on your honeymoon. Not only can you share beautiful memories, but you can share the same happiness you felt long ago.

Love Letters	Don't just reminisce about your early years. Be creative. Remember the time you made love in the bathtub surrounded by candles and bubbles? Remember when you greeted your husband at the door in a raincoat and nothing else? Remember when you ripped off each other's clothes in the kitchen? Relive it! You *can* go home again.

Intimacy Changes Over Time

Chris and Lois had become less intimate over time. They'd been married 25 years, and they wanted to plan a special anniversary gift for each other. They thought about having a party but then decided they wanted to go to the same resort in St. Thomas they'd gone to on their honeymoon. They were afraid, however, of spending all that money only to have their memories fall short.

I told them the memories are most important. Going to the same place they spent their honeymoon sounded very romantic, but it could be dangerous. The place they'd stayed in could be long gone or in disrepair. They would feel a lot of pressure to "perform" the way they did 25 years ago. They would feel compelled to have fun no matter what—which could end up making them resentful and angry at each other.

Instead, I suggested they try someplace new, a different Caribbean Island that had the same ambience, but be a place where they could create new memories.

It worked. The vacation rekindled their spark; they had a newfound intimacy. They had great sex they didn't have to compare with anything.

Romancing Your Marriage

It's true that a quick love note or kiss can be romantic, but once in a while, a grand gesture can be a real plus, especially if it's combined with acknowledgment.

One of my clients had been going through a difficult time; the wife had been working overtime for weeks. Her husband called her at work and told her to leave. They were going away for the weekend. When she started to find all the reasons why they shouldn't go away—who will take care of the kids, what about the dog—he told her that he'd already taken care of everything. All she had to do was go home, pack a few things, and meet him at the airport. He'd even arranged for a limo to pick her up.

Marriage Trap

It can be difficult to open up about sex—even when you've been married for a decade or two. But if you don't, there's a chance your intimacy will weaken and your sex life become nonexistent. If you're too embarrassed to talk face to face, why not try jotting down what you want in a note he'll see or e-mailing her what you want? Not only is it easier to explain what you'd like sexually, but it can be a turn-on to boot.

Don't Take Each Other for Granted

I know a couple who recently got divorced because things just got stale. After 12 years of marriage, they'd begun to take each other for granted. Unfortunately, when you believe that your wife or husband "will always be there," chances are he or she won't be, after enough time. Nobody wants to feel unloved.

And remember, your spouse is not a mind-reader. You need to compliment each other—whether it be the way a meal turned out or the way he looks, the way she handled herself at a client meeting, or the way he took charge of organizing the party.

Try the following exercise to understand your partner better, what he or she would like to keep your romance alive.

1. Spend 1 or 2 minutes each day thinking about what you like about your partner and then tell him or her.

2. Keep in mind that for a relationship to maintain a spark, you need to be positive to each other on a regular basis. Relationships go through many stages and need to constantly be worked on.

3. Make giving your spouse a compliment a positive habit.

4. Record how long it takes to do this short exercise, and the frequency in which you do it. Make notes whether you've worked on being positive, forgot to do it for a while, or simply went back to business as usual and ignored it.

If you want to keep your spark alive, you need to make giving a compliment a habit and not just an exercise you do once in a while.

Be Thoughtful

Fifty years ago, Emily Post was the queen of good manners. She told people how to drink soup, set a table, and make a lovely home. Rudeness was one of her cardinal sins. And she believed the golden rule: "Do unto others as you would have them do unto you."

Good manners are still important today, whether toward a stranger or someone you love. Treat your partner with respect. Be thoughtful of his needs, his mood, his time. Here are some suggestions for doing that:

- Leave an "I love you" card next to the coffee pot where he will see it first thing in the morning.

- Get tickets for a concert you know your wife will enjoy and surprise her with them.

- Send a text message just to say hello.

- Let him know you're aware he's under a lot of pressure, and ask him if there's anything you can do to help—and mean it!

- Give each other a compliment every day.

Being—and Feeling—Sexy as You Mature

Ask anyone who's not enjoying aging, and they'll tell you there's nothing sexy about growing old. That six-pack stomach gets a little soft. Those beautiful curves become cul-de-sacs. That beautiful head of hair gets thin— and starts growing where you'd rather it didn't.

Yes, it can be hard getting old. But how wonderful it can be to grow old with the one you love! Here are some ways to get into the mood when you're getting a little gray:

Remember spontaneity. Yes, there was a time when with one look, you were in the bedroom together with the door closed. But today, you don't even see your friends without it being scheduled two weeks in advance. Try to remember what it felt like to be free spirits. Take the remote out of your spouse's hand and lead her into the bedroom. Right now.

Get active—and I don't mean sexually. Take a walk around the block together. Put on some music and dance. Take a gym class together. When you get the blood flowing, you'll be more inclined to want sex.

Don't forget about quickies. Short and sweet can sometimes be all you can fit in during a hectic week. That's okay. Sometimes a fast schmooze right before getting dressed for work, or while the kids are preoccupied with their favorite TV show, is just what you need.

Make a date night—and keep it. Yes, planning ahead for a night of romance can take the spontaneity out of it, but it can also mean you'll be together at one restaurant or one movie theater, like it or not. And being together and having fun can put you in the mood.

Make a romantic mood. Maybe your bodies aren't what they used to be—so what! Inside, you're still the same people who fell in love all those years ago. But just to oomph up things, try putting on a sexy nightgown or a pair of silk boxers. Try making love in a bedroom filled with candlelight. Light some exotic incense. Put on perfume. Play some sultry music from your MP3 or CD player. I guarantee the sparks will fly.

Essential Takeaways

- It's not the frequency or the quality that counts; the important thing about sex is that you're in sync and you mesh in complementary ways.

- Don't be afraid to try something new. One of the nice things about being together a long time is that you can feel safe with each other.

- It's the little things that make an impact when it comes to romance: a note, a smile, or a quick kiss.

- Compliment each other at least once a day. Taking each other for granted can only lead to trouble.

Part 4

The Marriage Land Mines

Into every marriage a little pain will fall. It's as inevitable as the sun rising and setting or the heat in summer and the icy cold of winter. It's how you cope with that pain, how you handle it together as husband and wife, that makes all the difference in your marriage.

In Part 4, I go over the most common marriage trouble spots. These include the usual suspects, like raising children, dealing with money, coping with intimacy issues, handling the empty nest, and taking care of your own aging parents. I also offer strategies for the big sea changes—the ones that, unfortunately, some husbands and wives go through—from infidelity to bankruptcy and more.

To be forearmed is to be forewarned. It's my hope the following chapters provide the ammunition you need to face the trouble spots in your marriage head on—to overcome them and make your marriage last.

chapter 15

The Seven Deadly "I Don'ts"

Defensive downers

Saying too much

Relationship killers

Body language screams

Nobody's perfect. It's something you learn long before you hear wedding bells. We discover it in the classroom, on the playground, and at the dinner table. We realize that the parents we idolized might have flaws, that the teachers we respected aren't always right, and that sometimes beauty really is just skin deep.

Hopefully, by the time you get married, you have a good idea of most of your spouse's imperfections. As the years go by, you'll discover you can tolerate some more easily than others. What you thought was an adorable idiosyncrasy in the glow of "just married" may have become an excruciating behavior that drives you crazy now. And that doesn't even count the new and potentially irritating characteristics you encounter as your marriage evolves.

But annoying habits don't have to spell doom. In fact, they can sometimes be just that—bothersome quirks you learn to live with. On the other hand, they might become so impossibly irritating that you lose all perspective, and instead of communicating your displeasure, you react in ways that make things worse.

In this chapter, I discuss the seven worst behaviors I've seen destroy relationships if they aren't stopped.

Criticism: "You Never Do It Right"

There are reasons why words like *harping, nagging,* and *caustic* are synonymous with a certain type of criticism. Relationships thrive on acceptance and approval. A spouse who feels like she can't to anything right will eventually stop trying.

Criticism Versus Complaining

Think about these two sentences:

> "You always get it wrong!"

> "I wish you wouldn't get it wrong time after time."

On one level, they make the same point: one spouse is upset the other isn't doing something right and, frankly, never does it right! But on another level, they're very different.

The first phrase is accusatory. It leaves no room for discussion and it can make the recipient feel inept. The second phrase, however, leaves room for discussion. It isn't great to hear that you always seem to do something wrong, but at least there's room for discussion. A *complaint* can be addressed. *Criticism* just gets a person's hackles up.

Definition	**Criticism** is judgmental. When you criticize someone, you're making a judgment about him or her. **Complaining,** on the other hand, is expressing dissatisfaction about behavior—say, the way he never takes out the garbage.

Criticism Is Global, Not Situational

The very first time Elizabeth and George came into my office, I knew they were in trouble. When I went out into the reception room, they were arguing. George was yelling at Elizabeth because, "as usual, she was late." Elizabeth was fiddling with the strap of her pocketbook, muttering how sorry she was.

It didn't matter if I was an accountant, a maître d', or a therapist. George was criticizing Elizabeth because she was always late. And Elizabeth, accepting this truth, felt horrible.

The truth is, just as nobody's perfect, nobody's always imperfect. You can criticize about your spouse being late, but be sure you're discussing the situation at hand. In the scenario between Elizabeth and George, it was my office only—not a restaurant or a theater. Using the *always* word made Elizabeth feel awful. And, worse, it made her feel like there was no use in trying to be better. What was the point?

Avoid superlative words like *always, never, ever,* and *perpetually.* These don't give the recipient a chance. How can you argue about a situation when your spouse is being global? When you *never* do anything that's right, it means *never*—at home, at work, when you're watching TV, etc.

Contempt: "You Are a Jerk"

This one's a no-brainer. Treating your spouse as if he were a doormat or the village idiot doesn't make for a loving relationship. Love and positive feelings are severely injured when one partner believes the other is being patronizing and disrespectful. Contempt implies an underlying negativity about the recipient. It's difficult to have a good self-image when you're always being told how ridiculous you are.

A good marriage is based on a foundation of respect. You have to admire your spouse in order to fall in love. Without respect, a person can feel useless and just plain bad. The respect might come from something as mundane as the discipline he has to floss every night or as big as the dedication to work that got her the brand-new promotion, but wherever it appears, it reinforces your love for each other.

Laughing at Your Spouse's Expense: "You're Crazy, but I Love You"

It's true that a sense of humor can go far in healing wounds. Making a joke can ease a tense moment and break the ice. But some humor should be left to stand-up comedians. Biting sarcasm might be funny when you're listening to an act, but it can leave teeth marks when hurled at your spouse.

Take Jane and Bill, for example. They'd been married for 15 years and knew everything about each other—the good, the bad, and the ugly. Jane was known for a sense of humor that was usually at Bill's expense. Because she knew so much about him, she loved to talk about his every move—especially if she had an audience. "Watch," she'd say to a group of friends planning to carpool to the movies, "He'll come downstairs and ask me if I like his shirt."

Sure enough, as if on cue, Bill would come downstairs and ask Jane if she liked his shirt. Everyone cracked up—except Bill. "What?" he'd say, a half-smile on his face. He knew something funny had happened, but he didn't know what. He also knew he might have been the butt of the joke.

It became a habit. It didn't matter what the occasion was. If a group of friends were over for dinner, or for a Sunday afternoon brunch, or whatever, Jill was ready with a quip. "In a minute, Bill is going to ask me if we need anything at the store …." "Bill is going to come through the door saying the train was late …." "Bill is going to sneak upstairs after dinner so he can take a quick nap …."

Invariably, Jane was always right, but it was always at Bill's expense. Eventually, Bill realized that the laughter was directed at him. He became resentful of Jane; he got angry. She didn't treat him with respect.

"What is your problem?" he asked Jane when they'd come to my office. "Why are you always making fun of me?"

Jane's answer was "Because you're funny! You know I love you."

Bill wasn't so sure. It turned out that Jane had some deep-seated resentment about Bill; she hated that he was so nice to her, especially when she didn't deserve it. She lost respect for him and used passive-aggressive behavior not only to get back at him, but to prove even further that she wasn't a nice person.

Marriage Trap	A sense of humor is crucial to a relationship, but it's important to recognize that both of you have to think something is funny for it to have a positive impact. A joke is not a joke when it's at someone else's expense, especially your spouse.

Insults

Insults are easier to decipher. They're not buried under a joke. When you insult someone, it's loud and clear: "You're too fat." "You're an idiot." "You have the worst taste in wallpaper."

The problem with insults, albeit very direct, is that they erode respect. The more you insult your spouse, the worse he will feel. The more insults, the more pain. Period.

Dismissive Body Language

Insults are so direct and to the point, and you don't always want to hurl them. Maybe you love your spouse, but you're very angry with her. You want to yell and scream, but you're afraid of the repercussions. So instead, you bury your feelings and don't verbalize them. But feelings have a way of coming out anyway.

I tell my clients, "When you throw a pencil up into the air, it's going to fall to the ground every time." The ground, in this case, is body language. Instead of using your mouth, you use your body to demonstrate your anger, resentment, or boredom.

Let's take a look at some of the most common negative body language moves:

Throwing instead of passing. Instead of handing the style section of *The New York Times* to your spouse, you throw it his way and it lands on the ground.

Storming out of the room. You don't like what she said? Stomping away says it without words, especially if you slam the door behind you.

The big sigh. The louder the sigh, the more you're repeating: "I hate my life."

Self-grooming. Your husband is trying to create a budget for the family at a bad time. Instead of saying so, you flick away some imaginary lint from your sweater or, looking away, play with your hair.

The shrug. This particular body language is a double-whammy. When you shrug, you're not only discounting what your spouse is saying, but you, in turn, are saying, "Whatever …." That's one of the hallmarks of the passive-aggressive set.

The i device. Whether an iPhone, a BlackBerry, or the old-fashioned watch, being absorbed with something other than the conversation at hand "speaks" volumes.

Marriage Trap	*Boredom's* just another word for "anger." If you're bored, ask yourself if you're trying to cover up anger you feel toward your spouse. And if you're angry, ask yourself why.

Being Defensive: "Why Is It Always *My* Fault?"

It's easy to see how criticism and contempt can lead to defensiveness. After all, if you're bombarded with insults or judgments all day long, it's going to take its toll. Eventually, you'll fight back. But because your self-worth has been eroding, you're most likely not going to attack with insults of your own. Instead, you'll become defensive. You'll become a victim.

In many marriages, it becomes a ping-pong game. Sometimes the husband is the one hurling insults and the wife is the one to feel defensive. Other times, it's the wife who is full of contempt and the husband who becomes self-defensive. Either way, defensiveness is not good for your marriage!

Turning the Tables on Your Spouse

I call this type of defensiveness "the boomerang effect." Here's an example of a conversation Susan and Jacob had in my office:

> *Susan:* You never change the baby's diaper.
>
> *Jacob:* That's because you never ask me.

Susan: That's not true! Besides, why can't you ever volunteer, anyway?

Jacob: I'm not a mind-reader. If you want me to do something, you have to tell me. It's your fault, not mine!

Do you see how this works? If this were the boardroom, one of them might end up the new CEO. But this is a marriage—and confrontations like this have no place at home.

Making False Assumptions

If every husband and every wife were a mind-reader, we'd either have an idyllic paradise or a world where all men and women were divorced. Thankfully (in most cases), we aren't mind-readers. We can't always tell what our spouses want or what they're feeling. We need to communicate to each other to understand what's going on inside. (See Chapter 11 for more on communication in marriage.)

When we're defensive, however, not being a mind-reader goes to a new level, which I call "the anti-ESP syndrome." Here's an example of how it works, using new clients Claire and Tom:

Claire: Why are you mad at me?

Tom: I'm not mad at you. Why do you think I'm mad at you?

Claire: Yes, you are. I can tell. What did I do now?

Tom: I don't know what you're talking about!

… and it escalated from here.

Here's another example, from the same couple:

Claire: You don't want to watch this show. We can watch something else.

Tom: I never said I didn't want to watch it. It's fine.

Claire: No, it's not. Why don't you tell me the truth? I can tell that you're pouting.

Tom: I'm not pouting! It's fine. In fact, I'm not even going to watch TV now, so you can watch whatever you want!

Ouch! You can see that making assumptions about your spouse can lead to arguments. And when you're feeling insecure or defensive, the anti-ESP syndrome kicks into high gear.

MISC.

Don't Carry a Big Stick

Here's some advice from my Dr. Marty archives: the softer you speak, the louder you're heard. Add clarity to the equation, and any defensiveness, contempt, or anger will begin to disappear.

Denial: "There's Nothing Wrong!"

Denial is a big no-no in any marriage—or in life, for that matter. Unfortunately, it goes on all the time. I've had clients come to me and say they never thought their spouse was cheating, even though they found receipts in pants' pockets, lipstick stains, or the smell of a different perfume. And it makes sense. After all, who wants to admit his or her spouse is cheating?

But even on a less-dramatic scale, denial is something you draw on when you don't want to deal with something or you don't want to admit you're wrong. Unfortunately, like that proverbial pencil tossed in the air, you're going to hit the ground hard if you don't address it.

The truth is, you can deny on a daily basis a whole host of things—money, chores, social interactions, child-rearing, and more. Let's look at some examples:

You can see your bank account dwindling, but your husband says everything is fine. You need to believe him because the truth terrifies you. What do you do? Deny your circumstances.

Your husband gets upset because you haven't gone to the grocery store. You shout back that you never said you would—even though that morning you mentioned you were going shopping and asked if he wanted anything.

At a family gathering, your wife mentions that you lost your job. Later, you tell her that she hurt you, that you didn't want everyone to know. Her response? "I never said anything!" (Even though everyone, including you, heard her.)

Your daughter tells you, "Dad said I could go to the party" even though you said no earlier. You confront him later, and he says, "I never told her she could go. I wouldn't do that!" Unfortunately for your husband, your mother had been visiting and she heard him say "yes" loud and clear.

Reality Versus Need

Sometimes we deny a reality because we just don't want to face it. Like the woman who doesn't see the lipstick stains, we just don't want to think our spouse could be cheating on us. We need to believe our marriage is fine.

Need is a fierce emotion. When you feel insecure and defensive, it feels so much better to deny there's a problem.

Avoiding Responsibilities

Another reason you or your spouse may deny something is because you just don't want to take responsibility for it. Like the little kid who ate all the cookies, you don't confess because you don't want to be punished.

How do we avoid responsibility? Let me count the ways:

Making an excuse. It wasn't your fault you were late—there was a lot of traffic (while crossing your fingers your wife won't be listening to the traffic report).

Pointing the finger. It's not your fault. Your husband said he was going to fill up the car with gas.

Crisscrossing. Your husband claims you said you were going to take the dog for a walk. "No, I didn't," you say. You thought your husband said he would do it.

But ... butting. You asked your husband to pay the cable bill but he didn't do it. He says, "Yes, I said I would do it, but I was waiting for you to tell me when it was due."

No one likes whining. It's like nails on a blackboard: irritating, screechy, and annoying. When whining is combined with denying responsibility, it can be a very effective tool to stop an argument in its tracks—just to stop the noise. Unfortunately, it just stops the fighting temporarily. There's no resolution in whining—just maybe revolution!

Mentally Removing Yourself: "Huh?"

When one partner feels the other isn't listening or doesn't care, the fabric of the relationship begins to wear and tear. Sometimes this happens without either partner even realizing it. This often happens when one spouse becomes so involved with the children or work there's no time left for each other. The hurt partner's thinking may go something like, *If he loves me, why doesn't he want to be with me?*

No Reaction Is Not Staying Calm

Remember those scary movies where the husband ends up going postal and no one ever saw it coming? "He was so gentle," one neighbor says. Another says, "He was so quiet." The fact is, when your spouse isn't saying anything, it doesn't mean the discussion is over. It can mean that just below the surface, he's simmering in a nervous, anxious stew.

The best solution is for you both to talk. Sometimes that means arguing. Sometimes that means voices get raised. But at least feelings, thoughts— and even those nonproductive denials—are getting out. The pressure is relieved.

Muttering Is Not an Answer

No one can hear you when you grumble under your breath—and maybe that's what you want at times. But when you mutter something instead of saying it out loud, it's usually a sign you don't want to get involved, are being passive-aggressive, or are afraid.

None of these reasons provide an answer to a conflict. And they especially don't make for a strong marriage bond.

	Do You Love Me?
Misc.	An unfortunate side effect of removing yourself from a conversation is that your spouse can become needy. The more you push away, the more your spouse pulls you in. Before you know it, you can find yourself being smothered by a very insecure partner—a result that does not bode well for either of you.

Negativity: "We're Doomed"

No one likes a "Debby Downer," but no one likes an "always turning lemons into lemonade" person either. Yes, if your spouse is a Sally Sunshine who always wants to make lemonade out of lemons, it can get irritating—especially when there are real problems at hand.

Take Zoe and Craig. When Craig lost his job as an art director, he was grateful for Zoe's optimism. She told him he'd find another job soon. In the meantime, she could get more freelance writing assignments. They could cut back on their dinners out.

But when weeks turned into months, Craig didn't want to see Zoe's desperate attempts at being happy. Things were bad, and he needed to discuss a plan B with Zoe. But she refused to listen. Her optimism turned into denial, and it didn't do anyone good.

Catastrophic Thinking

Negativity is just as bad. It's contagious. If you think in black-and-white terms, you just might make a failed marriage a self-fulfilling prophecy.

Marriage Trap	There's no such thing as black and white in life. Situations, feelings, thoughts—they're all shades of gray. Sometimes they're lighter gray, and sometimes they're a darker hue, but in the same way no one is perfect, nothing is all doom and gloom or vice versa.

People who are depressed usually display a symptom called catastrophic thinking. It isn't rational; it's just their anxiety getting the best of them.

A form of therapy called cognitive therapy uses rationality as a way to combat catastrophic thinking.

For example, look at the following exercise. Write down what each situation means to you right now and rate it on a scale from 1 to 10 of how it makes you feel, with 1 being "not at all anxious" to 10 being "very anxious." Then take a deep breath and think about a fight in a more rational way. Write down the more rational expression, and rate that on a scale of 1 to 10, too. In most cases, when you think about a situation in a more rational way, your anxiety and fear will decrease. See the following examples to get a "feel" for this exercise and write down your own responses and ratings.

Taking Your Catastrophic Thinking Temperature		
Situation	*Feeling (1–10)*	*Reality Rethinking (1–10)*
A fight	Leaving me (10)	It's just one argument (5)
No call	Having affair (10)	Just got busy (3)
Not talking	Bored with me (9)	Purely focused on work (3)
Errand lost	Mad at me (9)	Simply forgot (2)
No to invite	Hates my friends (9)	Really has other plans (2)

Part of the Problem, Not the Solution

There's an old expression: "If you're not part of the solution, you're part of the problem." That can sound a little catastrophic, but the truth is, when you have the wrong reaction, you do become part of the problem. It doesn't solve anything when you deny something, when you get defensive, or when you start thinking all doom and gloom all the time.

Solutions always go back to communication and insight. If you understand why your spouse says what he says, you can react in a more constructive way. And by reacting in a constructive way, you can communicate much better.

Martyrdom: "It's Me, Not You"

There's nothing worse than playing the victim—regardless of whether you're wrong or right. "Poor me" just doesn't get you anywhere. You're miserable, and the person you're directing your martyrdom to is miserable. It's a no-win for everyone.

Playing the victim can also border on passive-aggressiveness. There's a joke I tell my clients: A husband asks his wife if she'd mind him going out to play poker tonight. She says of course she doesn't mind. "I'm sure I can find something to do—alone." Clearly, his wife doesn't want him to go out! But instead of telling her husband how she really feels, she gets coy. She sighs. She becomes a victim. If anything, playing the victim probably makes her husband want to go out and play poker even more!

If this situation really had happened, it would have probably started a fight. The husband would've felt guilty, which would make him defensive. He would start to yell, "I don't have to go if you don't want me to!" His wife would yell back, "What are you talking about? I told you to go!" And so on and so on ....

Yet the fight could have been avoided if his wife had just said the truth: "Can you go out next week? I'd really like to hang out with you tonight." The husband might not be thrilled by the answer, but he could compromise. He can play poker with the guys next week. After all, his wife needs him.

> **Keeping Her Word**
>
> **MISC.**
>
> A word of caution: the wife can't do this all the time. She has to keep her word and let him play poker next week. Otherwise, the husband may feel smothered.

Essential Takeaways

- Body language can speak volumes. Be careful what yours says to your spouse.
- No one likes a victim, so be honest and speak up.

- Avoid criticism; words can hurt.
- Making a joke about your spouse might be funny, but it also shows contempt.
- Listen when your spouse is speaking. Or simply ask if you can talk another time if it isn't convenient now.

chapter 16

And Baby Makes Three

Becoming parents overnight

Keeping love alive

Dealing with exhaustion

Taking breaks

Having children is a natural rite of passage in a marriage. We get married because we want to share our lives with another person, and in many cases, that means becoming parents. But let's face it: becoming a parent is a whole new level of responsibility. You go from thinking two to thinking three or more—forever. Children are a tremendous gift, and raising them is one of the joys of being together with the man or woman you love. But children can also drive a wedge into what once was a happy marriage.

This chapter explores the shift in thinking that comes with having children and shows you how your life can be enriched as it's enlarged when baby makes three.

Adapting to Change

You've had nine whole months to prepare. While waiting for the contractions to start again in earnest, you sit back and go through the list: The nursery is complete. The cradle is assembled. The rocking chair is in place. All the supplies are neatly stacked and awaiting duty.

You think you're in pretty good shape for the arrival of your baby. You have things under control for the day you come home from the hospital with your bundle of joy.

Wrong! Whatever you thought was going to happen, 9 times out of 10, you'll be mistaken. Your baby changes the equation completely, and these first few months you might have to be the most flexible, the most resilient, the most patient, and the most gentle you've ever been in your life—not only for yourself and the baby, but for your mate as well.

Shifts in Time Management

A newborn infant is an enormous responsibility, one that requires compromise with a capital *C*.

The first fact you have to face is that, try as you might, this baby makes his own—and yours by default—schedule. Whether you and your spouse have help or you only have each other, you will have to change the way you spend time.

When you have a baby, you say good-bye to the freedom of your early years as a married couple. If you're not prepared for relinquishing your independence, you'll be in for a rude awakening. Having a baby brings its own tremendous joys, but freedom is not one of them.

Coping with Fatigue

You'll do anything for your baby, sacrifice anything—including yourself— for her well-being. But remember this golden rule: you can't take care of anyone else if you don't take care of yourself! Here are some healthy lifestyle tips to deal with lack of routine, interruptions, and a complete overhaul of your previous life:

- Sleep! Many new parents take advantage of their baby's naptime by taking naps themselves.

- Eat a healthy diet. Fruits, vegetables, and whole grains give you the energy you need to care for a growing infant.

- Get enough exercise. When you're physically tired, you'll sleep better.

- Cut down on alcohol and caffeine. The first one will make you sleepy, and the second will make you wired. Either way, you might feel better for a little while, but you'll eventually crash.

- Keep to a regular schedule as much as possible. That means arranging for a sitter so you can go to work. It means rearranging both of your schedules so you can go to that yoga class. It means having friends and family over for dinner so your social life remains intact.

Misc.

Pot Luck Dinners

Everyone will want to meet your new baby, and having people around helps with your baby's socialization. But having guests does not have to mean polishing the family silver along with changing diapers. Ask your guests to bring a dessert or a side dish. No one expects you to do everything yourself.

Above all, give yourself a break! You have a new baby and, yes, it's stressful. You may not be at your best while you adjust. Change takes time. It's not easy, and it can be tiring. You're someone's parent, and that takes time to sink in.

Kids Come First

Many of my clients admit that when they got married with the intention of having children, they never realized exactly how much the focus of their lives would change forever after their children were born.

As one of my clients told me, "Holding my infant son for the first time made me feel how completely vulnerable I was. As a man I was confident. I could always take care of myself. But now? This baby is what I have to protect from the world. With all my heart."

Changing roles and changing dynamics in your marriage come as a big surprise to most new parents. It may seem strange to you that your first thought isn't about your partner anymore; it's about your baby.

Added Responsibilities

You've brought this new life into this world. You're responsible for sheltering, feeding, clothing, and keeping this life out of harm's way. You are the one responsible for her education, teaching her right from wrong … help!

But with these added responsibilities comes tremendous joys. Your baby's first smile. His first words. His first hug. And later, perhaps his graduation from college and his own marriage—all while you look on proudly. A baby will make love stronger, days shorter, nights longer, bankroll smaller, home happier, clothes shabbier, the past forgotten, and the future worth living for. The rewards far outweigh the heavy responsibilities.

Identity Shifts

When you think about it, our whole lives are about shifting identities. We are kids, then teenagers, then young adults. We become spouses and parents. Life is always changing, and our identity with it.

I remember a client who always began her sessions by talking about her previous lives. I thought she believed in reincarnation, but she was really talking about her life when she was a child!

From a Couple to a Family

It may have been difficult adjusting to being a married couple, but when a baby comes along, a whole new set of challenges take place. Now, more than ever, you need to communicate with each other. You need to compromise.

It's amazing how a simple cup of tea or coffee can change everything. It might just take 15 minutes out of your routine, but its positive effect can last a long time. If you're concerned about your baby, something about the current routine, or the way your spouse is handling something, just go into the next room when the baby is asleep. Discussing the problem will bring you closer as a couple and, ultimately, closer as a family, too.

Help Is Available

MISC.

The pressure is difficult enough when you have a healthy child, but if your child was born prematurely or has developmental problems, the challenges can be enormous. Remember, you don't have to do this alone. Seek professional help. Join a support group. Get the help you need.

Who Stays Home

In the black-and-white days of *Leave It to Beaver,* can you ever imagine Mrs. Cleaver coming home and asking, "Ward, honey, how was the Beaver today?" There was no question what the roles were in those days. That was the 1950s and 1960s—the last century! Today, there are no such hard-and-fast rules for who stays home with baby and takes care of the house.

Deciding who stays home is something you both hopefully discussed when you were first married. On the other hand, perhaps one of you has lost your job or prefers to stay home. Or maybe you want to share. The only important rule about "who stays home" is that it's a mutual decision, one that sits right with both of you.

Changing Routines

From the minute you bring your baby home, your life changes forever. Many couples find that they're socializing less and less with their single friends and their childless married friends. It's normal to gravitate to a new social circle.

Nor is it any surprise that you might have been a "party animal" when you were first married, able to burn the candle at both ends, but today? The most luxurious thing you can think of doing is changing into sweats and staying home. You spend more time at home, not only because you're tired, but because you want to spend time with your child. Instead of karaoke on Friday nights, it's Saturday morning play dates. That doesn't mean your life has gotten boring. It just means life is different.

The Joys of a Family

When you think of family, you might think of warm and joyful family gatherings and meaningful holidays with loved ones. That might well be your family—and you're lucky if that's the case. But the fact is that no one's family is perfect. And seeing that idyllic family on the movie screen may make us feel inadequate and, therefore, depressed. Why can't our family be like that?

There's one very good reason why: few families are or can be like that. A cartoon in *The New Yorker* once showed a banner proclaiming, "The Annual Functional Family Convention"—with one person sitting in the sea of otherwise empty auditorium chairs. Even in today's world, where dysfunctional families rule romantic-comedies, life on the screen isn't real. And after all, we go to movies to escape.

But that doesn't mean there's no joy in being a family. It's just more selective. Family jokes and conversations are unique and make you special. Family evenings can make you feel secure. It's just that they aren't perfect *all the time*. The moments are more fleeting, and we must be grateful for them when we have them.

Seeing your child take her first steps, say her first words, and just watching as this little person experiences the world are worth all the sleepless nights, the fuss, the worry, and the stress of parenthood—triple-fold! Those are the important things, not some unbelievably "perfect" get-together.

Sustaining Your Marriage as Your Children Grow

Throughout their lives, your children will have their ups and downs, their own challenges and joys as they navigate life.

At different stages, a child might go to her father for advice or affection; at other times, it will be her mom. Families are dynamic and always changing. As I discussed in Chapter 6, we don't stop being spouses when we become parents.

Avoiding Blame

You've seen it on sitcoms or maybe even heard it in your house: whenever a child does something right (like get all A's in school), he's *my* child. And when he gets into trouble, he's *your* son. Remember, there are two parents involved in raising a child, two to take responsibility, and two to share the blame.

This is a key point to remember to make your marriage a lasting one: don't blame your partner for the behavior of your child!

Take Time-Outs

Family vacations are important, but don't forget that a romantic weekend without the kids is important, too. Hire a babysitter, and go to a movie and get out together without the kids. You'll be better parents.

When Rose and David had their first child, they were in seventh heaven. Sure, it was difficult, but they knew there would be a transition. They had their sleepless nights, their 3 A.M. feedings, but they also delighted in their daughter—taking so many photographs their friends and family had stopped checking their Facebook pages.

But trouble begat trouble when their sex life went out the window. At first, they were too busy with their new baby to miss their time alone, but after several months, they found themselves snapping at each other. They were tired; there was less joy in the household.

They didn't want to go away. Rose's mother volunteered to watch the baby so they could take time off, but they didn't want to leave their baby for a long time.

They came up with the perfect solution: a local hotel. Sometimes they'd take a room and stay there just for a few hours. Sometimes they went overnight. But that time-out became important to them. It helped them be better parents—and better to each other!

Love Letters	No child was ever hurt by seeing affection between his or her mother and father.

Yes, having a baby has its pressures and its responsibilities. But with those tremendous pressures come tremendous joys that can last throughout all your years of marriage.

Essential Takeaways

- Having a baby changes your lives dramatically—individually and as partners.
- Be prepared to change identity, routines, and responsibilities after baby makes three.
- Avoid the blame game. You're both raising your child together.
- It's okay to show your love for each other. It sets a great example for your kids.

chapter 17

Money Changes Everything

Overcoming debt

Downsizing decisions

Wealth equals happiness?

Financial compatibility

A wise person I know once said, "Money doesn't buy happiness, but it can buy freedom." That's so true. You can have all the money in the world and still have a miserable life. On the other hand, you might be caught in a mind-numbing dead-end job and a windfall of cash could open up a world of possibilities, basically buying your freedom.

Here's the thing: money matters. Some people feel like it's crass to talk about money—and certainly good manners dictate we don't go around asking how much a neighbor paid for her house or how much a co-worker makes.

But there's a difference between crossing personal boundaries and talking cash. Keeping mum about money may not be crass, but it can be dangerous— especially if you're planning to get married and, more importantly, stay married. Read on to find out how finances can make or break your marriage and what you can do to keep your love alive no matter what your bank account holds.

Finances Are Not Static

Change is inevitable—and that includes how much money you have. Maybe you started out with very little, but over the years and several promotions later, the amount in the bank has grown. Or maybe it went the other way, when you had more money in the past than you do now.

Then there's the issue of the bank account itself. Maybe you have joint checking and savings all the way. Or maybe you keep separate accounts.

And what if you make more than your spouse? Is it equally both of yours to save or spend, or do you feel like you should be getting more of the cash at hand?

The subject of finances is wrought with change, differences of opinion, and evolving philosophies. A dollar might be just a dollar, but ask a couple what it represents, and you may get a very different answer.

Love Letters	Cash concerns change over the years, and it's vital that you and your spouse discuss finances frequently—at least once a month.

Most people think of money as a single concept: you either have a lot or you have a little. But cash is really twofold. On one hand, it represents freedom; on the other, security. Couples in long-term marriages have learned how to live in balance with both: using money for pleasure countered by savings in the bank and a 401(k) on the job.

Wealth Can Grow or Dwindle

Many couples struggle financially in the beginning of their relationships, especially if they marry young. But as their lives change and grow, as they have children and settle down, they might look back on those "salad years" of scrimping and saving with fondness, when life was simpler, there were no mortgages or college loans to pay, and love was always in the air.

There's no doubt your philosophy about money is a lot different when you walk down the aisle than it is after 10 or 20 years of marriage. Your children's education, preparing for retirement, caring for each other's parents—these are all issues that don't come up when you're first married, but they all can be financial speed bumps as you age together.

Ideally, your ideas about money and financial responsibility should be sorted out before you get married. You should know who the security sentinel is and who wants to take more risks—or if you're both equally divided.

But what if you didn't really discuss finances beyond your honeymoon destination or the amount of money each of you brings in from your job? What if neither of you is good with keeping within a budget? What if you resent your partner because you think he's cheap—or because she takes too many risks? The good news is that you can do something about it now—not 5, 10, or 20 years down the road.

Compromise, Not Sacrifice

Lesley and James had had the same financial goals when they first got married. They put some of their biweekly paychecks into their joint money-market savings account and used the remainder to pay their bills—with leftover cash to enjoy themselves. They even had the same ideas about saving for retirement versus saving for a vacation. It was perfect ... until it wasn't.

When they came to see me, life had changed. James had lost his job at an advertising agency and was doing sporadic freelance work; they never knew how much James would earn in a single month. They had stopped automatic bill payments just in case they didn't have the cash on hand. They started to dip into their savings account. They stopped going out to dinner, and disposable income had become a thing of the past.

MISC.

Facing Tough Decisions

Working together to create a harmonious financial life also involves some difficult discussions about wills and life insurance. No one wants to think about death, especially their own or that of someone they love. But if you don't put together a sound financial structure for the possibility, you may end up hurting those you leave behind.

Then their luck changed. James got a job as a creative director at a new ad agency, and the money began flowing again. But Lesley had built up resentment during James's unemployment, and she felt deprived. She wanted to spend some cash on a fabulous vacation. But James wanted to use the money to fix up the house; they needed a new roof and a new boiler. They started fighting, and there was no resolution in sight. Lesley had felt she'd sacrificed a lot and needed a reward.

I helped them see things more objectively. I suggested a compromise: a shorter but equally fabulous vacation for Lesley and a new boiler for James. It worked. Lesley no longer felt like a martyr, and James got to see the equity in their house grow. And as things progressed, James would get the new roof and Lesley would get another romantic vacation for two. It was a win-win!

The goal to any disagreement about money is compromise: deciding to postpone buying a new car until expenses eased up, for example, or, in Lesley and James's case, splitting the money so they can each get something for themselves—and for each other. Postponing a purchase or spending the money on something else might make you unhappy, but you'll still feel that your values and judgments are respected and you are heard.

When You See Different Shades of Green

In my experience, more men than women like to take risks with their money. They invest in start-ups, take chances with the stock market, and spend more money on major expenditures. Women, on the other hand, have more of a rainy-day mentality. Money is less about power and more about security. When money problems surface, women tend to be more scared. Of course, this isn't always true, and often it's just the opposite, but whatever your gender, you and your spouse need to complement each other.

Financial Endorsement

misc.

If your money problems seem insurmountable, I encourage you to read *Money Harmony*. An expert in the field of money management and relationships, author Olivia Mellon outlines the different "money personalities" couples have and how they can work out their money conflicts together.

This doesn't mean you have to think alike. And let's face it, opposites do attract. Free spirits are attracted to the logical, organized type and vice versa. You'd think this would create terrible money problems. After all, free spirits might have a devil-may-care attitude about money, whereas logical types may feel a pang every time they have to open their wallets.

But opposite views on money is not the problem. It's the "write-off" that hurts. If free spirits scoff at what they perceive as the logical type's cheapness, or if the logical type thinks the free spirit is flighty, I guarantee there will be a lot of fights about money. It might sound corny, but celebrating each other's differences helps when it comes to money. You need to give each other a voice, no matter how wide the money divide.

Creating a Budget Together

There's no time like the present! Even if you've spent a large portion of your married life calling a budget "the B word," you can mend your financial conflicts by facing them head on—and that means starting with a budget.

To start, make a list of all your expenses—and that means all of them. Don't forget visits to the drugstore or the dry cleaners. Use the following table as a guide to help you itemize what you spend each month.

Common Monthly Expenses			
Household	*Car*	*Necessary Personal Items*	*Fun!*
Mortgage/rent	Gas	Haircuts	Shopping
Property taxes	Parking	Dry cleaning	Dinners
Insurance	Tolls	Laundry supplies	Toys
Cleaning	Loan/lease	Medication	Gym fees
Utilities	Insurance	Drugstore needs	Gifts
Cable	Repairs	School supplies	Charity
Food		Health care	Vacation
Maintenance		Health insurance	Investments
Emergencies		Home office	Movies

Divide and conquer your expenses. Ask yourself what you can't live without, what you don't need, and where you can compromise. Do this exercise first individually. Then get together to discuss what you've both written down.

It also helps to create a monthly plan. Using your paychecks and any other incoming money, plan what you'll pay first, second, third, etc. For example, your mortgage should be at the top of your list.

Debt and More Debt

Sometimes couples come to me when their financial lives have gotten out of hand. Inevitably, one of them is furious that the other has gotten them into debt, and one of them is full of guilt that it happened.

The fact is, it did happen. It doesn't matter whether you did it together or one of you jacked up the credit card bills to insurmountable amounts. The problem is there, and you can either face it together or split up.

Realizing There's a Problem

It's hard not to face reality when a debt collector is calling you night and day, or when you're looking at a five-page Visa bill. Ask yourself if you're really surprised, or if you were looking the other way because you didn't want to deal with it. Chances are, there were probably signs—new clothes, new electronics, something that advertised "Look how much I'm spending!"

Getting Out of Debt

When you realize you're in debt over your head, the first thing you need to do is not panic. If you're not the one who spent all your money, you have every right to be angry—but don't act on impulse. Don't start screaming at your partner. That won't pay the bills any faster. Instead, follow these steps:

1. Take a deep breath and count to 10. Taking a quick time-out can stop you from saying something you may regret.

2. Either take out some paper or reach for your computer and spew out everything you want to say to your partner. Don't hold back! Write down all the awful, angry things you want to say.

3. Rip up the letter or delete the e-mail/document you just typed. Don't send it! Instead, now that you've gotten out your negative feelings, write a second letter or e-mail. This one should be more toned down. Gather your thoughts, and let your partner know how upset you are.

4. You can start the letter with something like, "I felt (horrible/furious/fill in the blank) when you (spent all our money/got us into debt/loused up our credit/fill in the blank)." Just remember that whatever you say will have the most impact if you don't make your spouse feel like he or she is being attacked.

5. Let your spouse have a chance to explain what happened. Work out the problem together. This might mean seeing a marriage counselor or a financial manager. It might mean some soul-searching. It might mean both.

6. Give yourself time. If nothing else, time gives you a chance to put things into perspective. Getting into debt is not the worst thing that can happen. (See Chapter 21 about the sea changes that can occur in marriages, including bankruptcy.)

Career Moves

Susan and Robert had had a good marriage for more than 20 years. But when Robert turned 50, he realized he hated his managerial job. He loathed going to the office every day. He despised the work he did. And he hated that he disliked it so much! Robert knew he was fortunate to be working, but he was miserable—and it was turning him into an unhappy person. He got depressed and was no longer the "Robert" Susan loved.

They had to make a change. After talking it over, they realized Robert could do something different. The kids were grown and there was no more college to pay for. The mortgage was almost paid off. The only problem with Robert quitting his job? Losing half of their income.

Susan and Robert had gotten used to an upper-middle-class lifestyle. They enjoyed traveling and giving their kids gifts. They enjoyed going out to dinner and going to the theater. If Robert went back to school to study something new, it wouldn't only mean losing money, but also spending money on tuition.

But they decided to go for it. Robert was depressed, and there was no point in a nice lifestyle if they weren't going to enjoy it! They could easily cut back. Fortunately, Susan also loved her job as a realtor, and she decided she could put in a few more hours a week to add to their income.

Robert went back to school to become a nurse. He was ecstatic with his choice, and Susan was so proud of him when he graduated. It was well worth the loss of money.

The moral of this story? If one of you wants to change careers midstream, it's important you discuss it together. Be sure you're both okay with the move.

> **Marriage Trap**
>
> Having a supportive spouse when you make a career move is a wonderful thing, so be sure you show your appreciation! The worst thing you can do is change your life and not thank your partner for standing by you. What was originally a happy compromise will turn into a bloody sacrifice.

Making Money Work with You, Not Against You

Over the years, I've found that one of the areas of greatest conflict couples have is money. Here are some ideas I tell couples who come to my office:

- Try to get together once a month to discuss outstanding bills and at least once a year to discuss financial goals.

- Some couples may have drastically different perspectives about how money should be spent. One way to handle those differences is to have three bank accounts: his, hers, and ours.

- Before spending money on what you believe is a major expenditure, talk to your spouse. Ideally, a major expenditure should be something you decide on together.

Marriage Trap   Don't hide major expenditures from each other. When your spouse discovers you've bought something without his knowledge, he may feel betrayed.

- Schedule a time to talk when a money issue comes up—either at a dinner out with just the two of you, or at the kitchen table. Just be sure you're both ready and willing to speak and there are no distractions to keep you from talking.

Essential Takeaways

- Money problems are a big source of conflict in marriage. Be sure you discuss any issues with each other to avoid letting a conflict get bigger.

- Take time every year to set up long-term financial goals. Goals change, and it's important you're aware of what each of you wants in your golden years.

- Don't go into attack mode if you find out your spouse has been spending too much money. Take time out before discussing it with her to settle down and gather your thoughts.

- It isn't the fact that one of you is a free spirit and the other hates to give money away that leads to financial problems. It's not hearing the other person. It's important that you respect each other's values even if you don't agree with them.

chapter 18

Intimacy Interference

Dealing with lowered libido

Making time for sex

Addressing intimacy issues

Rekindling the flame

How often have you heard a husband or wife say, "I just don't sleep as well when my spouse isn't sleeping next to me"? Maybe you've said it yourself a few times. It makes sense. We get used to the physical presence of our partner next to us: the space he takes up in the bed, the warmth of her skin, the rhythm of his breathing. Her body is almost an extension of your own.

This unconscious physical "completeness" we feel when our mate is next to us comes with time. Our mate is just there, like our hands or left ear.

Intimate Relations Can Erode with Time

The good news is that when you're in tune with your companion—so comfortable you can be completely yourself without any façade—you can experience a deep, satisfying intimacy. The bad news is that this feeling of comfort can, over time, give you a false sense of security. You can start to take your partner for granted and, instead of a growing intimacy, you begin to experience stagnation. Instead of feeling like one, you're both becoming an insolated two.

If you're beginning to think of your mate as "just there," the man or woman sleeping next to you, you're headed for trouble. Remember, a marriage takes work, even when both of you believe it's rock solid.

Familiarity Doesn't Have to Breed Contempt

I like to compare familiarity and contempt with job security. Are we ever really sure we can't lose our position? No matter how many years with a company, no matter what the accomplishments, promotions, awards, or how stable the company might appear, the fact remains that we could be without a job in a flash.

The best chance you have to keep that job is to keep working at it. That's why most of us work hard and don't mentally check out, waiting for Friday. If you can't take your job for granted, why would you do it with the most important relationship you have in the world—your marriage?

> **Marriage Trap**
>
> I've seen it many times: a CEO who would never consider sitting at his desk with his feet up, gazing out the window, doesn't think twice about his wife. Over the years, he becomes emotionally withdrawn from his marriage—and is completely shocked when his wife wants to discuss a separation.

But relationships don't have to stall after 10 or 20 or even 30 years. You just have to be aware that as close as you are with your significant other, you can't crawl into her head. As sensitive as you are, say, to her demeanor, her moods, or her quirks, there's still another part you can never know.

But you can talk to each other. You can check in with each other. Physical intimacy can do so much to make that connection.

Less Time for Sex

One lazy, rainy afternoon cuddling under the covers can seem like a two-week vacation, and you can come away satisfied and renewed. You feel connected with your mate, and you're better able to cope with the vicissitudes of life, its day-to-day humdrum and stress. Sounds perfect, doesn't it? And absolutely pleasurable. But there's one problem: time. A few hours with no agenda except to spend time with each other can be a hard thing to come by these days.

According to a 2010 Nielsen Media Research report, the average American household watches 8 hours, 15 minutes of TV in a 24-hour period. As soon as we click off the remote, many of us fall into bed with the sole thought of getting enough sleep to get up the next day and do it all over again. Sex is the last thing on our minds. It's easy to see why time for intimacy takes a low priority. Couples often find that sex becomes just another item on that long list of things that take a back burner in their hectic modern lives.

MISC.

No Time to Spare

A 2005 U.S. Census Bureau American Community Survey found that the average American spent 24.4 minutes commuting to and from work each way—that's an average of 100 hours per year, or the equivalent of more than 2 weeks of vacation. No wonder we complain there's not enough time for sex!

Life Problems Dampening Desire

Life is complicated, and the pace can be dizzying at times. That alone is enough to convert sex to a three-letter word in a crossword puzzle.

Add a life crisis—whether it be loss, family trouble, or a move to another town—and sex and intimacy can disappear altogether.

Do You Need More Time Together?

The following exercise is designed to help you focus on intimacy. If more than three of these statements ring true, you should sit down with your spouse and discuss the need for more intimate time together.

1. I always say no because I'm just too tired.

2. I never refuse my spouse's advances, but most times I'm too tired to enjoy it.

3. On the weekends the kids wake us and spend the mornings with us in bed.

4. We both want more sex, but we never seem to want it at the same time.

5. We never have time to "play" in bed anymore; we go directly to intercourse.

6. I often fall asleep on the couch with the television on long after my husband has gone to bed.

7. I don't see my wife in the morning because she gets up so early to go to the gym.

8. We've never taken a vacation or even spent a weekend without the children.

9. We watch a lot of television in our bedroom.

10. I haven't taken a personal day from work in years.

A lasting marriage is more than communication, respect, and deep love. You need sex to spice things up. Honor your intimacy. Understand the need. And make time—prioritize and even schedule it on your calendar if need be.

Marriage Trap	Sex can be like that yoga class you signed up for, the one you know would make you feel so good, so relaxed, so "at one with the universe" … if you went to it. Whether it's a client's unexpected visit or Tommy's science project that's due tomorrow, something always seems to take a higher priority.

When Desire Is Absent

When Lance and Beth came to see me, they didn't understand why their marriage had lost its luster. They didn't fight. They loved and respected each other. But they weren't having sex on a regular basis, and they were becoming more and more aware of the emotional distance that had replaced the intimacy they once shared. After talking to them for a while, I saw what had derailed this marriage of 22 years: life. Life had thrown more than one curve ball at this couple, and it was a testament to their love and commitment that they were in my office trying to figure out what to do next.

Lance and Beth met through a mutual friend when they were just out of college. After the first few dates, they both knew they'd found someone special and were married within a year. They both wanted children, but after trying for several months, it became apparent they had a problem. They went to a fertility expert and spent the next five years using almost all their time, money, and emotional energy on tests and procedures—only to be disappointed again and again. They decided to get off the fertility rollercoaster and adopted Jesse, who became the light of their lives. Jesse was a beautiful, well-adjusted child who grew into a lovely young woman, and Lance and Beth were very proud of her. When Jesse got married, her parents couldn't have been happier; they looked forward to becoming grandparents. Life was good—until it wasn't.

Jesse's husband was tragically killed in a car accident and, although Jesse remarried a few years later, the spark seemed to go out of their only child's eyes. Soon after, Beth developed a chronic illness that cut short her real estate career. Just when they thought things couldn't get worse, Lance lost his small manufacturing business to overseas competition. But with all this, Lance and Beth remained loving and loyal and came through their crises with a united front.

Right before they'd come to see me, things were looking up; the hard years were behind them. They'd become grandparents, Lance began a new career as a consultant, and Beth had learned to manage her illness and had become active in a local charity. So why was this couple in my office? Why weren't they stronger as a couple?

On the surface, they'd survived as a couple, more bonded than ever. But the crises had taken their toll. Instead of sharing their individual grief and fear, they gritted their teeth to be strong for the other one. They hadn't shared their fear, rage, and grief; they hadn't cried together. Now that life was better, they couldn't be physically intimate because they hadn't been emotionally intimate for many years.

The desire for intimacy and sex is a component of married life that should continue well into our sunset years. And if you don't limit the definition of sexual intimacy to the act of intercourse several times a week, sex doesn't have any age limitations.

Love
Letters

When life throws you a curve ball, you can be so busy focusing on surviving that fun, healthy habits—and yes, sex—are the last things on your mind. But you can combine all three with a few minutes of touch, be it a hug, kiss, or soft caress, that can make getting back to tackling your problems much easier and more productive.

Having regular sex doesn't mean you're intimate. It certainly improves the odds, but lasting marriages don't necessarily have hot sex five times a week. But they do have intimacy—a closeness that can be felt whether watching television, reading a book, or driving a car together.

Menopause

It's a fact of life that our bodies change as we age, and in order to live a good life through our senior years, we must adjust to those processes. As a woman approaches menopause and her hormone levels change, she can experience mood swings, flushing and hot flashes, and a decrease in libido. These symptoms usually diminish as menopause ends, but each woman's experience is unique: one woman may have intense night sweats, so much so she soaks the bed sheets, while another woman goes through her menopausal years with nothing more than a hot flash once in a while.

The decreases in *estrogen* during menopause can become a major problem for intimacy. Without enough of the hormone estrogen, the mucous membranes in the vagina thin and become less elastic. This change can cause vaginal dryness—which can make intercourse extremely painful.

Definition

Estrogen is a female hormone that promotes the development of female secondary sex characteristics. During menstruation, estrogen helps prepare the female genital tract for pregnancy. In menopause, estrogen production decreases.

Over-the-counter vaginal lubricants can help add moisture when having intercourse, and some can even add more "oomph!" to sexual satisfaction. There are also prescription estrogen-based suppositories that can increase moisture production in the vagina. The medications must be used regularly, and it can take time for you and your partner to adjust.

Estrogen isn't the only hormone that decreases in women when they approach menopause. Like men, women also lose testosterone, which can also lead to a lack of desire. Prescription testosterone medications can help, but they may bring some unwanted side effects, such as hair growth in the wrong places.

But there's a bright spot in menopause: birth control is no longer necessary, and monthly cramping and bleeding becomes a thing of the past!

Manopause

Although the changes males experience as they grow older aren't as dramatic as menopause in women, they, too, must also accept and adjust to their aging bodies. As men age, their levels of *testosterone* decrease. If these levels drop significantly, men may experience a loss of interest in sex.

Definition

Testosterone is the hormone that stimulates the development of male sex organs, male secondary sex characteristics, and sperm.

Older men may also have trouble getting or sustaining erections. They also tend to take longer to climax and ejaculate less semen.

The good news is that some solutions are available to help, including medication that helps men maintain an erection. It can also help to "get in the mood": candles, sexy lingerie, even x-rated websites can help keep things "hot."

Underlying Medical Problems

Medical conditions unrelated to sex, such as diabetes, obesity, high blood pressure, coronary artery disease, and depression, can also influence waning sexual desire. Adding insult to injury, the medications used to treat these conditions can also decrease sexual desire. It's important that you talk to your doctor about your conditions and treatments. Keep your partner in the loop. He or she needs to know it's not that you aren't in love anymore; it's a physical problem.

Chemicals of Desire

MISC.

Hormones are the chemicals that fuel sex drive in both men and women. These hormones fluctuate, especially as we age. Estrogen and testosterone are the ones generally associated with men and women, but other hormones that can also affect desire include thyroid hormones and prolactin.

Psychological Factors

After considering the physical reasons for lack of intimacy, it's important to look at the psychological issues that may be at fault, too. Stress, anxiety, insecurity, and other such feelings can affect your mood. Consider your responses to the following questions:

- Do you feel an inordinate amount of stress in your day-to-day life?

- Do you have financial concerns that seem to be escalating?

- Are you or your mate depressed, or is either one of you having some other mental problems?

- Are you having a family crisis?

- Are you facing a big challenge, such as a move to another city?

- Have you gained or lost weight recently and feel unattractive?

- Has privacy become an issue—either because of children or an aging parent who has come to live with you?

If you are having psychological problems, you may want to seek the help of a professional. He or she can help you through your current crises and help you connect to your partner again.

Each professional works in a different way. Sometimes, a therapist will want to speak to both of you together and then apart. I prefer meeting with couples at the same time, unless only one spouse is interested in my help.

Getting Back in the Groove

If you've been diagnosed with a physical problem that's causing your intimacy issues, there's good news. Help is available.

MISC.

Kegel Exercises

Kegels—pelvic floor exercises that tighten the vaginal canal and tone the muscles that control urine flow—can also enhance orgasms for a woman and her partner. Named for the physician who developed them, these exercises are simple, and a woman can perform them anytime, anywhere. After isolating the muscles that attach to the pelvic bone, tighten and then relax them for a count of five each.

Medication

Many medications can help treat sexual problems in men and women.

For menopausal women, hormone replacement therapy (HRT) pills, patches, or gels can help improve mood and sexual desire. Clinical studies have shown that HRT can increase the risk of breast cancer and heart disease, so many women are opting out of using HRT these days. Alternative solutions to reduce menopausal symptoms include herbal supplements, such as black cohash or wild yam. Please check with your health-care professional before using any supplement, including herbs.

Low-dose estrogen pills that have lower risk than HRT are available, as are suppositories or vaginally inserted slow-release estrogen rings that can help with sexual drive by increasing blood flow to the genitals. Again, check with your health-care professional before beginning any treatments for loss of libido.

Men may also opt for HRT, but with testosterone instead of estrogen. It can be given with an injection, orally, or by topical cream. If a man is experiencing erectile dysfunction, several prescription drugs are available. As always, talk over your options with your health-care professional.

Making Time for Love

I know couples who schedule sex and actually mark it on their calendars with a big "S!" Other couples may have an unwritten agreement that, say, Friday nights are date nights. They'll make sure the kids are at their grandparents' house or with a babysitter and make a reservation at a hotel or go out for a romantic dinner.

Whether it's an entry in an appointment book or an agreement between both of you, it's critical that you set aside time out of your busy lives for each other. How frequently? Where? When? That should be the fun part. Don't make it yet another obligation. Spice things up. Try new things. Use your imagination.

Where There's a Will, There's a Way

If you're having problems with desire and intimacy, it's important that you discuss your problems with your mate. You'll both feel much better if you can identify the cause or causes of your problem and work together to find a solution.

Once you've gained insight into your problem, you can be free of the negative thinking that can kill sexual intimacy. Thoughts such as *He doesn't want me because I'm not young and pretty anymore* or *She has such a high sex drive and I don't right now. She has to be going elsewhere for release* aren't only bad for your sex life, but also for your marriage as a whole.

As with everything else in a lasting marriage, communication and understanding are key.

Essential Takeaways

- Intimacy is not purely about sex. Yes, sex is important, but true intimacy can be found in a simple but loving touch or a smile.
- Talk over any problems you may have or think you have. That communication can provide insight and possibly a solution, too.
- Realize that in today's world, plenty of help is out there. Whether your problem is physical or emotional, you can find support and treatment.
- Scheduling time for sex can really work! Get out your date book!

chapter 19

The Empty Nest and Beyond

When the kids leave home

More leisure time

Growing old, growing apart

When the kids come back

Just when you think you've finally figured out everything—boom! Your adult children need to come back home to live. Or your kids have shuttled off to college and the house feels too big. And wait a minute: who's that stranger you shared the last 30 years with?

The golden years still have a lot to offer. And today, with 60 being the new 40, you need to be ready for anything. So enjoy, celebrate, relish your many years of marriage ... and fasten your seatbelts!

Just the Two of You ... Now What?

At this point in your marriage, you've figured out the real person you married. You've successfully dealt with all the different stages of life. You've had fun as a young couple, bought your first and subsequent houses, had and raised your kids, battled storms and came out the other side, and now ... well, now you have to figure out what to do next.

During these senior years, couples learn how and when to compromise, and they truly (read: not on the surface) accept areas of differences with minimum resentment. Hopefully, by the time you've been married for 20, 30, or 40 years, you've learned to appreciate and love each other and …

- Focus on what's right with each other.

- Give each other the benefit of the doubt in conflict situations.

- Successfully manage and truly accept any frustrations, disappointments, and hurts.

- Agree to disagree.

- Fully value each other—even if you're unable to completely see things the same way.

- Have a give-and-take sexual relationship on a regular basis.

- Learned how to communicate in such a way you each really listen to and hear each other.

- Can disagree with each other—and that's okay.

- Recover from your disagreements within a short period of time.

- Constantly find things to appreciate about each other.

- Spend time relaxing and having fun on a weekly basis.

- Spend time talking about any issues that come up in your relationship.

That's a long list of items, but you've had a long time living with each other and even if these elements aren't always present, they exist enough to make your marriage solid. Congratulations!

Revisiting Old Issues

Alicia and Thomas had been married 37 years. They had three children, five grandchildren, and three Beagles. They lived in a rambling old house in the country, and their children loved to visit. Alicia and Thomas looked forward to their visits; it was the highlight of their lives. Because now that they're retired, and getting up in the morning and going to sleep at night next to each other, going to the supermarket together, doing laundry together, and, well, just plain hanging out all the time with each other, if they were honest with each other, it wasn't so great.

What they realized after all these years, now that they were once again on their own, was that they didn't really know who the other was. Do you really believe that? How long? You never told me you liked Thai food! And on and on …. After all these years of marriage, they were headed for divorce.

That's when they came to see me, and together we worked out a blueprint for them getting reacquainted with each other. They needed to reconnect and remember what they loved about each other in the first place. They needed to go back to when they were young, during their first years together. It worked. By seeing each other with fresh eyes, they could really see each other—and love what they saw. Combined with planning their own activities individually (Tom loved golf; Alicia loved yoga), they didn't have to spend every waking moment together.

Simple Pleasures

MISC.

Growing old together can be one of the most beautiful times in a marriage. You don't have to go on a cruise or play golf at the country club. Going to the movies. Taking a walk. Having a picnic in the park. These are not only activities you did when you were young; they are activities you can do right now.

Are You Living with a Stranger?

Imagine this scenario: you wake to the sound of your alarm and squint at the clock. The glowing numbers tell you, yes, it's time to get up. You roll over to say good morning to your husband and … there's a total stranger staring back at you! What would you do? More than likely, you'd freak out.

And when the children are gone, along with all their activities, routines, requests, and chores, married couples do freak out when they realize, *Who are you? What have you done with the person I married and spent over a quarter of a century with?* It can be a shock when you're finally alone again.

But this time you aren't young and in love with your whole future ahead of you. This time, you're older, wiser, and comfortable with each other.

Some married couples are lucky. Although they miss the kids hanging around, they also love the solitude and the peace. They love turning their kids' rooms into offices or sewing rooms. They love the freedom of doing and saying whatever they want, whenever they want.

But other couples aren't as lucky. After the kids leave the nest, they find that they might not like each other very much.

Growing Apart

Chris, one of my long-married clients, describes these last few years of her marriage as, "It's like we're both in our own little boats that were once tied up along side of each other. Somehow they got untied, and they just floated apart. I could see it happening, and I'm sure my husband did, too, but it was like we didn't know how to get back … so we just drifted in different directions, just lazily bobbing and floating away."

For Chris and her husband, Tom, there were no big bombshells: no infidelity, money crises, health problems. Nothing but gently, slowly drifting away.

Tom told me, "There was nothing really wrong with our marriage. We just weren't a team anymore. And then I was alone. Just like that."

Chris added, "It was like Tom's boat was a tiny speck on the horizon, and then it just disappeared."

Your marriage doesn't have to drift away. These senior years can be an exciting time when you can become reacquainted with each other and fall in love all over again.

Living with Empty Nest Syndrome

If you stay married long enough, at some point it's going to be just you and your mate. You'll be left with the proverbial *empty nest*. After the kids are gone, after your neighbors move, and friendships run their course, it all comes full circle: you and your spouse who long ago said, "I do."

Empty nest is the stage of life when married couples are alone in the house after the children have moved out to start their own independent lives.

Definition

Avoiding Marital Burnout

It's hard to believe, but your marriage can be as fresh and exciting today as it was 20, 30, or 50 years ago. You don't have to become some grumpy old couple snapping at each other like a sitcom cliché. It does require some work, though. Yes, even after all these years, you still have to work on keeping your marriage viable.

It might sound strange, but one of the first things you need to do is become friends again. I've developed the following questions to help empty nesters reconnect. Answer each question as best you can, and ask your partner to do the same.

1. What do you think are the qualities of a good friend?

2. How good a friend are you with your partner now?

3. How good a friend were you with your partner at the beginning of your relationship?

4. Are you starting to drift away from each other?

5. If so, what do you think is causing the distance?

6. If so, what role did you play?

7. Given 20/20 hindsight, what else could you have done if you've drifted apart?

8. What can you do now to improve your friendship?

Like any other friendship, the one you have with your spouse may need some effort on both your parts to strengthen—or reconnect if you've drifted. The love you shared, and hopefully still share, will help it turn out well.

Some Grief or Loneliness Is Normal

Of course you feel sad when the children leave home: it shows the passage of time, of growing old. It can be bittersweet: you're happy your children have become healthy adults, but you also remember the first card they made for you at school, the first play, the hours spent on homework, and you're going to miss that.

Love Letters	Being thankful for what you have goes a long way toward feeling less isolated. Think about it: you've been married a long time, you're still together, and you've raised great kids. What else is on your list?

I don't want to make it seem that all you have to do is work on your relationship and your marriage will be a bastion of happiness that will carry you merrily into your sunset years. In reality, there are typically times when you'll feel like you're on your own or when you're sad. It's a part of life. It's normal.

Coping with an Empty House

Some of my clients started marriage with the hopes of having a large family as soon as possible. They had a five-year plan ready and waiting. Unfortunately, the idea of children was very different from the reality. They hadn't understood what it means to have a child: the responsibility, the compromise, the relinquishing of independence.

The good news? The couple concentrated on the love they shared for their baby. They took turns with chores. They delighted in their child's growth and sought out solutions to problems together. The 5-year plan did turn into the 10-and-a-half plan, but that was okay. They had learned to compromise.

The years as a family had their ups and downs, but they were happy years, and they flew by. Now, after all that energy, all that hard work, the children are gone, as they are meant to be. But what about you?

Your house—and your lives together—doesn't have to be a sad, lonely place. It can be wonderful. Now's your chance to do so many things. For example, you finally can take that watercolor class. You can learn how to scuba dive. You can learn Chinese. Take advantage of all this free time.

You can also create new goals. Instead of saving for college, save for that trip to Africa or the Far East. Or travel to see the next eclipse. Or do something as simple as working on your golf handicap.

A change of scenery might help. Redecorate. Change things up. Paint your child's room a peaceful shade of blue or a bright green. Add trim along the ceiling. Get the new light fixtures you've been wanting. Move in your desk or sewing machine, or turn it into a workout room.

You could even begin a new career. It's never too late to learn something new. Sure, you might not be able to get up on toe shoes and dance to Swan Lake, but maybe you can become a licensed nurse practitioner or write that book you've been dreaming of. Or maybe you could go back to school and finally get your Master's degree. For inspiration, consider Alfred Butts. The former architect was 85 years old when he changed courses and invented the board game Scrabble.

Just When You Thought It Was Over …

Vivienne and Jacob could finally relax. Their son, Elliot, had graduated college and moved to Chicago. He even took the family cat to live with him. Sure, Vivienne and Jacob were lonely for a little while, but they adapted. They loved changing Elliot's room into an office, and they planned to take a trip to Australia in the fall. They'd started going out on dates, just like when they were kids, and they found that they still had passion for each other. Things were great!

Great, that is, until Elliot came home. His girlfriend had left him; his roommate moved out of the apartment; he lost his account manager job. He couldn't afford the rent on his own.

Marriage Trap

Don't use your adult children as an excuse not to enjoy yourselves and become reacquainted. Nobody wins in this scenario.

Of course, Vivienne and Jacob welcomed Elliot (and the cat) back with open arms. They moved the computer out of his old room, and put back his bed. They postponed their trip to Australia in order to help support Elliot while he looked for a new job. Soon, it was like it always was: doing the laundry, cleaning up after Elliot, making dinner, and trying to find some peace and quiet while the football game blared.

Only this time, the family circle wasn't as joyous. Vivienne and Jacob were older, and they were tired. They loved their son with all their hearts, but the stress was mounting.

Then there were the parties. Elliot would invite his old friends over, and they'd take over the den. Vivienne and Jacob were forced to watch television on the small set in their bedroom. All this would have been fine except for one thing: Vivienne and Jacob started arguing with each other—over Elliot. Vivienne kept asking Elliot to do his own laundry. Jacob told her to leave him alone. Jacob asked Elliot how the job hunt was going every night at dinner. Vivienne told him to leave him alone.

By the time Vivienne and Jacob came to see me, they were beside themselves. They were angry, resentful, and full of guilt. They were fighting over their son—the boy they raised and loved!

It's never easy to see your kids come back. On one level, there's a sense of failure: maybe you didn't raise them well enough; they didn't know how to be independent. On another level, you're delighted to have them back.

But things are never the same. Here are the "golden oldie" rules I used to help Vivienne and Jacob—and Elliot, too:

First, welcome your child home. Be sure he always knows he can come home. You'll always be his parents, and he needs the safety net of your love.

It helps to establish boundaries. If you don't want your child to have parties in your house, tell her so up front. Be sure she knows she'll have to do her own laundry and help around the house.

Finally, make your child responsible for himself. In other words, stop acting like a parent. Let him see that he's the one who has to find a job, that he has to find a life. You can help, even suggest professional help, but he needs to know that he's an adult now and has responsibilities.

Welcome Home

Robert Frost once wrote, "Home is the place where, when you have to go there, they have to take you in."

Essential Takeaways

- Use your newfound freedom to do something you've been putting off—a trip, a class, or a redecoration project. You're never too old to try something new. Go for it!

- It's normal to feel sad when your adult children leave home.

- Make your adult child welcome if he needs to come home, but establish ground rules before he gets too settled.

chapter 20

The Parent Trap

Caring for aging parents

Clashing family needs

Making tough decisions

Finding solutions together

It seems like only yesterday when you'd share your day with your mother, when you'd go to your parent's house for dinner on a Friday night, when you'd ask your parents for advice on everything from finances to child-rearing. Or it might never have been like this for you. Maybe you and your parents grew apart as you grew older. Maybe you moved away and you only get an opportunity to see your parents once or twice a year. Or worse, maybe your parents meddle and don't know their boundaries. Your mother gives advice when it isn't asked for. Your father disapproves of the man you married. Or maybe it's your in-laws who cause you grief.

Whatever your parental situation, realize that all parents age. And at some time, you and your spouse might need to help them.

When Your Parents Grow Old

It's the circle of life: we're born, we grow up, and we have children, our children grow up and have children, we grow old and our parents grow very old, and eventually we die. And the cycle repeats, as inevitable as day follows night. A part of that cycle is falling in love, getting married, raising and educating children, and hopefully seeing them grow up and begin their own way in the world. Sometimes it feels like it happens too fast!

But along with seeing our children grow up is seeing our parents grow old. It can feel as if only a few short years separate the time when our children leave the nest and our parents start to decline. During that short stretch of time, we have fewer responsibilities before our roles change to something familiar but emotionally wrought—when our aging parents become our children. Whatever the circumstances, we must become more involved in our parents' well-being.

> **Marriage Trap**
>
> Sometimes couples have two sets of aging parents with very different needs. Sometimes you can be an only child, and sometimes siblings are around to help share the responsibilities. But whether you have one brother or four sisters, usually only one child becomes the primary caregiver. If that's you, it can create a great deal of stress on you, your family, and everyone involved.

Two Families for the Price of One

It wasn't long ago that a nuclear family would have included a grandmother or grandfather or both living under the same roof. It was a tradition and is still very much a way of life in some parts of the world. But as American culture changed, both children and their elder parents were financially able to maintain their own households. Seniors began to live longer and healthier. They were financially independent and enjoyed their own lives—especially when it came to visits from the grandkids. The new traditional family meant a mother, a father, and their children living together in one house, and grandparents living independently for as long as possible.

When you marry, you don't marry one person—you marry into a family. Your in-laws come with the territory. For better or worse, you must deal with them on some level—emotionally, financially, and physically—until the day they die.

The Desire to Do What's Right

It's difficult to see parents decline and fail. These are the people who raised you, who cared for and nurtured you, and who helped shape you into the person you are today. When your parents descend into confusion and dementia, it can be even more heartbreaking. The sobering fact is that aging parents can become a problem, and caring for them can become a situation that becomes more and more demanding—physically and emotionally.

Of course, you want to do the right thing for your parents, but now you also have your own family—a spouse and children to consider. But it's not always easy. Caring for your elderly parents can bring terrible feelings of guilt because you can become frustrated, lose your patience, and get angry. Or you can become depressed. Childhood issues, from quarrels with your siblings to those times your parents embarrassed you when you were a teen, can also surface, which can make an already charged emotional situation even more complicated.

And through it all, you just want to make the best decisions for everyone concerned. It's no wonder caring for an aging parent can make you feel overwhelmed and isolated and put a tremendous stress on your marriage.

> **Marriage Trap**
>
> *I will never put my parent into a home .... I'll always take care of my parents, no matter what .... She can move in with us ....* If you've maintained a good relationship with your parents over the years, you've probably had these thoughts over and over again. They're noble and true. They're what you believe is right. But reality can change your thinking, especially if your aging parents are putting your marriage in danger.

Taking Care of Aging Parents

The emotional aspect of taking care of your aging parents is one thing, but the practical, everyday logistics of the situation are equally important. Thanks to baby boomers, there are more seniors in the world than ever before. And these boomers want to be sure they're being taken care of properly in their old age.

To that end, the senior industry has been churning out solutions—from active retirement communities to home health aid, from assisted-living residences to daycare and senior-designated vacations.

If neither you nor your aging parent have enough money to help with their care, all is not lost. Good nursing homes can be paid for with Social

Security. Agencies can provide less-expensive part-time care, which helps to free up some of your day. Major corporations are also acknowledging the aging parent issue and giving employees "parent leave" in the same way they give maternity leave.

Making It Work with Your Family

It's rare in a marriage where the husband is responsible for his parents and the wife is responsible for hers. It just doesn't work that way. Your children, too, become involved, although on a less complicated level. There's nothing a grandparent enjoys more than an afternoon with his or her grandkids!

It's important to remember that your parents won't be around forever. Although taking care of them can be an enormous strain on your relationship, it's not forever. Enjoy your parents—or your spouse's parents—as best you can, and appreciate them for who they are. You don't want to be left with resentment or anger based on the way you both treated each other's parents after they're gone.

MISC.

Aging Statistics

People over 65 today have an average life expectancy 18.6 years more than it was in the 1990s. Half of all women age 75 and older live alone. The over-65 senior population will increase 36 percent by 2020, up to 55 million by 2020. Thirty-one percent of noninstitutionalized older Americans (about 11.2 million) live alone. One person in eight is an older American—12.8 percent of the population.

Making Hard Choices

As your parents age, you'll have lots to think about. If your parents live far away, will you or will they move closer? Do they sell the house and move into a *progressive-care facility,* where they can have as much independence as possible until they need nursing care?

Does your parent want to stay in her home? If so, will she have access to home care? If your parent can still live independently in her own home, you and your spouse will need to have signals that determine if she needs more around-the-clock care. Losing sight or hearing, an inability to walk around, or a loss of appetite might be some signs. But there are less obvious cues you may want to put on your "Is it time?" list. The following list can also point to depression—which can also become severe enough to be a concern:

- Excessive emotional behavior, such as inappropriate laughter or crying
- Falling asleep in a chair in front of the television every night
- An empty refrigerator
- A messy kitchen, with dirty dishes and pans, or bed sheets that haven't been changed in weeks
- Sleeping more than 10 hours a day
- Getting into a car accident or having too many tickets
- *Agoraphobic* behavior
- A lack of personal hygiene

> **Definition**
>
> A **progressive-care facility** offers a home in all stages of growing old. If your parent can live more or less independently, an apartment might suffice for her. As she ages, she'll be transitioned to more care facilities and hospitals—all under the same roof.
>
> **Agoraphobia** is an anxiety disorder that makes a person afraid to leave the house. He or she may be scared something will happen if they leave, or they may be terrified of interacting with others.

Hard choices can be made much easier if you're able to sit down with your parents while they're still physically and mentally healthy to discuss the future. This conversation enables your parents to make their wishes known—where they want to live, how they intend to finance it, and so on.

Planning is key. It frees both you and your spouse from making decisions on your own without knowing what your parents want. Spelling out as much detail as possible is a gift your parents can give you, their eventual guardian.

I also suggest having your parents sign a living will, advanced directives (whether or not he or she wants to be resuscitated when in a coma), and a power-of-attorney document so you can take care of things when they're no longer able to tell you what they want.

You can find a wealth of information on taking care of aging parents at the Administration on Aging website, www.aoa.gov.

Car Talk

Misc.

One of the most difficult decisions you can make about your aging parents is taking away the car. The ability to drive gives everyone a sense of freedom and independence. Taking away that ability can make someone feel helpless and hopeless. But if your parent is getting into a lot of car accidents, it may be necessary—before she hurts herself or someone else.

How Does Your Spouse Feel?

Claire and Donald had a wonderful marriage. They agreed early on that they didn't want children, and both were successful professionals. They were active socially and politically. They had a wide circle of friends and were the favorite aunt and uncle of Claire's brother's children.

Donald was an only child, and both of his parents had passed on. Claire's mother was a widow. Ursula was an active, healthy woman in her late 70s, financially and emotionally independent—or so it seemed.

Claire and Donald came to see me after Ursula had fallen down the stairs and broken her hip and spent a number of weeks at a rehabilitation center. During that time, Claire was shocked to discover that her mother was broke. Hadn't her father provided well for his wife? She always thought so, but she soon discovered her mother had spent all the money Claire's father had left. Ursula was on the verge of declaring bankruptcy because of credit card debt!

Seemingly overnight, Claire and Donald became totally responsible for Ursula. Even though Claire had two sisters and a brother, their contribution was minimal. They felt that because Claire and Donald had no children and were financially capable, they should care for Ursula. In fact, Claire's sisters didn't understand why their mother just couldn't move in with Claire and Donald.

Donald and Claire's marriage was in trouble—and there was more than one reason why they were sitting in my office. When the subject of Ursula came up, Donald's first statement was "I never signed on for this! I don't need this!"

Although Claire and Donald's experience may not be typical, it does illustrate the point that your family may expand to include older parents, and the best thing you can do to prepare for it is to discuss with your spouse your attitudes and beliefs about it before it becomes an issue—and an emotional crisis.

Devote Time to Discuss Events

What do you do if your husband wants your mother to be in a home and you're wracked with guilt about it? Talk about it. Bare your soul. Explain how you're feeling.

As difficult as it seems, discussing an emotional issue is very important. If you don't, resentment and anger can build to a point where your marriage is in danger.

Finding a Solution—Together

There's strength in numbers. And when it comes to making major life decisions, a united front is always stronger than two individuals. If you and your spouse are in disagreement about how to take care of an aging parent, it doesn't have to end in a stalemate. There are alternative solutions:

- See if there's a certified residence for seniors near your home. This makes visits to your mother or father more convenient. And you're only a few miles away if there's an emergency.

- See if your parent's supplemental Medicare insurance can help pay for home nursing care. It can take some of the pressure off you.

- Check out your town's real estate. Maybe there's a two-family house for sale where you can all live under the same roof—but with a lot more doors.

- Investigate adult daycare. They can be out of the house and enjoy themselves to boot.

Are You on the Same Page?

You might end up agreeing to disagree, but you and your spouse need to be comfortable with whatever decision you come up with. Be sure you've explored all the different living solutions.

Love Letters
An aging parent doesn't have to be—and shouldn't be—a deal-breaker. If you and your spouse can't agree on a solution, see if you can find a support group for children with aging parents in your area. Hearing how others have coped can offer some new insight.

Don't forget to be flexible. You can turn a page and discover that what seemed like the best solution a few months or a year ago may not be ideal today. Keep talking about it, and you'll probably find an answer.

Essential Takeaways

- Taking care of an aging parent can take a toll on your family, your marriage, and you.
- Plan to speak to your parents about their long-term wishes when they're still emotionally and physically well.
- Sometimes hard choices about your aging parents need to be made—especially when they're in danger of hurting themselves.
- Be sure you and your spouse are on the same page when it comes to taking care of an aging parent.

chapter 21

The Marriage Sea Changes

When an affair rocks your marriage

Overcoming addictions

Sticking through illnesses

Handling money trouble

Dealing with terrible losses

Into every life a little rain must fall. But in some cases, it can be more like a tsunami. Fortunately, many couples won't have to cope with infidelity, substance abuse, a debilitating disease, going bankrupt, or the unthinkable pain of losing a child, but some will. Can your marriage handle a rocky sea change? The answer is yes. And no.

Whether or not your marriage can weather the storm of a tragedy is partly due to how strong your marriage was before it hit and how you cope with the news. In this chapter, I go over some of the major upsets that can test a marriage and give you ways to work through it together.

Overcoming Infidelity

Cheating. There's no deeper sense of betrayal than to realize the person you share your life with, the person you love and trust, has had an affair. This is a hard one to come back from, but does infidelity signal the end?

Not really. The real reason couples divorce is that they feel distant from one another and don't know how to reconnect. They become so alienated, there's nothing else to do but end the relationship.

Many of the couples who come to see me are in the midst of the aftershock of infidelity. To help me help them, it's important that I understand the type of affair that's occurred. This way, the partner who's been cheated on can get valuable information as to how to proceed. The following sections outline the different types of affairs. See if you can identify which category fits your situation.

Infidelity Myths

If someone has an affair, the marriage is over. Not necessarily. Only 20 to 25 percent of divorces are caused by affairs, and 75 to 80 percent of couples stay together after the affair ends.

Most affairs are sexually driven. People have affairs for emotional reasons, not sexual. They feel ignored by their partner, not cared about, even angry, and don't know what to do with those feelings.

The Conflict-Avoidance Affair

This type of affair happens with couples who, on the surface, seem so nice. In reality, one of them will do anything to avoid conflict. In this situation, it's easier for the person to handle an unfaithful situation than to confront her partner.

My advice? If you want to continue your relationship, you need to speak up. You both have to learn how to communicate better with each other.

The Intimacy-Avoidance Affair

In this situation, one or even both partners builds an emotional wall for protection from the outside world. It's easier to have an affair than be emotionally exposed—even to your partner.

My advice? If a relationship is to survive after this type of affair, both individual and couples therapy should be considered.

The Sexual Addiction Affair

Here, one partner constantly has affairs and enjoys the chase. He or she will deny there's a problem—and may even be proud of the conquests.

My advice? If this relationship is to survive, it's important to determine the difference between sexual addiction and a loss of sexual intimacy. Therapy can help you both sort out the difference.

The Split-Self Affair

This affair is marked by what on the surface seems like a good relationship. However, feelings and needs aren't expressed or met, and communication isn't genuine. The unfaithful partner is torn between the positive history and the need to be himself. Sometimes, this means a change in sexual identification.

My advice? If this relationship is to heal, it's important that there be in-depth individual and couples therapy so each person can be open about his or her feelings. If it does turn out that a person has repressed his sexual identification, there might be nothing else to do but understand and accept the inevitable. Whether or not you remain married is something you need to decide together.

> **Marriage Trap**
>
> Sometimes an affair is really a way to get out. The unfaithful person wants to end the marriage on a conscious or unconscious level and will use an affair as an excuse to accomplish that.

Give Yourself Time to Heal

No matter how you define it, infidelity is a rejection. It's easy to see where the person who has been cheated on feels rejected. But the person who did the cheating, in most cases, feels emotionally or physically rejected, too. The key is working together to make things right.

As the cheated-upon partner, it's equally as important to realize that if you don't get the response you're hoping for, your partner may be consciously or unconsciously "testing" you to see if you're really committed to making a change and to help her feel more loved and welcome at home. Here, a sensitive balance is necessary. On one hand, trying to overcome your partner's infidelity by expecting the best is a good start. But on the other hand, you also need to accept the worst. If you don't get the response you hoped for, you need to accept the rejection—at least for the time being.

Infidelity Myth

MISC.

Once a cheater, always a cheater. It might feel that way at first, but many unfaithful partners are ashamed of themselves. They're often glad to be discovered. The affair is a symptom of a troubled marriage, and when the problems within are resolved, so is the roving eye.

The same holds true for the cheating spouse. He or she can be testing the waters to see if you've changed, if your marriage has a chance. True, the person who strays has the most to prove, but remember, there was a reason why this happened, and you both need to face it.

Barriers to Falling Back in Love

The partner who wants to make amends is always more focused on the need to restore the relationship rather than on negative feelings of anger, hurt, and·frustration. If you've been betrayed, you probably feel like you've been putting up with these issues for weeks, months, or even years—and you've reached the breaking point when you hear about the affair. In order for your marriage to be repaired, you need time to regain an emotional balance. It will take you longer to recognize any attempt from your partner to repair the damage.

Even though you show your partner you've changed by your behavior and actions, you still need to discuss your relationship and what happened. If your partner isn't yet ready to work things out, accept it with as much graciousness as possible. Honestly accepting rejection, not faking it, is a very powerful tool toward later reconciliation.

The Challenges of Substance Abuse

Addiction is a tough thing to conquer in a marriage. As the president of the Association of Professionals for Treatment of Problem Gambling, I've seen many marriages fall apart because of addiction, whether it be sexual, gambling, or substance abuse. But substance abuse has an extra dynamic: a physiological withdrawal that must occur even before emotional withdrawal and healing can begin.

Regardless of whether or not the vice is alcohol, drugs, sex, gambling, or the Internet, it's hard to have a partner who's an addict.

MISC.

Beating Addiction

We all have the potential to be addicted to something because it's human nature to move away from pain and move toward pleasure. People suffering from substance abuse, for example, first see it as a diversion, a relief from pain. But eventually, that relief turns to a panicky, negative, day-to-day existence fraught with danger and destruction—for the addict and those around him or her.

Helping Your Partner

If you're the nonaddict, you most likely believe that substance abuse—or any type of addiction for that matter—is best resolved by getting your partner to admit and deal with the addiction and participate in therapy.

A bigger challenge, however, is for you to think about your own needs and behavior. It's important for you to consider these questions before you can help your partner:

- What do you want and need from this relationship?

- How do you need to be treated?

- Are you being a good partner by being supportive (but not enabling) and understanding (but not rationalizing)?

- What are you going to do that doesn't depend on your partner's behavior?

Your answers are critical. They can determine how far you'll go to help your partner. And make no mistake about it; you *will* need to be involved right from the start. Substance abuse is a problem that affects everyone in the family.

Getting Through to a Troubled Child

If your child is the one who's addicted, the fallout is even more painful. Addicted children can pull families apart, and it's normal to react with denial: "No, not *my* child. He's just a little down." "No way. She just has a lot of energy." "Okay, maybe she's out a lot, but I know her friends. They're good kids."

Sound familiar? If your child is addicted, you'll need to seek therapy—individual, family, and possibly couples therapy, too. Time in a rehabilitation center might also be required for your child to get around-the-clock care and supervision.

Here's what you and your child can do to stop the addiction:

1. Set up a zero-tolerance policy, and stress that abstinence is critical. This may cause symptoms of withdrawal, but it's the only way a teenager can be treated effectively.

2. Get the family involved. Yes, this problem affects all of you, and all of you need to learn if you've been in denial or co-dependent. You all need to find relief from your pain via therapy.

3. Attend support groups. This is for you—not your child. Talking to other parents who are going through the same thing you are can be very healing.

4. Help your child see reality. One of the most important goals of therapy is for your child to realize and admit he has a problem.

Denial is a powerful drug in and of itself. An addict is very good at saying, "I'm not an alcoholic. I only drink wine or beer," or "I can stop whenever I want." Don't be fooled. Both of you need help for healing to begin.

5. Parents, teachers, and therapists must all work together to help the addict control her addiction; they must offer support and supervision.

6. Attend group therapy. It's important for your child to hear from former addicts. They offer hope that she, too, can change.

7. Seek individual therapy. Your teen needs support for a long while after he's stopped taking drugs. One-on-one therapy is critical for him to understand what led him to abuse in the first place.

Making Your Family Whole Again

Helping your partner or your child also means helping yourself. Melodie Beattie, a prominent expert in the field of addiction, popularized the term *co-dependent,* a nonaddict waiting for his or her partner to change.

Definition

Co-dependency occurs when an individual allows him- or herself to be controlled by someone else's behavior.

A co-dependent spouse might think, *What can I do? Joe is an alcoholic, and I can't get my life straight until he does something about his drinking,* or *I know Mary is abusing drugs when she's at school. She has to get treatment because she's ruining our family!*

The first step to making your family whole again is to assess whether or not co-dependency is an issue. Following are some symptoms of co-dependency. Do any of them ring a bell?

- Inability to identify what's "normal" in a relationship
- Difficulty in following through on a project
- Difficulty having fun
- Judging yourself and others without mercy
- Projecting low self-esteem onto others ("Why don't they get their act together?")
- Overreacting to change; an intense fear or an inability to act
- Inability to see alternatives to situations and, therefore, acting impulsively
- Constantly seeking approval and affirmation and compromising your sense of self to get it

- Feeling different from everyone else

- Being either ultraresponsible or irresponsible

- Lacking self-confidence to make decisions; powerless

- Denying feelings of fear, insecurity, guilt, hurt, or shame

- Isolation

- Hypersensitivity to criticism

- Addicted to drama

- Afraid of abandonment

- Lacking the ability to differentiate between love and pity

- Lying when it's just as easy to tell the truth

- Having rescue fantasies

If more than five of these apply to you, I urge you to seek individual therapy for yourself first, before you seek help for your partner. Co-dependency doesn't help anyone. If anything, it can prevent you from seeking help for your loved one. Instead, you continue to wait for him or her to seek help while you passively and helplessly watch things get worse.

> **Love Letters**
>
> Usually the nonaddicts seek help first. They have a more objective view of what's happening, they're more aware of the implications of the addiction on the family, and they themselves are feeling pain and anger. Don't wait. Seek help immediately. Waiting for an addicted partner to change is an invitation for disaster, and the longer you wait, the worse things will get and the harder it will be to deal with all the issues that develop.

Can you help your loved one through his or her addiction? Can life return to its preaddicted state? I've created the following Chances of Recovery Rating Scale based on my years of clinical experience that can help you determine if there's something you can do. Rate each of the following on a scale of 1 through 5, with 1 meaning "very little" and 5 meaning "a great deal."

1. Level of desperation

2. Severity of addiction

3. Level of motivation

4. Presence of dual addiction

5. Degree of damage the addiction has caused in addict's life

6. Personality

7. Work history

8. Work skill-set

9. Family support

10. Social supports

11. Quality of "meaningful other" relationship

12. Severity of addiction history

13. Resources for treatment (money, insurance, and so on)

Now add up your score:

> 75 to 65: Excellent chance of recovery
>
> 64 to 55: Good chance of recovery
>
> 44 or less: Fair to poor chance of recovery

A word of caution: this is just a general scale. Anyone can quit with the right support.

Coping with a Debilitating Illness

This sea change is painful, and one many of us have had to face with aging parents or with other people we love. But when it happens to you or your spouse, it can be devastating. You won't want to believe it at first. You'll deny the diagnosis. You'll cry and try to bargain with God. You'll get depressed, and eventually you'll accept what's happening and what will happen. Only then can you appreciate each day you have together.

Try to spend one or two minutes each day thinking about what you like about your partner, and be sure you tell him. Remember the good times you've gone through together.

Love
Letters

Keeping a journal can be a powerful tool to help you through a debilitating illness—whether you're the one in pain or the caregiver. Writing down your thoughts can be cathartic.

You're in This Together

A debilitating illness isn't easy to face, but unless you face it head-on, your relationship will drift apart—and getting through each day will be even more difficult.

Fear is a tremendous influence in determining whether people stay together in times of crisis. The unknown future can be so painful, you may find yourselves avoiding the topic altogether. Don't let this happen. Use these precious days to get your house in order.

Enlisting Help from Family and Friends

You may be determined to be strong and do whatever it takes to make your loved one comfortable. That's what Janice thought. Her husband, Jim, had been in a car accident and suffered a traumatic brain injury. He had difficulty walking, and his short-term memory was all but gone.

When Janice learned to accept the new Jim, she thought she could take him to his daily therapy sessions, work on his rehabilitation, and help him remember things. But it was now more important than ever for Janice to earn a living; she couldn't take care of Jim all the time. Their insurance paid for home health aides, but it was her friends and family who truly helped out.

A neighbor would make dinner one night. Another would bring over groceries. And still another would get Jim's medicine from the drugstore. Janice's family came and sat with Jim for a few hours every day, rotating shifts.

Not only did the support help ease Janice's responsibility, but it also helped her emotionally. She was able to take a break and care for herself—so she could better care for Jim when she was home.

Handling Bankruptcy

Marion and Louis came to see me when their money troubles had reached the point where there was nothing to do but declare bankruptcy. It was an old story: they hadn't been irresponsible or reckless. Louis lost his job, and Marion didn't earn enough to pay the mortgage plus all their bills. There was no choice if they wanted to keep their house.

A friend recommended a good bankruptcy lawyer, and they were able to work on a payment schedule for five years—and still keep their home. They had a second chance, and more time for Louis to find a job.

Stopping the "Blame Game"

It sounded like Marion and Louis had gotten a handle on their life and made it through the worst of it. But in reality, the worst was yet to come. Now that they were able to keep a roof over their heads, they had to deal with the emotional shock that comes from losing your credit and all your money.

Marion blamed Louis because he'd lost his job. It wasn't rational because it wasn't his fault, but she blamed him all the same. And Louis felt so guilty and full of shame, he blamed himself. Neither one was happy, and despite having gone through their bankruptcy crisis and come out the other side, they were headed for divorce.

They needed to discuss their feelings. They had to get their anger and pain out before they could begin anew. After several sessions where, under my guidance, they yelled at each other, cried, and yelled some more, they were able to get past their pain and rebuild their marriage and their lives.

Changing Money Habits

One of the first things a couple must do when they declare bankruptcy is build back their credit. They need to write out a budget and, more importantly, stick to it.

When couples are back on their feet, I suggest they take out a secured credit card, one that's attached to a savings account for, say, $250. They should use it every month and pay it religiously before the due date. This can go far in helping to re-establish their good credit.

Bankruptcy doesn't have to mean the end of your freedom—especially in tough times. Although it stays on your credit score for 10 years, it doesn't have to prevent you from getting a mortgage or making a major purchase. After a few years of paying your bills on time, banks will sometimes overlook the bad credit score because you're showing you're more responsible than you once were. You might not get the greatest rate, but you can probably get a loan for a house.

When the Unspeakable Happens: A Child's Death

I cannot think of a worse tragedy than losing your child. It defies the natural order of things. You, as parents, are supposed to go first, not your child.

Anger, shame, guilt, and profound pain—all of these emotions press down on both of you after such a great loss. It's no wonder the majority of couples who live through such a heartbreak don't make it. Just looking at each other brings back the rush of horror.

Sometimes the pain of what you're going through is so deep you can't speak about it. Instead of reaching out to each other for support, you turn away. You may still be living together, but you're no longer physically or emotionally connected—and you might even feel lonelier in your pain than if you were living by yourself.

Professional help is a necessity in this case, both individually and as a couple. If you have other children, they should see a therapist, too. I usually recommend families go together to a family therapist.

The Stages of Trauma Recovery

This section is designed to give you hope. Knowing others have gone through your pain and have healed successfully together can give you the confidence that you, too, can make it. Over the years, I've developed what I call "The Stages of Trauma Recovery."

Not everyone moves swiftly from one stage to another. A tremendous number of emotional issues spring up during the recovery process, and everyone needs to move along at her own pace.

The traumatic stage. At the initial blow, you'll feel a whole host of mixed emotions—rage, fear, sadness, inadequacy, guilt, and profound hurt and pain. You'll feel a sense of urgency to get things resolved as soon as possible so things can return to a semblance of what they were before the trauma, when you felt connected to your partner and not torn apart.

The understanding stage. The start of recovery begins with a logical understanding of why things happened so you can feel you have a sense of control again.

The repair stage. This is the stage when couples get an emotional understanding of what needs to be done on both sides of the relationship to feel hopeful.

The healing stage. Here, logical and emotional healing come together. Hope becomes healing.

The integration stage. At this stage, couples have developed a new type of relationship, one that connects and cares. This stage isn't easy, but it's worth the effort to save your marriage.

Essential Takeaways

- Sea changes can shake up a marriage—but they don't have to destroy it.
- People have affairs for many reasons, and very few of them have to do with sex.
- Addiction is a family disease, and all of you need to be involved in the recovery.
- Friends and family can offer support during turbulent times. Take advantage of the assistance they offer.

Part 5

Repairing, Reconnecting, and Renewing

Let's say the worst has happened: your partner has had an affair, you've lost respect for the one you love, or you no longer feel the love you once felt. There's been a break in your marriage, and mistrust and suspicion are on the loose. Does this mean divorce? Not necessarily. There are ways to successfully weather the storms of marriage. I know—I've seen them in action in my practice.

In Part 5, you'll find strategies to help you get over your anger and resentment, guidance for "falling back in like," and resources such as therapy and support groups to assist you if you don't feel you can do it alone.

The best part? I close the book with a chapter on renewing your commitment to each other, to toast the fact that you've come through everything together and intact, and to celebrate the future together with joy and, most importantly, a marriage that lasts.

chapter 22

Healing Old Wounds

Reestablishing trust

Having a little faith

Strategies for trust repair

Creating a trust plan

The worst has happened. Your spouse has cheated on you, or you cheated on him. She took money from your joint bank account for a secret gambling addiction. You almost wiped out your savings buying jewelry online. Or maybe it's less extreme: your spouse hid a secret passion for Internet porn. You did a little harmless flirting at work. You lied about how much those shoes cost.

Whether extreme or something a little more along the lines of a white lie, lying and cheating don't do great things for your marriage. In this chapter, I share techniques I use in my practice to help rebuild trust and repair a relationship that's been damaged.

Repairing Deteriorated Trust

When partners are struggling because the original trust they shared is lost, the work to repair it can be difficult.

I Cannot Tell a Lie

misc.

A 2010 *Redbook* magazine survey of couples found that 36 percent of the men and 40 percent of the women have lied to their spouse.

Arthur and Elaine had been married for 23 years. They'd gone through the early lean days, the birth of their two daughters, college, and becoming grandparents together. By any stretch of the imagination, Arthur and Elaine had a good life, a happy life. They were some of "the lucky ones" whose marriage endured.

But looks can be deceiving, and when the couple came to see me, they were, in reality, ready for a divorce. Arthur had recently gotten in touch with an old flame on the web. They'd gone to college together, and she had been his "first." Arthur had broken it off with her when he met Elaine. Elaine knocked him for a loop; she was everything he ever wanted: beautiful, smart, kind, and easy to be with. They always had a great time together.

But over the years, their sex got a little lackluster. Alone time gave way to social events, dinner dates with friends, vacations with friends, Sunday afternoons with friends. They no longer touched each other. They had a routine down pat: they'd both come home from their jobs and watch TV for a few hours while they ate take-out. Then one of them would say "I'm done" and get into bed to read. Invariably, he or she was asleep when the other came into the bedroom. Life had become boring. Love was taken for granted.

So when Alicia, Arthur's old girlfriend, found him on Facebook, it was like a cool glass of water for a thirsty man. He felt a zing when he saw her name pop up. He wrote her back. Soon they were talking to each other about their respective spouses, their kids, their grandkids. They began to exchange photos. It seemed harmless enough—except for the fact that Arthur never told Elaine about Alicia. Now, when he came home from work, he didn't watch TV. He went straight to his computer in the den and chatted with Alicia.

Things became more serious in a matter of months. Soon they were sending sexy photos to each other; they started in with "What are you wearing?" questions. And they decided it was time to meet. They planned on a Saturday, but before their encounter, Elaine stumbled upon Arthur's Facebook romance. It was horrible; she felt betrayed.

When Elaine confronted Arthur, he swore nothing happened. And it hadn't. But in Elaine's mind, he'd already violated their trust. He'd already cheated.

Elaine was ready to leave Arthur. And Arthur was full of guilt and regret. He really did love Elaine; he was just playing. But right now? They came to see me as a last resort.

Love Letters	Believe it or not, you *can* learn to trust your partner again—truly. People trust in stages. As time goes by and they see that their unfaithful partner is really working on becoming trustworthy again, things can start to change. Trust takes root again, and if both partners are willing to put in the effort, trust can grow and become solid again.

Rebuilding Trust Takes Time

The process of healing takes time—sometimes a long time. When couples understand what went wrong and what to do about it, they can then work on recapturing the closeness they once had. It isn't easy, but it is possible.

Building trust in a relationship requires time and contact with your partner; you can't trust someone you don't know. When you and your partner first met, you most likely spent a great deal of time together—and thought about each other when you were apart. However, typically, like with Arthur and Elaine, everyday life takes over and time is spent focusing on jobs, careers, children, and other people.

The operative word here is *together*. You did spend time together; you did want to spend time together. There was an attraction that initially drew you together, so it's possible that spark can be rekindled.

The following sections offer four strategies for rebuilding trust that I used with Arthur and Elaine, as well as hundreds of other clients, with great success.

Spend Time Together

There's no substitute for sharing interests and enjoying activities together. Familiarity strengthens emotional connection, and you want your partner to associate being with you as a positive, happy experience.

Spending time together and enjoying yourself gives you the opportunity to talk about things, to resolve issues important to the relationship, and to give or get emotional support for problems the two of you are facing in the outside world.

Use Positive Self-Talk

I teach my clients "self-talk." Even though when you see your unfaithful spouse, you might be thinking, *You cheating @#$&,* talk to yourself and make yourself remember a time when you really were glad to see him. Say something positive about him to yourself. Being glad to see your partner goes a long way in getting you to feel better about him—as well as getting him to feel less guilty and good about seeing you. The result? More trust over time.

Share Your Thoughts

It's a fact: people tend to trust us when we let them see our vulnerability. One powerful way to develop closeness with the partner you've wronged is to let him know what's on your mind, what's worrying you, and how you feel full of remorse over what you did.

> **Love Letters**
>
> Sharing a mistake you haven't yet corrected, or some issue you're still working on, demonstrates that you don't think you're always right and your partner is always wrong. Honesty and openness are key in rekindling trust.

Letting your partner know you identify with a situation she's struggling with can go far in the trust department. Speak up and tell her about your own experiences in a similar situation. It doesn't have to be about the trust issue at hand. It's about getting close again.

For example, if your partner has lost motivation because her friend has become ill, you could say, "I remember when my sister got sick. I was worried that she was going to die, and I didn't feel like doing anything but curling up on the couch."

A word of caution when sharing a similar experience with your spouse: be careful not to talk too much about yourself. This current situation is about your spouse—not you!

Acknowledgment

Acknowledge your partner for something she did or said that you appreciate. Acknowledging positive behavior and communicating your appreciation goes a long way in building back trust.

Acknowledgment doesn't have to be spontaneous. Think about it. Look for and mention—in a genuine way—some struggle your partner is going through.

For example, Arthur recognized that Elaine was struggling with a deadline at work on top of everything else. He told her, "Elaine, I really appreciate that you haven't given up on your job, especially with all you're going through. I know you're under a lot of pressure and, despite everything, you're making a real effort to make things work. I think you're awesome— and I'll bet they think so at work, too."

The Role of Faith

Twentieth-century essayist H. L. Mencken once said, "Love is the triumph of imagination over intelligence." If you really, truly love someone, you can find it in your heart to forgive. You can take a leap of faith and try afresh.

Of course, this doesn't happen overnight. Over time, however, if the spouse who hurt you keeps his promises, if he's consistent and open, if he shows his appreciation and love for you, it can happen. The fact is, "forgiving and forgetting" isn't black or white. There are shades of gray. If your marriage is worth saving, take a deep breath and jump.

An Effective Replay Technique

For people to truly forgive, they must believe future actions and attitudes will be different. They want emotional insurance that if they forgive this time, they won't be hurt again. In order to get your partner to believe you, it's important that you develop new understandings and behaviors. You must have a clear idea of how to say and do things differently.

This replay technique was successful with Arthur and Elaine, and hopefully will be successful for you, too. It offers you a new way to approach your partner and make her feel there's hope for the relationship and that you're really prepared to work at making things right.

Set Aside Two Hours

Two hours might sound like a luxury, but remember that this is an investment in your marriage—which makes it a necessity. By clearing your schedule and making time for each other, you're already making a positive move to restoring your happy marriage. You are ...

- Showing each other that you value the other.
- Declaring that your marriage is worth saving.
- Taking the exercise to save your marriage seriously.

Identify Problem Issues

When you do the replay technique, you'll rehearse, rethink, and refine your understanding of what you can do to change the way you previously approached a situation or conversation.

The first step to healing old wounds is to identify exactly where your problems lie. It might be a good idea to go over your definition of trust with each other (see Chapter 10). Share your feelings and thoughts. If you're feeling angry and hurt, say so. Don't be afraid to raise your voice. For this technique to be successful, you have to be honest with each other.

Being honest is important, but there's a right and a wrong way to approach it. If you feel your spouse has let himself go, don't say, "How could I be attracted to someone who's a slob?" Instead, be tactful. "Let's not take each other for granted. I will start a healthier lifestyle if you are willing to do so, too," is a much better route.

Identify an Insight

Think about what you did and why you did it. Were you bored? Were you feeling neglected? Were you totally stressed out and ready to snap at the slightest provocation?

Rather than making excuses for your behavior or expecting your partner to figure out the answers, dig deep inside to see what was going on with you that impacted your behavior. It also helps to communicate this insight in a way that demonstrates your understanding and doesn't blame the other. Say "I was cranky and irritable because I was tired and wasn't thinking clearly," rather than, "You know I'm tired by Friday evenings, so of course I was cranky!"

Recognize What Really Hurts Your Partner

As you identify issues or situations that have been a problem in your relationship, also think about what you would do differently if the same situation or conversation happened again.

Spend some time exploring what specific actions or words angered or hurt your partner, and communicate it. You might say something like, "I know I shouldn't have yelled at you in front of our friends because it embarrassed you—and you wouldn't have treated me that way."

When Arthur and Elaine did the replay technique, he told her, "I know what I did was awful. I wasn't thinking. Next time I hear from an old friend, you'll be the first to know."

What Could You Have Done Differently?

Don't expect your spouse to do something differently—that expectation will only reignite the fire in your fight. Instead of healing an old wound, it will create a fresh one.

Actions speak louder than words and, right now, you can only change yourself. You can't change anyone else. More importantly, your partner has to see these changes coming from you. Later on, when you've reconciled, you can be sure you both change.

If Elaine counted solely on Arthur's word that he wouldn't go back to Facebook-flirting, trust would have been difficult to rekindle. Instead, she focused on the love they shared with each other and their long history together, and she made sure they spent some romantic time together.

> **Love Letters**
>
> It's important to realize that the spouse who was wounded is often looking for a reason to heal the relationship. Give her a reason to start letting down her guard and begin accepting you again: discuss, communicate, and validate.

Arthur, on the other hand, acknowledged when Elaine did something exemplary or when she looked great. He tried to make their romantic nights extra special by making reservations at a favorite restaurant or buying tickets to a show.

Develop a Plan

Together, create a plan to deal with the situation if it happens again. For example, you might say to your partner, "I have to be more aware of when I'm tired," or "When we're out and I'm struggling to stay awake, I'll ask if we can leave soon."

Your spouse, on the other hand, can say, "I realize you're cranky on Friday nights, so I'll try not to make plans," or "I'll leave you alone on Friday nights so you can destress."

A plan is only good if it's used. When you and your spouse work out your differences and create strategies for next time, don't leave it at that. Work the plan! If necessary, set up another two-hour meeting to go over your issues again.

Three Scenarios: An Exercise for Healing

The following table lists three issues or situations that have caused difficulties in relationships. Maybe some are true for you. If so, describe your conversations and behaviors at the time of the conflict. Keeping the advice in this chapter in mind, identify a possible new approach for each one.

Replay Technique Scenarios Example

Scenario	Old Approach	New Approach
He flirted on Facebook	Emotionally withdraw	Discuss why he did it
She told them my secret	Angry outburst	Discuss why she did it
He's cranky on Fridays	Push him to talk anyway	Respect his feelings and give him privacy

After you've thought through a different approach, replay the original conflict situation in your head, but substitute your new response or approach. This exercise gives you an opportunity to rehearse and become comfortable with responding in a different way from your usual pattern.

MISC.

Audition Time

Eventually, you'll want to try out your new approach to conflict on your partner. Pick a time when things are going well or the flow of communication has improved, because your partner will be in more of a receptive state of mind.

Essential Takeaways

- Rebuilding trust cannot be rushed or forced. It needs to be demonstrated—by both people's actions.
- Sometimes you need to take a leap of faith. If your marriage is important to you, don't be afraid to jump.
- Set aside quality time to discuss your problems—even if you have to take a day off from work. Saving your marriage is not a luxury.
- The replay technique is an effective tool for healing old wounds.

chapter 23

Falling Back in Like

Remembering the good things

Validating your partner

Honesty matters

Get reacquainted

Enduring marriages aren't the perfect ones. I don't know one marriage wherein life is always rainbows and roses. Let's face it, life can be difficult at times. There are ups and downs to any relationship. But what counts isn't the situations themselves; it's how you react to them.

When you drift apart, it doesn't mean the curtain has to drop. You can get back together again. You can fall back in like. This chapter helps you rekindle what you once had.

A Complicated Emotion

It has defied scholars, poets, and Nobel Prize winners. It's called love, and when it happens you know it, but you don't always know why. Nor does "why" matter. In those first heady years, life is good. No, great! It's what happens later on that separates a lasting marriage from one that fails.

When you hit a rough patch, you have choices. You can …

- Get a divorce.

- Become emotionally divorced—you live together, but you don't share anything; you're removed.

- Have business as usual. I think of this as the "default setting." You eventually get a real divorce, get an emotional divorce, or have an affair.

- Repair. This means time for negotiating, talking things through, and getting professional help.

The best way to survive a bad time in your marriage? Don't deny it. You'll only make the chasm bigger. Try the exercises in this book. Communicate. Validate and respect each other. You can repair the damage if you really want to!

Back to the Beginning

Repairing a marriage and ensuring it will last takes genuine effort. If you feel you're at fault, you need to make a real apology. And if you don't think you're to blame, you need to listen without a chip on your shoulder. Remember, you both need to see each other's point of view. There are several ways to go about this.

Marriage Trap	Be careful about apologizing if you don't feel it. Reconciliation is difficult, and you'll probably only have one chance. Pretending to be sorry is not only ineffective, but cruel.

Take Responsibility for Your Actions

When you're ready to apologize and truly realize you made a mistake, tell your spouse. Admit wholeheartedly that you were wrong in what you did and how you regret hurting her.

When you apologize and your partner wants to speak, be quiet and listen. Let her talk because she needs to express her feelings. Part of the process of forgiveness and repair is for both of you to be open and willing to listen to each other.

But this is just the first step. There's still a long way to go to make things right again.

Explain the "Why"s

It's crucial for your partner to hear an explanation of why you did what you did. One of the greatest fears a wronged partner has is, *If I forgive him, will he hurt me again?*

If you can't give a proper explanation about why, say, you maxed out your credit cards, it will make your partner feel powerless in trying to prevent any further occurrences.

The Devil's in the Details

If your partner wants the details of, say, an affair, you should openly respond to him. This might be difficult for you, but imagine what he's going through! The more you hold back, the more he'll feel something else is going on.

> **Love Letters**
>
> For your marriage to last, each of you must have peace of mind. You both must believe in each other again. Honesty goes far in achieving this.

Analyzing the Situation

Understanding the problems in a relationship can help correct them—and make your marriage stronger. The following quiz helps you determine if you know what makes your spouse happy, and whether you're giving him what he needs.

Rate the following statements on a scale from 1 (false) to 5 (true):

1. My partner thinks we spend enough time together.

2. My partner really likes it when I buy him little things.

3. My partner likes when I tell her on a regular basis how much I care.

4. My partner thinks I'm interested in what's important to him.

5. My partner thinks I'm sensitive to her feelings.

6. My partner believes I am supportive of him, especially in light of the stress he's facing.

7. My partner knows me pretty well.

8. I do what my partner asks of me on a regular basis.

9. My partner thinks I am affectionate on a regular basis.

Think about your answers. If you found some of these items important to your partner, are you doing what you need to show him you respect, understand, and love him? If you aren't doing enough—or anything—think of ways you can correct your behavior.

Let's look at an example using the first statement, "My partner thinks we spend enough time together." Say you scored a 1 or 2. That means you need to figure out a way to spend more time alone with your partner.

Finding Solutions

Here are some ways to help demonstrate to your partner what you're willing to do to bring you both closer together:

- Figure out a way to spend more time alone with your partner—a dinner out or a quiet movie night at home.

- Buy a small gift for your partner, whether it's that book he was looking for or that gourmet pesto sauce she couldn't find in the supermarket.

- Tell your spouse what you appreciate about her and the positive way it makes you feel.

- Take more of an interest in things that are important to him.

- Be more aware of her feelings so you can be there if she needs to talk. Be a better listener.

- Find ways to help your partner with issues he's facing. Sometimes all your spouse wants is for you to listen and to understand him.

- Talk to her about your feelings on a regular basis.

- Finish projects or take care of chores your spouse would like you to do.

- Touch him in a caring, nonsexual way at least once a day.

Now, think about your partner's three main complaints and why you think he feels that way. Try to figure out how you can respond to your spouse's complaints in a positive way. Be a partner—not an adversary. The purpose of this exercise is to help you to better understand your partner so you can be more sensitive to his needs.

Love Letters

Sometimes repairing a marriage takes a lot of hard work, but the outcome is worth it many, many times over.

Using Positive Self-Talk

It's important to understand how you got yourself worked up and agitated. Many times, it's caused by what you say to yourself and the dialogues in your head—and you might not even be aware of them. The following three questions are designed to give you a good idea of what you're telling yourself. The way you respond can help you identify the messages you're sending yourself—and help you see if you're being your own worst enemy in your marriage.

1. What do you say to yourself when you think about your partner?

2. What do you say to yourself when you actually see her? (Think of the last time you actually saw your partner.)

3. What feelings are triggered when you think about seeing your spouse? Do you feel frustration, anger, futility, or powerlessness? Or are you excited to see her?

If you're angry with your spouse, you've most likely responded to these questions with very negative and angry answers. Your goal with positive self-talk is to change the messages in your head—which will automatically change your attitude and how you approach your partner. This change gives you the best chance to start the ball rolling in a more positive direction.

The following table provides some examples of negative self-talk and alternative positive self-talk for you to use instead.

Turning the Tables on Negative Self-Talk	
Negative Self-Talk	*Positive Self-Talk*
"Larry isn't going to listen to me."	"I'm having a hard time talking to Larry."
	"I'm worried about his response."
	"I understand that Larry's frustrated dealing with me."
"She just doesn't get it."	"She is seeing things from a different perspective from me."
	"I'm frustrated, but so is she."
	"She must really feel like I did something to her."
	"How can I understand why she doesn't get it? She's bright, so what am I missing?"

Now think about your responses to the three questions you answered earlier, and turn the tables on your own negative self-talk. Explore new statements you can say to yourself that are more positive and will help move you away from negative self-talk.

If you're having problems with your relationship, you need to reinforce as many positives as you can. As much as you may want the relationship to work out, there will be times when you get frustrated, upset, angry, or overwhelmed. During those difficult periods, it's important for you to find a reason to hang in there. Research has found that the more motivated we are, the more we tend to stick with a task. Thus, the more committed you are to finding a solution for your marital problems, the more likely you are to find one!

While you're thinking about this, here's another point to keep in mind: you need to not only correct what's wrong, but also remember the good times. The positive self-talk steps are designed to help you stay focused and motivated. Following the steps outlined here provides the *self-reinforcement* you need and helps you generate the energy necessary to continue your journey toward building a new relationship.

Definition

Self-reinforcement strengthens your resolve to do something. Reinforcement occurs when you know there's a reward on the other end—in this case, a lasting marriage!

Remember What You Loved About Your Partner

A great way to start increasing your positive self-talk is by focusing on the good qualities in your relationship. Think about what first made you fall in love with your now-spouse. Was he kind and generous? Did he laugh at your jokes? Was he funny? Did he make you feel safe and secure? Make a list of the things you like about your partner.

Remember a Time When You Were Happy

Two things can significantly strengthen a relationship: having a conflict that resolves itself in a positive way, with both of you feeling accepted and understood, and going through a crisis together with a positive end result.

Choose to remember and focus on either a positive experience you shared with your spouse or a situation that involved a disagreement with your spouse but turned out to be a good experience.

Visualize the Memory

Now, find yourself a comfortable chair and think about the experience by going through the following questions. Put on some music, light some candles, or do whatever it takes to let your mind go back to the experience and put you in the right frame of mind.

This experience should take at least five minutes. Don't rush it. Once you've really captured "the movie" in your head, touch the tips of your ring finger and thumb together to reinforce the experience. Repeat this with a second positive experience you remember. It's helpful to have two positive experiences "anchored" so you can call them up as needed.

1. Describe the experience you remembered. What did it look like?

2. Describe the conversation between you and your partner. What was the tone? What words were used?

3. What did you say to yourself during the experience? What words did you use?

4. What did the temperature of the room feel like? Or what was the weather like outside?

5. During the experience, did you notice any smells? (Aromas are very powerful memory triggers.)

6. How did your body feel? Were you tense, energized, or relaxed?

7. Do you remember the emotions you felt? Recapture your feelings as best you can.

By completing this exercise, you've started to take a deeper look at yourself. You can also visualize that happy time in your marriage and pull it up whenever you need a refresher of those early feelings.

Working with a Positive Mind-Set

Now that you're feeling better about yourself, your spouse, and your life together, you can discuss your problems in a less heated manner. You can speak more coherently. You can speak with love.

Ideally, it would be great if your husband or wife could go through the four stages of positive self-talk. This way you're both in a place where reconciliation is not only possible, but desired. But if you need to do the exercise solo, you can still create an environment of calm and love.

Dr. Marty Fortune Cookie

MISC.

Be careful. It's a quick step from being right to being self-righteous.

Acknowledge Your Partner's Value

One of the basic rules of a good partnership is to never say anything that makes your partner feel devalued. Instead, look for things to say and do that make her feel appreciated. Catch him doing something right and tell him.

The following sections offer several ideas of how you can start getting your partner to like you again.

Have a Positive Experience

Think about how often you talk with your partner. How much of your conversation is a positive, pleasurable discussion? How much is about problems or disasters? If you end up discussing a problem every time you talk, you'll find yourself thinking before the conversation, *Oh darn, here comes another problem!*

While this association may not be conscious, you can bet it's present. To prevent this from happening, find ways to have a positive experience with your partner. This is called a positive *anchor.*

Definition

Anchoring is more than keeping a ship at port. In psychology, anchoring is holding to a steady course. It helps keep you grounded.

And don't be in a hurry when you're interacting with your husband or wife. For example, if your spouse calls you at work, try not to sound short and rushed, even if you're under a deadline. Sounding rushed gives the message that, "I'm squeezing you in. You're not worth my time and full attention." That's the opposite of a positive experience.

Speak Positively Without Patronizing

Some people don't trust positive statements because they think someone is trying to manipulate them. They can also be uncomfortable with praise. When you want to say something positive to your partner, be sure it's genuine and said from the heart.

Notice if your partner's response to your efforts is positive. Continue your conversation on a positive note if the response you see is a good one. But stop if you're met with negativity or skepticism, and try another time.

Reinforce Good Feelings

Think about your partner's positive qualities, and remind yourself what you like about her. It's easy to get caught up in being frustrated about a situation at hand and forget about the good stuff.

The best part? The more you reinforce your good feelings, the more good feelings you'll have! In turn, the better your spouse will feel, too. It's a win-win situation.

Perform Random Acts of Kindness

Buddhists live their lives with a very simple rule: be kind to all. When you do small, random acts of kindness, people feel good. When you do something nice for your husband, it reverberates. He feels loving toward you. He appreciates you even more.

I'm not talking about going out and buying him a car. I'm talking about making his favorite dish for dinner. Or picking up his shirts from the dry cleaners. Or even something as simple as filling up his car with gas. The intermittent reinforcement in a random act of kindness is very, very powerful.

Essential Takeaways

- Use positive self-talk to help repair your marriage.
- Remember a happy memory about your spouse and what you love about him or her.
- Practice being thoughtful and kind with small gifts or actions.
- The more positive actions and discussions you have, the more you reinforce your love for each other.

chapter 24

It's Okay to Ask for Help

When it's time to see a therapist

Qualities of a good marriage counselor

Other types of therapy

Counseling—help or hindrance?

You've tried talking things out. You've read the manuals, and you've talked to close friends. You've tried to forgive and forget. But it isn't working. Your resentment continues to build. Your anger is threatening to take over. You're beginning to feel overwhelmed. Worse, you're afraid your marriage is falling apart—and maybe you even want it to end. If you feel as if you're at the end of your rope, don't despair. Help is out there, and there's no shame in seeking professional help.

I can attest to the hundreds of marriages I've helped save because the couples wanted things to get better. They didn't wait until the chasm was so big there was no way to put it back together—and, unfortunately, I have seen my share of couples in that situation, too. In this chapter, I tell you everything you need to know before seeking help, including how to find a good therapist who can work with both you and your spouse and, ultimately, make your marriage a lasting one.

When to Seek Couples Therapy

Think of a marriage or couples therapy as the last port in a storm, the place to go when you've tried everything to make your marriage last to no avail.

When Brian and Iris came to see me, they weren't sure if I could help them. Since their kids had left home, they'd grown further and further apart. Brian was spending long hours at work, and Iris was afraid he was having an affair and didn't believe him when he tried to reassure her. Iris, on her part, felt very isolated and alone. She'd worked as a medical assistant at a thriving group practice, but in her heart, she was a mom first. She doted on her children and raised them well. But now that they were gone, she didn't have a clue as to what to do with the rest of her life. Instead of trying to take a class or pursue a hobby, she became more and more clingy—which distanced Brian even more.

Things were going from bad to worse. In fact, Brian and Iris made up their minds that their marriage was failing and they were only going through the motions of trying therapy.

Iris was the one who suggested they come to me. Brian agreed, but as soon as they came into my office, I could tell he was there against his will. He was defensive and sullen.

Iris was stone-faced as well. Brian wanted a divorce, but she didn't want him to go. As soon as she said those words, her composure failed and she started to cry. Brian moved farther away from her on the couch.

The energy in the room was palpable; there was so much anger, disappointment, and rejection it had to be overwhelming for them. How could they begin to repair their marriage when their emotions were strangling them?

> **Love Letters**
>
> You can't control what someone else does, but you can be proactive in changing your own behavior.

I think we all know relationships are difficult to sustain and even more difficult to repair when damaged. But I also believe that it's possible to fix troubled relationships and that a good marriage counselor can help couples save, improve, and move their relationships forward.

Although each couple and each story is unique, there are three basic situations in which a marriage counselor can help:

- Your partner has left and you'd like to win her back.

- Your partner is saying he wants to leave, but you want to work things out.

- You are worried your partner doesn't love you anymore and wants to leave you.

When Your Relationship Is Falling Apart

The reason you're reading this chapter is because you want to save something very special. You realize there are significant consequences when a relationship comes apart:

- If you have children, it will change your relationship with them.

- Your financial lives will be split apart, from salaries and pensions to savings and portfolios.

- A divorce will be a sizeable financial investment—divorce lawyers don't come cheap.

- Your day-to-day life, that comfortable pace you had for so many years, will never be the same again.

- You will need to pick up the pieces and start a new life; and, if you have the energy, you will have to enter the dating game all over again.

- Most importantly, the person you walked down the aisle with so many years ago, the person you were going to love for the rest of your life, will be gone—and you will be alone.

It makes sense to try to make your relationship work before you end it! As I told Brian and Iris, you can fix your marriage, but it will take a lot of work on your part.

Some Good News About the "Last Resort"

Believe it or not, when you're afraid your marriage is ending, you may have more time to fix it than you realize!

Like Brian and Iris, if you're seeking the help of a marriage counselor, then you're struggling with your relationship. Your partner may be sleeping in a different room or not living in the same home. In Brian and Iris's case, Brian had already filed for divorce, and Iris had been forced to speak to an attorney.

But as I told Brian and Iris, even then, you can still repair your marriage. The complete process of divorce takes time, and during those weeks and months, you can give you and your spouse a chance to save your marriage.

I know from having done thousands of hours of counseling that often partners who want to leave the relationship are really very reluctant to do so. They actually feel desperate and hopeless, and believe their partner will never change. In fact, for the majority of couples, it's only out of desperation that divorce becomes the chosen option.

Here's some good news: you don't have to do everything right, and you don't have to do it all at once. But you do have to do enough so your partner believes you're sincere about wanting to change. You don't have to be perfect, but you do need to convince your partner by your actions that you're moving in the right direction.

Years from now, you'll be able to look back at this time with a sense of pride in having done your best to heal the relationship. Always keep in mind that you cannot fail if you do your best, and you cannot succeed if you don't try.

> **Marriage Trap**
>
> Remember, if you continue to do what you've been doing, you'll get the same results as before. A marriage counselor can help you learn to approach your relationship issues in a different way, which will, in turn, help you avoid repeating patterns that will ultimately have the same result: potential divorce.

So if you need to make that call to a therapist, by all means do it.

The Rejection Factor

There's one very specific dynamic that occurs before you come to see a marriage counselor—rejection. This is something you'll definitely encounter in yourself or in your spouse as you work toward repairing your marriage.

Rejection walks a very fine line between wanting things to get better and being terrified they won't. Without understanding rejection, you may not be able to read any positive signals your partner is sending. You may lose an opportunity to make things better—and he may, too.

It's not going to be easy to convince your partner to change his mind about your relationship, especially if he was the one to reject you. Both in the beginning and during the therapy process, there will be times when things will be touch and go, when your partner will say nasty, hurtful things or tell you he doesn't want to be with you anymore. For example, every time Iris reminded Brian they had a therapy appointment, he would start to yell. "Why are we spending good money on this?" But here's the thing—Brian went. As I've said earlier in this chapter, no one, not even the person who wants a divorce, is completely willing to let go.

We are all human, and we all get discouraged when our efforts are rejected. Learning to deal with rejection is one of the hardest things to accomplish while trying to rescue your relationship.

Even in Rejection, There Is Hope

It's likely that even though you're ready and probably anxious to make things better, your partner is not. That doesn't mean the situation is hopeless. Each of you may be ready to forgive, but at different times. Your partner may be considering lowering the barriers and opening her arms, but she may also still be cautious and doesn't want to appear too vulnerable. In fact, you may want to give up just when your partner is looking for confirmation of your new commitment and change!

On the other hand, you don't want your partner to feel pressured or, worse, stalked. Give him space; let him see that your interactions and behaviors are different and you're not just telling him. Your partner will be far more impressed by your new perspectives and personal changes if he discovers them on his own and realizes you've refrained from continuous pestering.

Men and Rejection

Research has found that men are three times more likely than women to give up on a relationship. They are also less likely to try different techniques to repair the situation.

Rejection Testing

It is also important to realize that if you don't get the response you're hoping for, your partner may be consciously or unconsciously testing you to see if you're really committed to making a change.

When you come into a therapist's office, a sensitive balance between hope and reality is necessary. On the one hand, going into a situation expecting the best is a good start. But on the other hand, being able to accept the worst is also critical. If you don't get the response you hoped for, if it doesn't look like your marriage will be repaired, it's extremely important to accept that rejection. Remember, different people have different timetables for forgiveness.

The partner who wants to make amends is always more focused on the need to restore the relationship than on any negative feelings of anger, hurt, and frustration. The partner who wants out, however, probably feels like he's been putting up with these issues for weeks, months, or even years and has reached a breaking point. This person needs time to regain emotional calm, and it will usually take him longer to accept any marriage repair attempts.

For several weeks, Brian and Iris seemingly made no progress in their sessions. Brian kept pushing Iris away, and she kept trying to reel him in. But the insights Iris gained in therapy began to sink in; she became calmer. She showed Brian that she didn't have to be clingy, that she didn't want to be needy. By acting this way, Brian was able to see that Iris was really trying to change—for him. He began to feel a glimmer of hope. Maybe he'd been too aggressive and judgmental himself.

Even though showing your partner how you're changing is better than simply telling him, you will, at some point, need to discuss your relationship.

When Your Spouse Isn't Ready

One of the biggest mistakes the *in partner* can make is to wait for the *out partner* to go for counseling. If continuing the relationship is really important to you, act now and make an appointment for yourself. Waiting for your partner to be ready can reduce your chances for success.

> **Definition**
>
> The **in partner** is the spouse who wants the marriage to work, the one who initiates marriage counseling. The **out partner** is the one who wants divorce and doesn't want reconciliation.

Going for counseling on your own gives your partner three clear positive messages:

- I care enough about our relationship to do something to make it better.

- I am willing to take a hard look at my role in the problems we're having.

- I finally "hear" you and understand that for a long time you've been saying you're unhappy and the relationship is in trouble.

In addition to these positive messages, couples therapy can still work with just one person present. It can help you …

- Better understand your partner and learn to see the world from her perspective.

- Take an impartial look at yourself.

- Figure out the best way to approach and talk to your partner.

- Avoid accidentally stepping on land mines and blowing up the relationship.

- Trust and appreciate a counselor's impartial perspective derived from years of professional experience in seeing what works and what doesn't work in relationships.

- Lessen the tension in your relationship.

Relationships are like two hands holding a rubber band. If both hands pull in opposite directions on the rubber band at the same time, it will snap. If one hand moves toward the other, the tension decreases and the rubber band doesn't snap. Learning to put less stress on your marriage can stop it from snapping into divorce.

No One Is an Island

Misc.

You can't always tell what's real and what isn't. A therapist can offer objective insights you'd never be able to get on your own.

What to Expect from a Marriage Counselor

Seeking therapy can help you repair a marriage that's in deep trouble. I can also tell you that you need to be sure you see a good therapist, one who ...

- Makes you feel comfortable.

- Speaks with tact and kindness.

- Tells you honestly if she can help you.

- Has accreditations and diplomas prominently displayed, or hasn't hesitated to tell you his background.

- Is consistent; he doesn't keep switching or missing appointments.

- Explains the basics during your first meeting: cost, time, and personal boundaries.

- Is trustworthy; she doesn't discuss other clients.

- Doesn't try to persuade you to come back. If you're getting a bad vibe or feel "pushed," trust your gut and interview someone else.

Time Well Spent

Designing a house, cooking a meal, learning a language, or taking a course takes time and energy. So will trying to save your marriage. But like many things that take time and effort, it's worth it!

A Safe, Comfortable Environment

If you don't feel safe, you're not going to open up and talk. One of the most important things a therapist can do is to make you feel at ease: soft lighting, comfortable seating arrangements, calming art—all these can help put you in a better frame of mind.

A safe environment also involves a good relationship between you and the therapist. If you feel comfortable with him or her, you will feel safer, and it will be easier for you to open up.

Problem-Solving Techniques

When I first saw Brian and Iris, I welcomed them to my office. I told them I realized it's difficult to come for marriage counseling, and I gave them each a clipboard with an exercise on it. The purpose of this exercise was to make it easier for the three of us to discover their real issues quickly. I give it to all my first-time clients. It might help you with your relationship concerns, too. Here it is:

What do you and your partner have disagreements about? Rate the following list of common hot spots with the level of concern you have for that issue, from 1 (very little) to 5 (a great deal):

1. Money

2. Parents

3. In-laws

4. Faithfulness

5. Sexual intimacy

6. Addiction

7. Child-rearing

8. Violence

9. Anger issues

10. Time spent together

11. Dependability

12. Satisfaction with the relationship

Feel free to include any other issues you've noticed in your marriage in the list, too.

Once we pinpoint the issues hurting this marriage, we can go about finding solutions. Through talk, written exercises, and homework based on the tools and information I've shared throughout this book, we're able to come to a resolution. More times than not, I'm happy to say it turns out well!

Finding a Good Therapist

Countless therapists are out there available to help you, but unfortunately, not all of them are good ones. A lot of what makes a therapist right for you is the chemistry you both feel. Successful therapy is based on relationships; if you like the person you meet the first time, that's a step in the right direction. But how do you find that person? Here are some suggestions:

- Ask family and friends for any recommendations.

- Ask another professional whom you trust—your physician, accountant, or lawyer.

- Check with your health insurance company.

- If your workplace offers it, contact your employee assistance program.

- Nearby colleges and universities may be a good resource.

- Go online, but only use reliable sites, such as www.PsychologyToday. com or www.WebMD.com These sites require therapists who list with them to have advanced degrees and experience in their field.

- Check out professional organizations, such as the American Association for Marriage and Family Therapy at www.aamft.org.

Support Groups: You're Not Alone

If you have a problem, I guarantee there's a support group in your area that addresses it. From families of alcoholics to eating disorders, from depression to divorce, the majority of communities have groups made up of your peers who may be able to help you.

I've recommended support groups to some of my clients as an additional tool to help them through marital troubles, but always as an addition to our couples therapy—not as a substitute. Although legitimate support groups are supervised by a professional, the sessions themselves are hosted by people without professional training.

> **Solid Support**
>
> MISC.
>
> A good support group is supervised by an expert; he may not be there at every meeting, but it's still his responsibility to ensure no problems arise.

Sam and Grace had been seeing me for several months, and their marriage had begun to revive. Their major problems were behind them, but they still had some residual resentments and some issues with communication. I recommended they join a support group because they could discuss these residual issues with others in the same situation. They could speak openly without risk. At this point in their therapy, I didn't think Sam and Grace still needed the formal atmosphere of our sessions; they could go further in a group of their peers.

There's safety in numbers, as the saying goes, but there's also *comfort* in numbers. When you're in a group situation, with people just like yourself, it can help ease your pain.

Realizing others are out there in exactly the same situation as you can go far in repairing your marriage. Sure, you can read magazine articles and watch TV commentary, but there's something about sitting next to someone who's in exactly the same situation that makes a tremendous impact. There are people out there who understand for real—they're going through the same feelings, pain, and fears as you.

In a support group, you can speak about your experiences without risk. You don't have to censor your emotions and your words as you would with your family or your friends. The best part? Instant understanding, empathy, feedback, and advice from people who've been there!

To find a good support group in your area, check with your local hospitals, community centers, and counseling associations. You can always check out a support group with no strings attached. If you don't feel comfortable at one group, try another one. They shouldn't cost anything, although many groups ask for a small donation to cover coffee and snacks.

Do You Need Sex Therapy?

Couples often think that if they can resolve their problems with their marriage, the sex will take care of itself. Or if they have better communication or trust, the attraction will be recharged. Unfortunately, this isn't always true. Sexual problems often need additional help. If you're having problems with intimacy, whether they be emotional or biological, a sex therapist may be able to help.

Just as a pediatrician is better qualified than a cardiologist for children's issues, a sex therapist is better qualified to help with sex issues. Sex therapists don't take the place of marriage counselors, although they can be licensed therapists. They usually do have more training in the sexual arena and are more qualified to deal with the physiological aspects of sexual issues than your family physician or counselor.

Sex therapists often work in conjunction with marriage counselors to help couples revitalize their intimate relationships. But they're not there to mold someone into what his or her spouse wants. If one of you wants more sex than the other, the sex therapist may delve into possible physiological issues and emotional issues. But if one of you has different needs, you both have to learn to live with it—or not.

Marriage counselors can help with intimate conversations, feelings, and beliefs, but sex therapists can help with the physical act of intimacy itself.

MISC.

Certified Sexuality

Sex therapists can become members of the American Association of Sexuality Educators, Counselors, and Therapists, an organization dedicated to enhancing sexual health. You can find out more at www.aaasect.org.

Sex therapists can help with any number of sexual problems, from lack of interest to an inability to have an orgasm. But before they can do their work, you, as a couple, need to have resolved the problems that had initially led you to a marriage counselor. Any residual trust or respect issues, anger, or insecurities must be addressed, not by the sex therapist, but by your couples therapist.

However, once you've resolved your intimacy issues and the sexual problems still remain, a sex therapist can help. She may give you exercises to do on your own time, or she may take a detailed history of your emotional life and your physiology. One thing a sex therapist never does is ask you to perform any sexual activities while you're in his office. Any intimate exercises are done on your own time.

Essential Takeaways

- Seeking professional help shouldn't be seen as a stigma.
- You can expect empathy, kindness, and objectivity from a good marriage counselor.
- Marriage counselors will see you alone if your spouse isn't ready yet.
- A support group can help you share your experiences with other couples who have been in your shoes.
- If necessary, your marriage counselor can refer you to a sex therapist.

chapter 25

Renewing Your Commitment

Celebrating as a couple

Second honeymoons

Creating vows

Reaffirming your love

I believe marriage should be celebrated whenever and wherever you feel like it. If you're together, whether it be 1 year or 30 years, it's a testament to the love you share.

But certainly, the big milestones—25, 35, or 50 years—are joyous occasions, and I know many married couples who have decided to have second weddings or vow renewal ceremonies. If you've sustained your love through better and worse, richer or poorer, what better way to share your happiness with those you love? Or maybe a quiet husband-and-wife-only romantic getaway is more your speed.

Whatever your style, it's time to celebrate!

Celebrating Your Life Together

In this world where divorce is as much the norm as a long-lasting marriage, the couple who stays together through the rites of passage in a life together—the early salad days, the birth of your children, your new home, the day you became grandparents, your retirement, and everything in between—deserves a party and a champagne toast.

The Good Times, the Bad Times

Ellen and Steve's twenty-fifth anniversary was fast approaching, and they wanted to do something special. They'd been through so much together, especially in the past few years, when they had to deal with their aging parents and a daughter who went through a painful divorce after only two years of marriage.

But what to do? They'd come to see me when their daughter's marriage started getting rocky; it seemed like every time they started a conversation with each other, it ended up in a fight. I helped them through their rough patch, and now they were happy. When they were young, their families couldn't afford an elaborate wedding. Instead, they got married at City Hall, and Ellen never got to wear a wedding gown.

MISC.

One Is Silver, the Other Gold

As the years go by, anniversary milestones increase in value. The first year might be paper, but if you have made it to 25 years, you deserve silver. And 50? Definitely gold!

Ellen was watching a reality TV show about picking out a wedding gown, and she thought the brides looked so beautiful. The dresses were pure fantasy with beading and lace. And then it hit her: she could buy a wedding dress! Nothing was going to stop her. Sure, she wasn't a youngster, so maybe she wouldn't choose an off-the-shoulder body-clinging number, but why not a long-sleeve vintage ivory dress? Or a strapless gown in pale pink? And what about a long veil?

Ellen was on a mission. She discussed the idea of a second wedding with Steve, and they both agreed it would be a lot of fun. They started with the various venues near them—The Golden Manor and The Regency Crown— and ended up with a devil's food, mocha-topped wedding cake. They even hired a band and a photographer.

Their only problem was what they should say to each other. What would they write for their vows? They ended up sharing a simple phrase, said to each other before a kiss: "Thank you for my life."

Reasons to Renew Your Vows

There are several meaningful reasons to recommit. Maybe you were never legally married. Or maybe your first wedding was at the Justice of the Peace or you were broke the first time around and this time, you want to "do it right." Or maybe you have reason to celebrate: you've weathered a lot of crises in the past couple years, and you want to rejoice at having come through them. And perhaps the best reason of all: you want to renew your commitment to each other and to your marriage.

There are no rules or guidelines about wanting to renew your vows, just the desire to reaffirm your love.

Marriage Trap

The wrong reason to renew your vows: to have a party. Renewing your vows is a sacred event. The commitment you're celebrating with each other is the highlight—not the dress, the flowers, the band ....

Finding the Words

Elizabeth Barrett Browning wrote, "How much do I love thee? Let me count the ways." You don't have to write or even recite poetry for your vows, but if your words are true and from your heart, they'll be beautiful.

Here are some questions to ask yourself to get the creative juices flowing:

- What did you feel the first time you saw your partner?
- What do you have in your life now that you would not have if you hadn't been married to your partner?
- When did you first realize you were in love?
- What are some special moments from your life together you remember most?
- What do you miss most about your partner when you're apart?

- Do you have a favorite song or movie? Something that's very romantic and personal to you both?

- What quality do you most love about your partner?

To Quote

Another source of inspiration for writing renewal vows is the web. Sites like www.thinkexist.com and www.great-quotes.com offer thousands of quotes on a variety of topics.

Vow Renewals "I Don'ts"

The nice thing about a vow renewal ceremony is that you don't have to stand on ceremony. Unless you weren't married legally the first time around, there's no need for a license, a blood test, or an officiator. But there are some "I don'ts" you need to keep in mind.

Nix the bridesmaids. Even if you didn't have attendants the first time around, it won't be just the dresses that feel tacky. Your children, of course, can be in attendance, if you so choose.

Forget gift registries. It would be fun to register online for gifts, especially if you were married before the Internet existed. But a vow renewal isn't about getting you your first blender.

Avoid gifts. This party is for you, with your friends and family as witnesses to your love. It's not an excuse to get gifts. If you're also celebrating an anniversary, gifts are permissible, but only if you want them.

Skip the elaborate invites. Your vow renewal invitation is not a wedding invitation, complete with RSVP card and onion paper inserts. You can certainly have invitations printed, but keep them unfussy: "Please join us as we renew our wedding vows" is a good way to start the invitation.

Don't throw wife-ette or husband-ette parties or showers. The hangovers belong in the past, along with your initial wedding.

Finally, don't confuse an anniversary party with a vow renewal ceremony. Parties are great, and an anniversary is a wonderful event to celebrate. But a vow renewal ceremony is more serious; it's a sacred reconnection between two people who love each other.

Romantic Renewals

Renewing your commitment to each other doesn't have to take place in front of your friends and family. It doesn't have to be catered or take place in a lavishly decorated tent on the lawn.

Marilyn and Ted wanted to celebrate their 35 years together, but they didn't want to spend the money on a big wedding and reception. Instead, they took a trip to Paris for the weekend, sitting at cafés, walking on the Seine, enjoying a view of Paris turrets from their boutique hotel room.

Is there a place you'd want to go to renew your love? Maybe it's a trip to a place you've never been, such as the Far East or India. Or maybe you'd like to go back to the same place you had your honeymoon. Renewals can be as individual and romantic as you want them—it's up to you.

Marriage Trap

It might sound romantic to go back to The Bahamas where you spent a glorious week on your honeymoon, but beware. The hotel you stayed in might not exist anymore, or it might have become a fleabag. Do your homework beforehand. Check with a travel agent or on the web.

Daily Affirmations

Of course, vow renewals don't have to be a special occasion. In fact, the best marriages renew their vows daily—without even realizing it. A smile, a compliment, a touch—these are all daily reminders of how you feel and how much you love your spouse.

Trust, honor, and respect are not just words in a wedding vow. They should be a way of life. Every day, show an interest with your partner's activities, hobbies, or work. Hug each other daily. And be sure to say "Thank you." Showing appreciation is an important affirmation. Finally laugh! There's nothing like humor to make you feel close—and loving—to your spouse.

Marriage can be one of the most precious and beautiful elements of life. And a lasting marriage is the most precious and beautiful of all. Celebrate your love!

Essential Takeaways

- Renewing your vows can be as grand as 100 guests or as intimate as a candlelit dinner.
- Your renewal vows don't have to be elaborate and poetic. Just say what you feel.
- Reaffirm your love for each other each day, every day.

Glossary

abuse   More than a physical blow to the face or a despicable sexual act, when you neglect a loved one, that's emotional abuse. When you create an unsafe environment, that, too, is abuse.

acceptance   One of the fundamental pillars of a good marriage. When you accept a person, you leave judgmental thinking behind and love him or her "warts and all."

accommodation   The time during a marriage when roles are established, expectations are set, and compromises are made. This can occur early in a marriage or in the later years, depending on the couple and their life experiences together.

adage   Another word for a saying or a proverb. If used enough, it becomes a cliché.

anchoring   In psychology, anchoring is holding to a steady course. It helps keep you grounded.

arbitrary   When something is arbitrary, it means it's someone's opinion only. It's not absolute. It's a random judgment, feeling, or thought.

bipolar   A mental disorder caused by chemical imbalances in the brain. Here, a person swings from being very manic (spending money, not sleeping, being "over the top") to very depressed.

clinical depression   Different from the normal ups and downs people go through in life, clinical depression is a chemical imbalance in the brain that can make a person feel helpless and hopeless to the point where she can't get out of bed.

co-dependency   Occurs when an individual allows himself to be controlled by someone else's behavior.

cognitive   Another term for thinking. It involves the front part, or frontal lobe, of the brain that can solve problems and finish tasks. If damage is done to the frontal lobe, you can become cognitively impaired.

complementary goals   Goals that work in sync with each other. For example, if one of you prefers to work at home while the other needs an office, you both have goals that work together.

compromise   An agreement reached without any resentment, anger, or sense of sacrifice on either side. Both parties should feel as if they got something they wanted.

criticism   Being judgmental. When you criticize someone, you are making a judgment about him.

dopamine   One of the chemicals in the brain responsible for pleasure. The more dopamine, the better you feel, and the more you'll want sex.

ego repair   A term used when a person's feelings are hurt and her self-esteem is damaged and needs to be fixed.

empty nest   The stage in a marriage when the children have left home to start their own independent lives and you and your spouse are home alone.

eroticism   A term used for the sexual quality, or person, object, or situation that brings on desire.

estrogen   A female hormone that promotes the development of female secondary sex characteristics. During menstruation, estrogen helps prepare for pregnancy. In menopause, estrogen production decreases.

flexibility   Being able to go with the flow and postpone or amend your desires or wishes.

honeymoon stage   The first few months of marriage while the sex is still hot, before routines become boring. It's the time when marriage is more consumed by fantasy than reality.

hormones   Chemicals released in the brain when triggered by outside stimuli such as a kiss. Hormones are also automatically released when triggered by the body, such as hormones that dictate monthly menstruation.

in partner   The spouse who wants the marriage to work, who is the one who initiates marriage counseling.

Kegel exercises   These pelvic-floor exercises for women tighten the vaginal canal and tone the muscles that control urine flow; they can also enhance orgasms for a woman and her partner. Named for the physician who developed them, these exercises are simple and a woman can perform them anytime, anywhere. After isolating the muscles that attach to the pelvic bone, tighten and relax them for a count of five each.

land mine   A dangerous situation that comes at you unawares. Just like stepping on an actual hidden land mine can kill you, saying or doing something that pushes your relationship over the edge—however innocently—can be a land mine, too.

law of reciprocity   A behavior in which you give freely, with no strings, which makes the recipient want to do the same in kind, also freely and without strings.

leap of faith   Believing in something that hasn't yet been proved. It's a belief in someone or something despite contrasting evidence.

longitudinal study   A study that researches the same people over a long period of time.

out partner   The spouse who wants a divorce and doesn't want reconciliation.

passive-aggressive behavior   A psychological term for doing something that's not overtly aggressive. Instead of provoking a fight, for example, you fill the house with flowers—knowing your spouse is allergic to pollen.

pheromones   Chemicals triggered by a powerful response—such as sexual attraction and a belly laugh with someone you're attracted to. The more pheromones that are released, the more attracted you become.

progressive-care facility   A housing alternative that offers placement in all stages of growing old. If your parents can live more or less independently, an apartment might work. As seniors age, they're transitioned to assisted-care facilities and hospitals—all under the same roof.

testosterone The hormone that stimulates the development of male sex organs, male secondary sex characteristics, and sperm.

tolerance Accepting the things that make your mate happy or are really important to her.

validation When you validate someone, you give him substance. You show him that he has value.

Appendix B

Resources

If you'd like to learn more about how you and your spouse can build and maintain a marriage that will weather all the storms, the following books, websites, blogs, and organizations may help.

Books

Bernstein, Jeffrey, with Susan Magee. *Why Can't You Read My Mind? Overcoming the 9 Toxic Thought Patterns That Get in the Way of a Loving Relationship.* New York, NY: De Capo Press, 2003.

Bloom, Linda. *101 Things I Wish I Knew When I Got Married: Simple Lessons to Make Love Last.* New York, NY: New World Library, 2004.

Bloom, Linda, and Charlie Bloom. *Secrets of Great Marriages: Real Truth from Real Couples About Lasting Love.* New York, NY: New World Library, 2010.

Bufala, Nelly. *Marriage, Are You Ready for It? Secrets to a Long-Lasting Relationship.* CreateSpace Publishing, 2010. www.createspace.com.

Gottman, John, Ph.D., with Nan Silver. *Why Marriages Succeed or Fail ... and How You Can Make Yours Last.* New York, NY: Simon & Schuster Paperbacks, 1994.

Gottman, John M., Ph.D., and Nan Silver. *The Seven Principles for Making Marriage Work.* New York, NY: Three Rivers Press, 1999.

Gray, John. *Mars and Venus Together Forever: Relationship Skills for Lasting Love.* New York, NY: HarperPaperbacks, 2005.

——. *Men Are from Mars, Women Are from Venus: The Classic Guide to Understanding the Opposite Sex.* New York, NY: HarperPaperbacks, 2005.

Lister, Pamela, and the Editors of *Redbook Magazine. Stay in Lust Forever: 10 Secrets Every Couple Needs for a Long-Lasting, Passionate Relationship.* New York, NY: Hearst Paperbacks, 2007.

Perry, Susan K., Ph.D. *Loving in Flow: How the Happiest Couples Get and Stay That Way.* Naperville, IL: Sourcebooks Casablanca, 2003.

Saban, Cheryl. *Recipe for a Good Marriage: Wise Words and Quirky Advice for Happy, Long-Lasting Relationships.* London: Ryland Peters and Small, 2006.

Schwartz, Richard, and Jacqueline Olds. *Marriage in Motion: The Natural Ebb and Flow of Lasting Relationships.* New York, NY: De Capo Press, 2002.

Wilkov, Jennifer S. *Dating Your Money for Couples: How to Build a Long-Lasting Relationship with Your Money and Each Other in 8 Easy Steps.* ESP Press Corp., 2007.

E-Books

Hart, Henry. *The Newlyweds Guide to a Lasting and Happy Marriage: The Must Have Guide to a Long Life Commitment to Happiness, Kindle Edition.* www.amazon.com.

Tashman, Martin, Ph.D. *The Relationship Rescue Manual: What to Do When Your Relationship Is Falling Apart.* www.yourmarriagecounselor.com.

——. *Helping Relationships and Marriages Heal from the Trauma of Infidelity.* www.yourmarriagecounselor.com.

Websites

American Association for Marriage and Family Therapy (AAMFT)
www.aamft.org
A national site for professionals and couples looking for advice.

American Counseling Association (ACA)
www.counseling.org
A comprehensive site for professionals and people in need of a therapist.

American Psychological Association Help Center
www.apa.org
A helpful resource on relationships and mental health.

International Association of Marriage and Family Counselors
www.iamfc.org
A division of the American Counseling Association.

Marriage Counseling
www.mayoclinic.com/health/marriage-counseling/MY00839
Advice from the famed Mayo Clinic.

National Council on Family Relations (NCFR)
www.ncfr.org
A website for professionals.

National Institute of Mental Health (NIMH)
www.nimh.nih.gov
A site that offers resources and links for mental illness, marital problems, and more.

Your Marriage Counselor
www.yourmarriagecounselor.com
Advice for putting the spark back into your relationship.

Blogs and Forums

Life Challenges: The CyberCenter for Living Creatively with Life's Challenges
www.ridinggrace.com/lifechallenges.html

MentalHelp.net
www.mentalhelp.net

SelfhelpMagazine
selfhelpmagazine.com

Talk About Marriage
talkaboutmarriage.com

Index

A

acceptance (spouse acceptance)
  challenges, 84-85
  circumstantial, 85-86
  common courtesies, 82-83
  flexibility factor, 80-81
  golden years, 73-75
  "Positive Partner Awareness Inventory" exercise, 87-88
  signs, 88-89
  tolerance, 81-82
  validation, 80
accommodation stage, 47-55
  avoiding disillusionment, 49-50
  financial and career changes, 51-52
  Maslow's Hierarchy of Needs, 53-55
  mortgages and parenthood, 52-53
  setting emotional goals, 50-51
acknowledgments, healing strategy, 245
addiction challenges
  sexual addiction, 227
  substance abuse, 228-233
    children, 230-231
    co-dependency, 231-233
    helping spouses, 229
adult children, empty nester challenges, 213-215

affairs
  conflict-avoidance affairs, 226
  healing tips, 227-228
  intimacy-avoidance affairs, 226
  marriage myths, 27
  sexual addiction, 227
  split-self affair, 227
aging considerations, 71
  fantasies, 72
  golden years and marriage, 69-70
  mortality fears, 72-73
  romance and sex, 161
  vulnerability and temptation, 72
aging parents, caring for, 217-224
  depression, 221
  emotional strains, 218-219
  spouse considerations, 222-224
  tips, 219-222
agoraphobia, 221
anchoring, 259
anger and fighting
  anger buster techniques, 135
    clarity, 137-138
    laughter, 138-139
    listening, 136-137
  energy use, 134-135
  reasons for
    depression, 132-133
    feeling unloved, 130-131
    helplessness, 131-132
    passive-aggressive behaviors, 133-134

tips, 139-144
    avoidance of demeaning words, 143-144
    avoiding hurtful behaviors, 141
    communication, 140
    deep breathing, 142-143
    time-outs, 140-141

B

bankruptcy challenges, 235-236
behaviors
    avoiding hurtful behaviors, 141
    destructive behaviors
        contempt, 167
        criticism, 166-167
        defensiveness, 170-172
        denial, 172-174
        dismissive body language, 169-170
        insults, 167-169
        martyrdom, 177
        mentally removing yourself, 174-175
        negativity, 175-176
bipolar disorder, 28
body language, dismissive, 169-170
boundaries, establishing, 95-97
    importance of space, 96
    quiz, 96-97
budgets, creating, 191-192

C

careers
    financial and career changes (accommodation stage), 51-52
    financial implications, 193-194
catastrophic thinking, 175-176

challenges, 15
    avoiding disillusionment, 49-50
    bankruptcy, 235-236
    caring for parents, 217-224
        depression, 221
        emotional strains, 218-219
        spouse considerations, 222-224
        tips, 219-222
    death of child, 236-237
    debilitating illnesses, 233-234
    destructive behaviors
        contempt, 167
        criticism, 166-167
        defensiveness, 170-172
        denial, 172-174
        dismissive body language, 169-170
        insults, 167-169
        martyrdom, 177
        mentally removing yourself, 174-175
        negativity, 175-176
    early danger signs
        denial, 23
        emotions, 22
        excuses, 23
        silent treatment, 21-22
    empty nesters
        adult children, 213-215
        avoiding burnout, 211
        coping tips, 212-213
        grief and loneliness factors, 212
        overview, 207-208
        reconnecting with spouse, 208-210
    "facing life's challenges" stage
        balancing home and work, 61-62
        building home and community, 62-63
        crises, 58-59
        daily life, 59-60
        expectations, 57-60

extended family issues, 66
goals, 63-65
parenthood, 65-67
financial issues, 16-17, 188
  career moves and, 193-194
  compatibility concerns, 190-191
  compromising, 189-190
  creating budgets, 191-192
  overcoming conflicts, 194-195
  overcoming debt problems,
   192-193
health, 18-19
in-laws, 19-20
infidelity, 225-228
  conflict-avoidance affairs, 226
  healing tips, 227-228
  intimacy-avoidance affairs, 226
  sexual addiction, 227
  split-self affairs, 227
intimacy issues, 197-206
  desire challenges, 200-204
  exercises, 199-200
  familiarity and contempt, 198
  timing sexual encounters,
   198-199
  treatments, 204-206
personal hygiene habits, 20-21
spouse acceptance, 84-85
substance abuse, 228-233
  children, 230-231
  co-dependency, 231-233
  helping spouses, 229
world views, 19
children and parenthood
adaptations, 179-182
  fatigue, 180-181
  responsibilities, 182
  time management, 180
avoiding blame, 185
dealing with death, 236-237
family joys, 184
happy marriage factors, 6
identity shifts, 182-183

substance abuse challenges,
  230-231
time-out periods, 185-186
circumstantial acceptance, 85-86
clarity, anger buster techniques,
 137-138
co-dependency, 231-233
commitment renewals
  daily affirmations, 279-280
  romantic renewals, 279
  vow renewal ceremonies, 275-279
communication tips, 126-127
  effective communication, 115-120
  fighting, 140
  meetings
   law of reciprocity, 125-126
   preparations, 124-125
  men versus women, 121-124
  sex and intimacy issues, 154-157,
   206
community, building, 62-63
compatibility concerns, 6, 190-191
complaining versus criticism, 166
compromising
  "facing life's challenges" stage,
   66-67
  financial issues, 189-190
  golden years, 70
conflict-avoidance affairs, 226
contempt
  destructive behaviors, 167
  intimacy issues, 198
  overcoming, 102-104
coping tips, empty nester challenges,
 212-213
counseling
  expectations, 268-270
  finding therapists, 270
  rejection factor, 265-267
  sex therapy, 272-273
  solo sessions, 267-268
  support groups, 271-272
  when to seek, 262-264

couples therapy
   expectations, 268-270
   finding therapists, 270
   rejection factor, 265-267
   sex therapy, 272-273
   solo sessions, 267-268
   support groups, 271-272
   when to seek, 262-264
criticism
   destructive behaviors, 166-167
   versus complaining, 166

D

danger signs
   denial, 23
   emotions, 22
   excuses, 23
   silent treatment, 21-22
dating
   classes, 149-150
   event planning, 148
   hiking dates, 150
   hobbies and sporting concerns,
      150-151
   scheduled date nights, 148-149
death, dealing with child's death,
   236-237
debilitating illness challenges,
   233-234
debt, overcoming, 192-193
deep breathing tips, 142-143
defensiveness (destructive behaviors),
   170-172
denial
   destructive behaviors, 172-174
   early danger signs, 23
depression, 28
   aging parents, 221
   anger and fighting connection,
      132-133

   passive-aggressive behaviors,
      133-134
desire challenges (sex and intimacy),
   200-206
   medical conditions, 203-204
   men, 203
   menopause, 202-203
   psychological factors, 204
   treatments, 204-206
      communication, 206
      medications, 205
      timing, 205-206
destructive behaviors
   contempt, 167
   criticism, 166-167
   defensiveness, 170-172
   denial, 172-174
   dismissive body language, 169-170
   insults, 167-169
   martyrdom, 177
   mentally removing yourself,
      174-175
   negativity, 175-176
disillusionment, avoiding, 49-50
dismissive body language, 169-170
divorce statistic myths, 26-27
dopamine, 41

E

early danger signs
   denial, 23
   emotions, 22
   excuses, 23
   silent treatment, 21-22
effective communication tips, 115-120
emotional concerns
   caring for parents, 218-219
   early danger signs, 22
   setting emotional goals, 50-51

empathy, showing toward spouse
    different points of view, 91-93
    importance of influence, 100-102
    moods and needs, 97-100
    overcoming contempt, 102-104
    respecting opinions, 93-95
empty nester challenges
    adult children, 213-215
    avoiding burnout, 211
    coping tips, 212-213
    grief and loneliness factors, 212
    overview, 207-208
    reconnecting with spouse, 208-210
energy use and anger, 134-135
establishing boundaries, 95-97
    importance of space, 96
    quiz, 96-97
estrogen, 202
excuses, early danger signs, 23
exercises
    boundaries, 96-97
    healing strategies and trust,
        248-249
    intimacy issues, 199-200
    lasting marriages, 11-13
    "Positive Partner Awareness
        Inventory," 87-88
    "Qualities of a Good Relationship,"
        99-100
    trust, 109-111
expectations
    couples therapy, 268-270
    realistic expectations (lasting
        marriage considerations), 10-11
extended family issues, 66

F

"facing life's challenges" stage
    balancing home and work, 61-62
    building home and community,
        62-63
    crises, 58-59
    daily life, 59-60
    expectations, 57-60
    extended family issues, 66
    goals, 63-65
    parenthood, 65-67
faith and healing, 245
familiarity, intimacy issues, 198
family joys, 184
fantasies
    golden years, 72
    sexual fantasies, 156-157
fatigue and parenthood, 180-181
fighting
    anger buster techniques, 135-139
        clarity, 137-138
        laughter, 138-139
        listening, 136-137
    energy use, 134-135
    honeymoon phase, 43-45
    marriage myths, 30
    reasons for
        depression, 132-133
        feeling unloved, 130-131
        helplessness, 131-132
        passive-aggressive behaviors,
            133-134
    tips, 139
        avoidance of demeaning words,
            143-144
        avoiding hurtful behaviors, 141
        communication, 140
        deep breathing, 142-143
        time-outs, 140-141
financial issues, 188
    bankruptcy challenges, 235-236
    career moves and, 193-194
    compatibility concerns, 190-191
    compromising, 189-190
    creating budgets, 191-192

financial and career changes
(accommodation stage), 51-52
marriage challenges, 16-17
overcoming conflicts, 194-195
overcoming debt problems,
192-193
sharing and trust issues, 111-112
flexibility factor, 80-81

G

goals
emotional, 50-51
"facing life's challenges" stage,
63-65
happy marriage factors, 4-5
golden years and marriage, 69
aging considerations, 71-73
fantasies, 72
mortality fears, 72-73
vulnerability and temptation, 72
compromising, 70
empty nester challenges
adult children, 213-215
avoiding burnout, 211
coping tips, 212-213
grief and loneliness factors, 212
overview, 207-208
reconnecting with spouse,
208-210
marriage rebirth, 75-76
spouse acceptance, 73-75
guidelines (marital guidelines), 42-43

H

happy marriage factors
compatible children views, 6
complementary goals, 4-5

religious beliefs, 8
sense of humor, 6-7
shared values, 5-6
healing strategies and trust, 241
acknowledgments, 245
exercises, 248-249
infidelity, 227-228
plan development, 248
positive self-talk, 244
replay techniques, 246-247
role of faith, 245
sharing thoughts, 244-245
spending time together, 244
health conditions
debilitating illness challenges,
233-234
marriage challenges, 18-19
hiking dates, 150
hobbies, date concerns, 150-151
home
balancing home and work, 61-62
building, 62-63
honeymoon phase
fights, 43-45
idealizing mates, 41-42
marital guidelines, 42-43
overview, 37-38
passion and romance, 38-39
separation anxiety, 40-41
sex, 41
hormones, mood-affecting hormones,
155-156

I

idealizing mates (honeymoon phase),
41-42
identity shifts (parenthood), 182-183
in partners, 267

in-laws
    handling extended family issues, 66
    marriage challenges, 19-20
infidelity
    conflict-avoidance affairs, 226
    healing tips, 227-228
    intimacy-avoidance affairs, 226
    sexual addiction, 227
    split-self affairs, 227
infidelity challenges, 225
influence between spouses, 100-102
insults (destructive behaviors), 167-169
intimacy issues, 197
    changes, 158-159
    desire challenges, 200
        medical conditions, 203-204
        men, 203
        menopause, 202-203
        psychological factors, 204
    exercise, 199-200
    familiarity and contempt, 198
    timing sexual encounters, 198-199
    treatments, 204-206
        communication, 206
        medications, 205
        timing, 205-206
intimacy-avoidance affairs, 226

judgmental thinking, avoiding, 94-95

kindness, random acts of kindness, 260
Kinsey Institute for Research sex study, 157-158

lasting marriage considerations, 8-13
    change factor, 10
    exercises, 11-13
    love definitions, 9
    realistic expectations, 10-11
laughter, 145
    anger buster techniques, 138-139
    aphrodisiac qualities, 146
    closeness factor, 147
    power of, 147
law of reciprocity, 125-126
listening, anger buster techniques, 136-137
loneliness, empty nester challenges, 212
love
    evolving definitions, 9
    rekindling, 251-260
        giving details, 253
        taking responsibility, 252-253
        troubleshooting problems, 254-255
        using positive self-talk, 255-258
        valuing your spouse, 259-260
    renewing marriage commitment
        daily affirmations, 279-280
        romantic renewals, 279
        vow renewal ceremonies, 275-279

marriage
    accommodation stage, 47-55
        avoiding disillusionment, 49-50
        financial and career changes, 51-52

Maslow's Hierarchy of Needs, 53-55
mortgages and parenthood, 52-53
setting emotional goals, 50-51
challenges, 15-21
   financial, 16-17
   health, 18-19
   in-laws, 19-20
   personal hygiene habits, 20-21
   world views, 19
early danger signs
   denial, 23
   emotions, 22
   excuses, 23
   silent treatment, 21-22
"facing life's challenges" stage
   balancing home and work, 61-62
   building home and community, 62-63
   crises, 58-59
   daily life, 59-60
   expectations, 57-60
   extended family issues, 66
   goals, 63-65
   parenthood, 65-67
golden years, 69-76
   aging considerations, 71-73
   compromising, 70
   marriage rebirth, 75-76
   spouse acceptance, 73-75
happy marriage factors
   compatible children views, 6
   complementary goals, 4-5
   religious beliefs, 8
   sense of humor, 6-7
   shared values, 5-6
honeymoon phase
   fights, 43-45
   idealizing mates, 41-42
   marital guidelines, 42-43
   overview, 37-38

   passion and romance, 38-39
   separation anxiety, 40-41
   sex, 41
lasting marriage considerations, 8-13
   change factor, 10
   exercises, 11-13
   love definitions, 9
   realistic expectations, 10-11
myths
   affairs, 27
   common interests, 29
   divorce statistics, 26-27
   fights, 30
   mental problems, 28
   sex, 26
renewing commitments
   daily affirmations, 279-280
   romantic renewals, 279
   vow renewal ceremonies, 275-279
martyrdom (destructive behaviors), 177
Maslow's Hierarchy of Needs, 53-55
medical conditions and intimacy issues, 203-204
medications and sexual problems, 205
meetings (communication tips)
   law of reciprocity, 125-126
   preparations, 124-125
men and intimacy issues, 203
menopause, 202-203
mental problems
   bipolar disorder, 28
   depression, 28
   marriage myths, 28
money issues
   bankruptcy challenges, 235-236
   financial issues, 188-195
      career moves and, 193-194
      compatibility concerns, 190-191
      compromising, 189-190
      creating budgets, 191-192

overcoming conflicts, 194-195
overcoming debt problems, 192-193
sharing and trust issues, 111-112
mood-affecting hormones, 155-156
moods (spouses), respecting, 97-100
mortality fears, 72-73
mortgages (accommodation stage), 52-53
myths
    affairs, 27
    common interests, 29
    divorce statistics, 26-27
    fights, 30
    mental problems, 28
    sex, 26

needs
    communicating sexual needs, 154-157
    respecting spouses, 97-100
negativity (destructive behaviors), 175-176

opinions, respecting, 93-95
out partners, 267

parenthood
    accommodation stage, 52-53
    adaptations, 179-182
        fatigue, 180-181
        responsibilities, 182
        time management, 180
    avoiding blame, 185
    compromise, 66-67

family joys, 184
    identity shifts, 182-183
    rules and expectations, 65-66
    time-out periods, 185-186
parents, caring for, 217-224
    depression, 221
    emotional strains, 218-219
    spouse considerations, 222-224
    tips, 219-222
passion (honeymoon phase), 38-39
personal hygiene habits, marriage challenges, 20-21
pheromones, 146
playtime considerations
    dating
        classes, 149-150
        event planning, 148
        hiking dates, 150
        hobbies and sporting concerns, 150-151
        scheduled date nights, 148-149
    laughter, 145-147
        aphrodisiac qualities, 146
        closeness factor, 147
        power of, 147
"Positive Partner Awareness Inventory" exercise, 87-88
positive self-talk (healing strategy), 244
psychological factors, intimacy issues, 204

"Qualities of a Good Relationship" exercise, 99-100
quizzes
    boundaries, 96-97
    trust, 109-111

random acts of kindness, 260
realistic expectations (lasting marriage considerations), 10-11
rebirth (marriage rebirth), 75-76
rejection and counseling, 265-267
rekindling love, 251-260
    giving details, 253
    taking responsibility, 252-253
    troubleshooting problems, 254-255
    using positive self-talk, 255-258
    valuing your spouse, 259-260
Relationship Satisfaction Scale. *See* RSS
religious beliefs (happy marriage factor), 8
reminiscing, romance and sex, 158
renewing marriage commitment
    daily affirmations, 279-280
    romantic renewals, 279
    vow renewal ceremonies, 275-279
        reasons, 277
        tips, 278-279
        wording vows, 277-278
replay techniques (healing strategies and trust), 246-247
resentment, minimizing, 74
resources
    couples therapy
        expectations, 268-270
        finding therapists, 270
        rejection factor, 265-267
        sex therapy, 272-273
        solo sessions, 267-268
        when to seek, 262-264
    support groups, 271-272
respecting spouses, 74
    importance of influence, 100-102
    moods and needs, 97-100
    opinions, 93-95
    overcoming contempt, 102-104

responsibilities of parenthood, 182
romance and sex, 153
    aging considerations, 161
    benefits, 155
    communicating needs, 154-157
    honeymoon phase, 38-39
    intimacy changes, 158-159
    Kinsey Institute for Research sex study, 157-158
    mood-affecting hormones, 155-156
    reminiscing, 158
    romancing tips, 159-160
    sexual fantasies, 156-157
romantic vow renewals, 279
RSS (Relationship Satisfaction Scale), 30-33

scheduled date nights, 148-149
self-acceptance, 83-84
self-reinforcement, 257
self-talk, rekindling love, 255-258
self-trust, 107-108
sense of humor (happy marriage factor), 6-7
separation anxiety (honeymoon phase), 40-41
sex
    communicating needs, 155
    honeymoon phase, 41
    intimacy issues, 197-206
        desire challenges, 200-204
        exercise, 199-200
        familiarity and contempt, 198
        timing sexual encounters, 198-199
        treatments, 204-206
    marriage myths, 26

romance and sex, 153
    aging considerations, 161
    benefits, 155
    communicating needs, 154-157
    honeymoon phase, 38-39
    intimacy changes, 158-159
    Kinsey Institute for Research
        sex study, 157-158
    mood-affecting hormones,
        155-156
    reminiscing, 158
    romancing tips, 159-160
    sexual fantasies, 156-157
sex therapy, 272-273
sexual addiction, 227
shared values (happy marriage
    factor), 5-6
sharing
    healing strategy, 244-245
    trust issues
        money, 111-112
        space, 112
signs
    early danger signs
        denial, 23
        emotions, 22
        excuses, 23
        silent treatment, 21-22
    spouse acceptance, 88-89
silent treatment (early danger signs),
    21-22
space, sharing and trust issues, 112
split-self affairs, 227
sports, date concerns, 150-151
spouses
    acceptance
        challenges, 84-85
        circumstantial, 85-86
        common courtesies, 82-83
        flexibility factor, 80-81
        golden years, 73-75
        "Positive Partner Awareness
            Inventory" exercise, 87-88

        self-acceptance, 83-84
        signs, 88-89
        tolerance, 81-82
        validation, 80
    establishing boundaries, 95-97
        importance of space, 96
        quiz, 96-97
    playtime considerations
        dating, 148-151
        laughter, 145-147
    reconnecting with (empty nester
        challenges), 208-210
    respecting, 74
    showing empathy toward
        different points of view, 91-93
        importance of influence,
            100-102
        moods and needs, 97-100
        overcoming contempt, 102-104
        respecting opinions, 93-95
    trust
        building, 108-109
        developing, 109
        importance, 105-107
        past influences, 108
        quiz, 109-111
        self-trust, 107-108
        sharing issues, 111-112
    valuing, 259-260
Stages of Trauma Recovery, 236-237
substance abuse challenges, 228-231
    children, 230-231
    co-dependency, 231-233
    helping spouses, 229
support groups, 271-272

T

temptation, golden years, 72
testosterone, 203
therapists, finding, 270

therapy
  expectations, 268-270
  finding therapists, 270
  rejection factor, 265-267
  sex therapy, 272-273
  solo sessions, 267-268
  support groups, 271-272
  when to seek, 262-264
time management, 180
time-out periods
  fighting tips, 140-141
  parenthood, 185-186
tolerance, spouse acceptance, 81-82
treatments, sex and intimacy issues,
  204-206
  medications, 205
  timing, 205-206
trust
  building, 108-109
  developing, 109
  healing strategies, 241-249
    acknowledgment, 245
    exercises, 248-249
    plan development, 248
    positive self-talk, 244
    replay techniques, 246-247
    role of faith, 245
    sharing thoughts, 244-245
    spending time together, 244
  importance, 105-107
  past influences, 108
  quiz, 109-111
  rebuilding strategies, 245
  self, 107-108
  sharing issues
    money, 111-112
    space, 112

validation (acceptance), 80
valuing spouses, 259-260
vow renewals
  ceremonies, 275-279
    reasons, 277
    tips, 278-279
    wording vows, 277-278
  daily affirmations, 279-280
vulnerability (golden years), 72

wedding vow renewals
  ceremonies, 275-279
    reasons, 277
    tips, 278-279
    wording vows, 277-278
  daily affirmations, 279-280
women, menopause and intimacy,
  202-203
work, balancing home and work,
  61-62
world views, marriage challenges, 19